Where the Sun Rises Square

Where the Sun Rises Square

Mass Incarceration and the Binds of Reform in Brazil

DAVID C. THOMPSON

STANFORD UNIVERSITY PRESS
Stanford, California

Stanford University Press
Stanford, California

Library of Congress Cataloging-in-Publication Data
Names: Thompson, David C., author.
Title: Where the sun rises square : mass incarceration and the binds of reform in Brazil / David C. Thompson.
Description: Stanford, California : Stanford University Press, 2026. | Includes bibliographical references and index.
Identifiers: LCCN 2025008480 (print) | LCCN 2025008481 (ebook) | ISBN 9781503641921 (cloth) | ISBN 9781503644564 (paperback) | ISBN 9781503644571 (ebook)
Subjects: LCSH: Criminals—Rehabilitation—Brazil—Rio de Janeiro. | Resocialization—Brazil—Rio de Janeiro. | Prisoners—Brazil—Rio de Janeiro—Social conditions. | Prisons—Brazil—Rio de Janeiro. | Mass incarceration—Brazil—Rio de Janeiro.
Classification: LCC HV9335.R56 T46 2025 (print) | LCC HV9335.R56 (ebook) | DDC 365/.6610981—dc23/eng/20250429

LC record available at https://lccn.loc.gov/2025008480
LC ebook record available at https://lccn.loc.gov/2025008481

Cover design: Lee Friedman
Cover photograph: *Frei Caneca prison complex, ca.1960s.* From the digital archives of the Escola de Gestão Penitenciária (School of Penitentiary Management), Rio de Janeiro, Brazil.

The authorized representative in the EU for product safety and compliance is: Mare Nostrum Group B.V. | Mauritskade 21D | 1091 GC Amsterdam | The Netherlands | Email address: gpsr@mare-nostrum.co.uk | KVK chamber of commerce number: 96249943

To my parents.

Contents

Abbreviations

APAC: Associação para a Proteção e Assistência aos Condenados (Association for the Protection and Assistance of the Convicted); alternately, Amando o Próximo, Amarás a Cristo (Loving Your Neighbor, You Will Love Christ). The two names refer to the same organization.

GRP: Guia de Recolhimento à Prisão (Guide for Delivery to Internment)

LEP: Lei de Execução Penal (Law of Penal Execution)

ND: não declarado (not declared)

NUSPEN: Núcleo do Sistema Penitenciário (Penitentiary System Nucleus)

PROJUDI: Processo Judicial Digital (Digital Judicial Proceedings)

PRONASCI: Programa Nacional de Segurança com Cidadania (National Program of Security with Citizenship)

RG: Registro Geral (General Register), a national identification number.

SEAP: Secretaria de Estado de Administração Penitenciária (State Secretary of Prison Administration)

SEI: Sistema Estadual de Identificação (State System of Identification)

TCP: Terceiro Comando Puro (Pure Third Command)

TFD: Transcrição de Ficha Disciplinar (Disciplinary Record Transcript)

TJRJ: Tribunal de Justiça do Estado do Rio de Janeiro (Rio de Janeiro State Justice Tribunal)

UNDP: United Nations Development Programme

UPP: Unidade de Polícia Pacificadora (Police Pacifying Unit)

VEP: Vara de Execuções Penais (Court of Penal Execution)

Where the Sun Rises Square

Prison Is Just a Question of Time

Hi my friend, or better yet, my new friend, David. It's around one in the
morning and I can't sleep because of the heat, but I've been thinking about
your workshop until today, everything that we talked about. Anyway, I
hope everything's well [. . .]

David, I believe in my ideas, because I know that many never had a
chance, but some day someone will come to recognize me, and just like God
brought us together that day, I believe that I will be in front of someone who
can listen to me, who will believe in my dreams and who will give me all
that I need—a chance! I don't mean to get out of here, I committed a crime
and I have to pay for it, but a chance to invest in my project and a chance
that my work will be felt in the destroyed society that we see today, and
you know what else David? Prison is just a question of time, the forgotten
people on this side of the wall are going to be tomorrow's society, and if
nobody changes the way that they live and think, when they return they
will be even worse.

[. . .]

Sincerely,

Your new friend, Diogo

"Even when everything goes wrong, God is in control"

I got this letter a few days after it was written. I was at a daylong event that the
psychology department of Rio de Janeiro's prison administration had organized

to reflect on the successes and the current state of a volunteer program called Project Life, which aimed to promote "health and citizenship" among the incarcerated population. As usual, the head of the administration failed to appear for his scheduled presentation. In his place, we had just heard from Colonel Gilson,[1] the "Subsecretary of Treatment," who spoke about new initiatives to be implemented at some unspecified later date. The Colonel's speech started with a refrain that I heard many times over the course of my research, mostly during events like this one:

> Here in Brazil we have no death penalty and we have no life sentence. Every person inside prison, *every single one*, will leave one day. It is our responsibility, together, to make sure that they leave in a better state than when they entered, and that they have an opportunity to prove their worth to our society.

This is a lie. Rio's police enforce a de facto death penalty in the thousands that they kill every year. Hundreds also die while held in the state's prisons. Based on the administration's own data, those incarcerated in Rio are six times as likely to die of infectious disease than the general population.[2] But the repetition of the phrase was important. It suggested that the project of incarceration and the work of those of us sitting in the audience—mostly white, mostly women, mostly trained psychologists and social workers—were united by a responsibility to cultivate human potential, to reform those in prison for the sake of a better tomorrow.

There was a short coffee break after Colonel Gilson's talk. Pastor Bruno, who was sitting a few rows in front of me, stood up and came over. He was a white man in his early forties who had worked for years as a prison missionary; now he was volunteering in a men's unit that I will call René Dotti, where he ran *cultos* (worship) and Bible study each week. This was the same prison where, one week ago, I had met Diogo during a Project Life workshop that I facilitated. Diogo's letter started a correspondence that ultimately lasted two years, as we wrote to each other between my visits to René Dotti and discussed my project, his own work, and the questions that lay between them. Diogo had passed it to Bruno the day before. Bruno handed it to me; I sat reading during the break while the other attendees gathered around the coffee table.

Something was shared between Diogo's letter and Gilson's speech, some future moment that they saw on the horizon. Both had their gaze firmly planted on the date of release as the point from which incarceration should be oriented and judged. If prison is just a question of time, the Colonel had made this question a rallying call. But Diogo, writing in the heat of a crowded prison cell at night, had carved it into a threat.

Resocialization

About thirty-five years ago, during Brazil's most recent transition to democracy, the country embarked on a massive project of carceral expansion. Its prison population, estimated at 90,000 in 1990, reached over 650,000 in 2024, with another 220,000 confined under some form of house arrest.[3] We can call this project mass incarceration, but only if we recognize that punishment discriminates. Those caught in the criminal justice system's expanding orbit are disproportionately young, Black, and residents of urban peripheries—people like Diogo. Today, they are held across hundreds of jails, prisons, penitentiaries, and other units scattered across the country—places *where the sun rises square* (*onde o sol nasce quadrado*), according to the Brazilian adage. Virtually all of them are severely crowded beyond their official maximum capacities. These are institutions where forms of solidarity between imprisoned people have consolidated into new collectives; where everyday violence sometimes erupts into something more spectacular, spilling into city streets and international headlines; and where every morning tens of thousands line up—mostly Black, mostly women—as they wait to visit their loved ones.

The transformation of punishment took a specific shape in the state of Rio de Janeiro.[4] Successive governments decommissioned penitentiaries in the urban center and the once infamous, now touristy island of Ilha Grande. In their place, a ring of prison complexes emerged around Rio's urban peripheries. Both the scale and scope of policing expanded through a set of security policies that governments and media justified in the name of building a new Rio, ready for its global debut at the 2014 FIFA World Cup and 2016 Olympic Games. Black, windowless vans known as *camburões* crisscrossed the city's new thoroughfares every day as they trafficked hundreds from police stations into the prison system. But when they arrived at their destinations, each van would pass through a gate emblazoned with the promise and the mandate to "Resocialize to Conquer the Future" (Ressocializar para o Futuro Conquistar).

This phrase, the ever-present motto of the prison administration, seems out of place. It insists on a sense of optimism in the midst of a notoriously violent and punitive set of institutions. It justifies imprisonment as an intervention into the lives and futures of those held in custody, an attempt to transform them from criminal-objects into citizen-subjects. I don't think that anyone believed that it was the main function of imprisonment. And yet resocialization was stamped on gates, walls, and official letterheads; it was cited by judges to justify another denied parole application; it was a constant, yet elusive talking point among those whose work in prison fell under the broad umbrella of "treatment." It circulated, seeping into disparate areas of prison life and governance, while people like Diogo and Colonel Gilson took the idea and the aspirations that it represented and put them to use.

This is a book about what is made and unmade under resocialization's sign. My claim is that resocialization animates Rio's prisons, that it continues to shape a punitive landscape that appears detached from and often antithetical to any coherent project of reform. It marks out and codifies a trajectory of reform against which those held captive are classified and judged. At the same time, prison workers and incarcerated people mobilize its vision of change to make meaning of the positions they are forced into, or to mark out new ones for themselves. As a concept, resocialization holds out the possibility of a future within the violence of the present. As a set of practices, it fractures and bends this possibility toward different ends. As an institutional critique, it somehow both attacks and affirms the project of incarceration in Brazil. The collective hopes and anxieties that stick to those in prison, as well as fundamental questions about the nature of human change and the possibilities for individual and social futures, all coalesce around resocialization and the domains of punishment that it calls forth.

Another way to say this is that Rio's prisons are anticipatory machines. They continually anticipate a moment—release—and a subject who is both worthy and capable of inhabiting it: the resocialized person. These horizons stalk the present, setting up a field of intimacy, suspicion, and hope that encircles the institutions and their captives. Speaking from radically different points within this field, Colonel Gilson and Diogo oriented themselves toward this mode of anticipation, where the promise and the supposedly inevitable fact of release made the imperative to reform self-evident. But something also slipped between the two. Gilson's speech recruited his audience into a fight against crime. Diogo's letter was a dispatch from a fight for survival. Those two projects met among the legal and discursive ground of reform, brought forth by federal legislation and by a longer history of tutelage, colonialism, and redemption in Brazil.

By following resocialization, I move through Brazil's unfolding landscape of punishment, oriented by the question of how the future has become a resource within the carceral present. The result is just one among many possible stories about confinement. But it reveals the variegated and often perverse relationship between prisons, punishment, and hope, a relationship that deserves to be interrogated. It was not always as explicit as Diogo's letter or Gilson's speech. Sometimes it appeared in behavioral classification regimes, or in the collective concern over the wording and punctuation of a report. Sometimes it emerged in a psychologist's warning that any discussion of structural violence could serve as an excuse for imprisoned people to avoid their personal responsibility to change. Sometimes it was held in the anxious tenor of a mother worried if her son was "ready" to leave prison. Sometimes it wrapped around a recently released man as he tried to sleep in a van outside the hospital while waiting for the birth of his child.

The word *resocialization* is never far from these spaces, but it doesn't bear their weight alone. It sits within a broader family of reformative narratives, including recovery, social reintegration, and redemption—what Diogo once described to me in a letter as a "philosophy of 're.' "[5] Both in conversation and in writing, he showed a profound ambivalence to these ideas, painfully aware of their hypocrisies even as he remained invested in the futures that they laid out. At the same time, these were the only futures—or at least, the only ones held up by the institution—that remained tangible for him within a space of confinement. Resocialization was both a part of his captivity and a pathway out of it.

Punishment and Optimism in Brazil

At the time of writing this book, there are forty-three jails, prisons, and penitentiaries operating in the state of Rio de Janeiro. Each one holds anywhere between two hundred and five thousand people. Just over half stand within a single prison complex—formally known as Gericinó, but still mostly referred to by its older name, Bangu—sandwiched between an environmental conservation area, a military training zone, and a landfill site in Rio's West Zone. Others are scattered across the urban peripheries (as seen in Figure I.1), with a handful located in smaller cities across the state. Collectively, these units are administered by Rio's State Secretary of Prison Administration (Secretaria de Estado de Administração Penitenciária). Those who worked or volunteered in prisons referred to it by its acronym, SEAP. Incarcerated people, their families, and their communities mostly called it "the system" (*o sistema*).[6] In 2014, when I began my fieldwork, scholars and activists expressed alarm that the state's prison population had surged past forty thousand. By the time I returned in 2016, it had passed fifty thousand and was operating at about 170 percent of its official capacity.[7] This was a period of exceptional growth, but the overall expansion of Rio's prison population has largely lined up with that of Brazil as a whole since 1990. The explosion in imprisonment does not map onto rates of crime. Instead, it points to a fundamental shift in security politics following the end of Brazil's military dictatorship and return to democracy in the mid-1980s.[8] The importation of War on Drugs rhetoric from the United States, combined with a newfound sense of insecurity at home, provided justification for massive investments in policing and a series of punitive sentencing reforms. Politicians across political divides began to campaign as representatives of law and order, while criminal judges, styling themselves as guarantors of public security, responded to an influx of cases with increasingly harsh punishments.[9]

One of the most critical shifts in Rio de Janeiro was the implementation of Police Pacifying Units (Unidades de Polícia Pacificadora or UPPs), which transformed the scope of policing in the city. Starting in late 2008, the program saw militarized police "retake" favelas—informal, impoverished neighborhoods in Brazil's cities and icons of the nation's startling inequality—by establishing permanent occupations of these communities. These units were justified as an effort to both "liberate" residents from the de facto control of organized crime networks known as factions (*facções*)[10] and to fold the favelas back into the broader urban fabric. The World Cup and Olympic Games provided further justification for establishing UPPs across the city and pouring resources into policing. Coming after the sustained economic growth of the previous decade, particularly under the first presidency of Luiz Inácio Lula da Silva, the two events were planned and publicized as the culmination of an optimistic tale of national development in which Brazil would, finally, emerge as a modern, transformed

FIGURE I.1. Map of prisons within the municipality of Rio de Janeiro (highlighted) and surrounding municipalities.

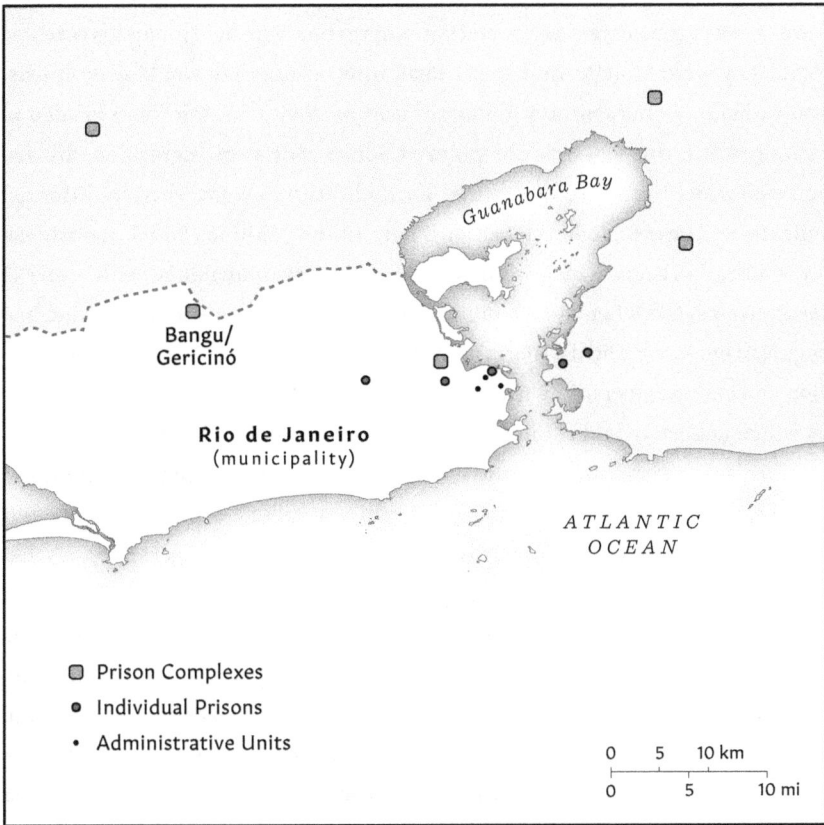

country. In some cases, UPPs served as a pipeline for new infrastructure, social
projects, and government services, at least in the first few years of their operations. But they also extended the reach of state security into areas that had
previously been subject only to sporadic police operations. Despite promises of
peace, many UPPs also terrorized neighborhoods through armed conflict, ex-
posing residents to state violence and drawing them into the orbit of courts and
prisons.[11]

The project to produce a new, modern Rio de Janeiro was the dream of a security state, one that funneled tens of thousands into prisons. The incarcerated
people with whom I worked were part of this wave of arrests and convictions.

They had been apprehended by UPP police, or else by the patrols that increasingly occupied tourist areas in Rio's center and South Zone. From there, they were taken to the nearest police station, where they were held for up to two days. Next, they were brought into the "triage" unit, where they would wait at least a week before being sent to yet another unit to await trial. For those headed to men's prisons, this was also the point at which they were segregated, divided between units that were designated for and internally governed by different collectives. These include the factions, paramilitary militias,[12] and the ostensibly "neutral" prisons, which were destined for those unaffiliated with either of these groups, but where a new organization known as the People of Israel had begun to emerge.[13] The division was not based on an incarcerated person's previous formal membership within these groups. Instead, it was largely decided by which collective laid claim to the neighborhood where they had lived. From that first moment of confinement, it could take anywhere from three months to a year to finally receive a court hearing and a sentence.

Those most directly exposed to the mix of legal and extralegal strategies that constitute "security" in Rio are young and Black. In the state of Rio de Janeiro, 72 percent of those held in prisons are identified by SEAP as *preto* ("black" or dark-skinned) or *pardo* ("brown" or mixed), compared to 51 percent of the state's general population.[14] Their families and communities also bear the economic and social costs of captivity. But prisons do not just act on a preexisting racial order; they create and maintain it by marking out Blackness as a sphere of rightlessness and by reinforcing racial boundaries.[15] Most of those whose lives and deaths are quantified in incarceration statistics are legally identified as male, and 92 percent of Rio's prison population are confined in units designated for men.[16] These numbers obscure the criminalization of trans people and travestis—who cultivate and inhabit feminine subjectivities but do not necessarily identify as trans or as women—who are rendered invisible in statistics. At the same time, the rate of incarceration for those the state identifies as women rapidly grew in the decade leading up to my research. Black women, in particular, are also caught by the system as family members of those held captive, and as prison visitors subject to strip searches and other routinized assaults in the name of preventing contraband.[17]

This convergence of urban renewal and anti-Black violence is nothing new. As anthropologist João Vargas argues, what unites the different permutations of national optimism across Brazil's history are their commitments to the eugenic project of whitening the nation.[18] But even as I began my fieldwork in 2014, the future that Rio was apparently pulling itself toward began to crumble. First came a wave of popular discontent and protests against the incumbent government and its president, Dilma Rousseff. Then the combined weight of a deep economic recession and political turmoil turned hopes inside out, producing a deep national pessimism. The undoing of these aspirations was on display for the world when Rio's new buildings and infrastructure literally buckled under the weight of the Olympic Games. By this point, a narrative of crisis had already been well-established within the country. *Crisis* captured the sense of collapse as unemployment, homelessness, and gun violence—all ostensibly markers of the "old" Rio—returned to permeate daily life in the city. The term *crisis* also signaled the vacuum that stood on the horizon as the aspirations of Brazilian families, communities, and governments suddenly seemed unviable.

In the following years, a rising authoritarian movement, led by Jair Bolsonaro, would come to occupy and (for a time) monopolize this space with a new vision for Brazil's future. But the period of my fieldwork was still entrenched in both the reality and the rhetoric of crisis. What it might mean to imagine and pursue a future for oneself, and to prove that one was "ready" for this future, was far from clear for many, if not most, Brazilians. But this is precisely what the nation's prisons and courts demanded of their captives.

Unfulfilled Promises

The word may appear on the front gates of every prison in Rio de Janeiro, but resocialization is not an obvious point of entry into the system. The violence of these institutions, their intense crowding, and the unending succession of mismanagement and corruption scandals all point to a disregard of, if not an active hostility toward, any project or principle of reform. The people I worked with routinely reminded me of this during my fieldwork. When I introduced myself and identified my research topic, the most common and immediate reply I received was that "resocialization does not exist" (*a ressocialização não existe*). People did not always mean the same thing by that phrase. Some were pointing out that rehabilitative programs had dried up in the last two decades, as the pressures of mass incarceration left no room for therapeutic or educational work. Others were trying to tell me that resocialization was always a rhetorical cover for the project of incarceration, a way to gloss over its harms, or a form of "makeup," as one social worker put it. But the claim that resocialization was missing, in some fundamental sense, was ubiquitous.

The axiom "Resocialization does not exist" was firmly established in Rio long before I began my research. I heard it most from those who were directly charged with a responsibility to reform: social workers, psychologists, public defenders, missionaries, and other staff or volunteers whose labor fell under the broad umbrella of "treatment."[19] Incarcerated people and those who had recently left prison would also repeat the phrase back to me. Nobody was waiting for a foreign anthropologist to demonstrate what had already become an article of faith. In fact, many prison workers were already well-versed in the history and the social science of punishment, both of which trace a transformation over the last century in which the rehabilitative impulses that had first justified the construction of the penitentiaries were gradually abandoned in favor of punishment and containment.[20] Rio's social workers and psychologists used this literature to make sense of their position within prisons and to maintain a critical distance from the institutions they worked for. Social work interns would read theorists of punishment including Loïc Wacquant and Erving Goffman as part of their training to work inside prisons.

But even when they argued that resocialization did not exist, nobody claimed that it was meaningless, unimportant, ineffective, or undesirable. In fact, by denying resocialization's existence, these actors continually reaffirmed it as an ideal. "Resocialization does not exist" only works as a critique of prisons if you assume that it *should* exist, that any functioning or "humane" prison *must necessarily be* a rehabilitative one. In fact, there was little doubt among prison staff and volunteers that resocialization was both desirable and effective, that properly organized and funded projects could transform the life trajectories of those in prison. The value of resocialization as a social good and a practical goal was never in question. Instead, the gesture toward its absence was an attempt to make prisons and courts accountable to their own objectives, holding out hope for some future model of imprisonment that would be legitimate precisely because it was, *finally*, reformative.

At the same time, my interlocutors also continually ran up against the explanatory limits of resocialization's nonexistence. The formerly incarcerated author Samuel Lourenço Filho exemplifies and confronts this dilemma in his book *Resocialized in the City of Chaos*, a reflection on his experiences during and after the twelve years he was held inside Rio's prisons.[21] Across the account, Lourenço grapples with the inadequacy of claiming either that resocialization exists or that it does not, even veering between positions within the same sentence: "It seems like this resocialization business doesn't even exist. If it doesn't exist, let's end it here—but it doesn't end, let's debate this term. And if it does exist, when does it begin?"[22] That tension drives the account forward, as he continually cycles between describing resocialization, critiquing it, denouncing its nonexistence, and offering a kind of ironic detachment from the concept. There is no resolution. Instead, the author lets the contradiction hang, turning it back onto the reader with the provocation to "answer me, before the end, was I resocialized or not?"[23] As Lourenço's narrative reveals, and as I describe here, resocialization routinely failed—failing to work, failing to cohere into anything close to a framework of support or care, and failing even to exist. But it did many other things. So much of Rio's prisons operated as if the concept were both real and viable that its presence, phantom or otherwise, defined how confinement was governed and experienced.

This is resocialization, not as a substantial program of support but as a set of unfulfilled promises. On the one hand, it offers a defense of the incarcerated person, affirming them as worthy of care, respect, and support not because of who they are but who they might become. That future person becomes the justification for the present one's claims to humanity, citizenship, and rights. They look a lot like a wage laborer, a responsible parent in a nuclear, heterosexual family, and a churchgoer—but above all, like someone who has turned their back on the "world of crime"[24] and built a stable life within the bounds of social respectability. The person in the present is essentially an incubator, the keeper of a potential waiting to be discovered, cultivated, and brought out into the world. This is the promise that self-actualization and security are fundamentally the same thing, that the two might have diverged, but could still rejoin at some point on the horizon, if only the prison system could properly prepare them for this reunion.

Then there is the promise of incarceration itself, the insistence—almost two centuries after the construction of Brazil's first penitentiary, and forty years after legislation marking a new, "progressive" model of punishment—

that the continuing, systematic violations of law in Brazil's prisons, as well as the harms it has dealt to its captives, their families, and their communities, are not evidence of its failures or its true purpose but signs of its unrealized potential. It is the stubbornly persistent quest for the prison yet to come, for a better, more "humane" kind of captivity, constantly frustrated but always renewed; the insistence of a prison psychologist that, if only she had the resources to do her job, she might actually make a real difference to the lives of her imprisoned clients; or the placard reading *The System Must Be Resocialized*, held in the grip of the mother of an imprisoned man as she marched in protest around Rio's Justice Tribunal, surrounded by other family members holding up citations of prison law.

These promises also bring forth a demand: that the incarcerated person continually prove their commitment to becoming the version of themself that law, bureaucracy, and prison staff have foretold. Judges, prosecutors, public defenders, and staff repeat this demand in different forms. It both fuels and feeds off their concern that they might be duped, that their imprisoned clients or patients are just putting on a show, following the script of resocialization without ever meaningfully dedicating themselves to it. Demands and doubts are wired into penal bureaucracy through a set of psychosocial instruments that claim to measure, analyze, and evaluate the incarcerated person's aptitude or willingness to change. To be imprisoned in Brazil is to be caught by these instruments, to be taken hostage by the promises of reform.

To understand this, we might begin with the basic shape of a prison sentence itself, the way that people move through and out of captivity in Brazil. This is the typical path that someone follows as they "progress" through their imprisonment. Figure I.2 represents, in a simplified form, the basic stages of a sentence in Brazil. After the criminal trial, most are assigned to either a "closed" or "semi-open" prison unit, a decision that rests on length and nature of the sentence. From that point until the end of parole, their sentence is characterized by a slow "progression" through successive stages that ostensibly relax the binds of confinement, in accordance with the law's vision of "harmonious social integration."[25] None of these movements are automatic; instead, they rely on the incarcerated person's capacity to demonstrate that they have reformed, that they no longer present a danger to society.

This is Brazil's version of "progressive" imprisonment, a model that finds

FIGURE I.2. Typical stages of "progression" through a prison sentence. Source: Author.

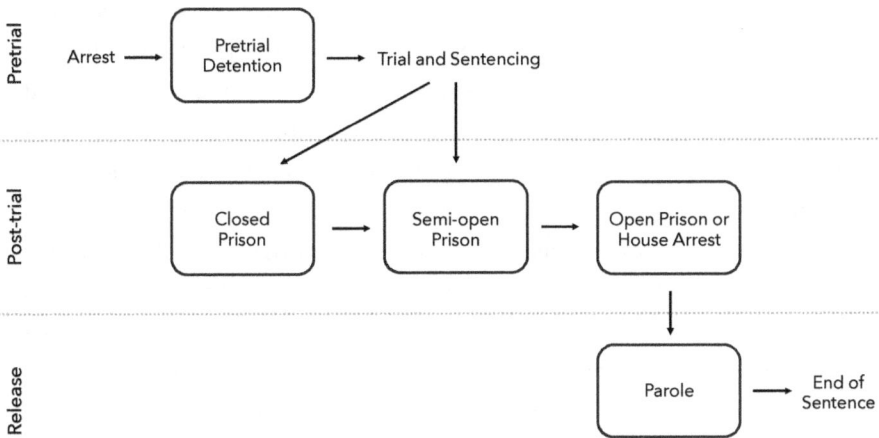

other expressions across most prison systems in the world. While some of its elements were established in Brazil before 1984, that was the year they found their most cohesive expression in the Law of Penal Execution (Lei de Execução Penal, or LEP), which attempted to modernize the administration of punishment across the country. Chapter 1 explores the idea of progress and the impact of the LEP in more detail. For now, I will highlight that this law cemented the presence of a set of actors who were responsible for both evaluating imprisoned people and providing "assistance" to them, "with the objective of preventing crime and orienting the return to coexistence with society."[26] Social workers, psychologists, and psychiatrists had been employed within prisons across the country before this point, but the LEP was the first legislation that outlined their professional responsibilities and mandated their presence. The new guarantee of religious freedom within the LEP also brought in a stream of evangelical missionaries who reshaped the landscape of punishment in the country. Finally, the LEP reinforced the right of imprisoned people to legal representation, giving Brazil's Public Defense Office a clear mandate for work within the system.

In this book I sometimes use the phrase *resocialization workers* to refer to the group of actors recruited into Brazil's prisons by the LEP. There is a limit to its utility, since it glosses over critical differences between the professions. Social workers, psychologists, and psychiatrists—collectively referred to as "technicians" (*técnicos*)—were paid employees of Rio's prison administration, and their work was split between treating and evaluating imprisoned people, although the demands of the latter often pushed the former to the sidelines. Public defenders worked inside prisons but were not employed by the administration itself, and their responsibilities largely involved advocating for their clients within a progressive sentencing model. Religious assistance was volunteer-based and largely untethered from any legal responsibilities, although it still fell under the auspices of "treatment" and was overseen by social workers. Across these positions and the traditions of knowledge or intervention that were unevenly distributed between them, fault lines emerged over both the nature and the stakes of reform. But despite their differences, they converged at two key points. First, all worked under the LEP's mandate for providing "assistance" to incarcerated people. Second, they shared a sense of solidarity with one another as defenders and advocates of both imprisoned people and the project, or at least the idea, of resocialization.

The fact that those charged with reforming imprisoned people would also be personally invested in such a mission is hardly surprising. But for someone caught in the system like Diogo to do the same—to speak of himself as an unfulfilled promise, to couch his own humanity in the invocation of a future, reformed self—poses a different kind of problem. When those in prison seem to share, even partially, in the self-proclaimed objectives of their captors, scholars often describe these dispositions with discomfort, isolating them in a cocoon of qualifiers before attempting to explain them away.[27] Some suggest that any positive meaning found within prison indirectly reflects a trauma suffered outside its walls, an injury so great that confinement provides a sanctuary against it.[28] Others have argued that attachment to redemptive narratives represents an almost desperate attempt to rescue something of value from the otherwise mortifying experience of imprisonment.[29] Then again, these expressions of penitence and rehabilitation might also be a learned and enforced "script" that those in prison reproduce and potentially subvert for their own purposes.[30]

Such interpretations maintain a distance between the incarcerated person and rehabilitative discourse, attempting to "rescue" the former from the latter. They also mark a refusal on the part of the researcher to be seduced by rehabilitation, an effort to build analysis outside the self-serving categories and frames of reference served up by governments, prisons, and courts. They therefore rely on what we might call, following Paul Ricoeur, a "hermeneutics of suspicion"—an approach to knowledge that takes the form of uncovering hidden truths from the veil of misrecognition.[31] These analyses hold back on any endorsement or affirmation of the commitments that some people in prison make to projects of self-transformation or reform, and instead search for truth against the grain of what they say and do. But in doing so, they also replicate, in both form and content, the incredulity that animates prisons themselves. Criminal justice demands to know the captive person but can never entirely believe the confessions that it extracts.[32] To understand rehabilitation as a façade, something that must be seen past or beyond, reproduces that disbelief, drawing us into the same modes of suspicion that emerge out of the concept itself. This is the same stance taken up by lawyers, judges, prison psychologists, and parole officers, who study incarcerated people's narratives of self-transformation for markers of insincerity or misplaced confidence in an attempt to uncover the person hiding underneath.

In highlighting these similarities, I am not building an argument for, or an endorsement of, resocialization. This book makes no claim about whether Brazil's prisons are "truly" reformative, nor does it evaluate the successes and failures of specific projects and protocols. It takes its cue from decades of prison abolitionist work that has pushed us to think through the uses of reform beyond the question of whether it "works." This scholarship has underscored how the historical back-and-forth between "more reform" and "more punishment" is underwritten by a common refrain—*more*—that has justified a continued investment into punishment.[33] At the same time, rehabilitative, educational, and therapeutic programs have been deployed within prisons to preempt and blunt more radical demands for change by channeling outrage into ameliorative policies.[34] Rehabilitation also inevitably forces a triage, cleaving between those who are deemed worthy of redemption and those who are punished for their supposed incapacity to change.[35] My aim is to build on these insights with a focus on the routine processes of punishment, grappling with resocialization as it unfolds from one moment to the next. I chart a path through Rio's prisons to understand what resocialization *does*—the temporalities that it folds into the operations of punishment, and the predicament of those bound by its promises and its demands. I don't think that resocialization is an as-yet unrealized vision that, upon its arrival, will either free us or redeem us from the violence wrought by incarceration. Instead, I am grappling with a different kind of problem: namely, that resocialization is already here.

Held in the Breach

About six months after I met Diogo, I was back in René Dotti, sitting in front of a stage in a large yellow room known as the "education hall," a space we will return to a few times in this book. I had been invited to a special event: a performance that Diogo had organized and directed over the last few months with a theater group called Project Overcome (Projeto Superar). A minute after I arrived, the director of the prison's small school picked up the microphone that was lying at the front edge of the stage and, without concealing her impatience, announced to nobody in particular that the event's allotted time was limited, that the show had to start immediately. Most of the audience was already seated, with about eighty incarcerated people present, although the front row of plastic chairs was reserved for outside visitors like me. So when the orange curtains parted, I had a close-up view of the stage, which stood a few feet above the audience.

The action began below, on our level: Two actors walked down the central aisle of the audience toward the stairs leading up to the stage, where another pair, playing the role of prison guards, patted them down.[36] This same action was mirrored above, as the play's protagonist, a young travesti, entered from back-stage and raised her arms to receive a body search from a third guard. The three found each other at the front of the stage, now transformed into the visiting area of a prison, and embraced. The acoustics of this hall were awful, and while some actors were able to project their voices, others were lost in the whir of the fans mounted along the side walls, even for those sitting at the front row like me. But the audience followed the gist of the story through the words that pierced the buzz, the actors' expressions, and their familiarity with the scene itself. Luana, the protagonist, had recently been imprisoned. In this opening scene, we were witnessing the first visit of her parents, who held their arms over her shoulder and tried to comfort her. But for the moment, Luana was inconsolable at the prospect of serving her twenty-three-year prison sentence, and pushed back their words of encouragement, her own voice crackling with despair.

After a short while, they left (and were patted down again by the guards waiting at the bottom of the stairs) while Luana sat in the center of the stage, alone and struggling with her own despair. Diogo and another actor emerged from the curtains on either side and began to circle her, hissing out her own internal monologue: "It's hopeless"; "You have nothing to live for"; "Why don't you just kill yourself?" But Luana picked up a book from the floor and used it to wave them off, blowing them back behind the curtains. Then she opened its covers and started reading in silence. Gradually, a smile came over her face. In the final scene, Luana's mother came up the stairs and joined her in the visiting area. Luana told her that she had begun to hope again, not only that she could change but that she could also transform other people. The two sat down in the same place onstage where Luana had once broken down; she opened the book, and they began to read together.

As the audience applauded and music began to play, the other actors returned to the stage and began to dance energetically, facing us. Once the noise died down, they stood off to the sides—except for Diogo, the director, who wiped tears from his eyes, thanked God for the opportunity to be present today, and expressed his gratitude for our attention. "Who would have thought," he asked, "even two years ago, that this little Black kid from the favela would be here today, writing, making theater? Everyone here, every single person, has the capacity to change." When he finished speaking, he hugged his fellow actors, and a band set up in front of the stage to play "The Girl from Ipanema." A few hours later, back in my apartment, I would write in my field notes that the music "seemed liberatory in a way that was completely out-of-place with the space." But the moment didn't last for long. The school director took the microphone again and told us all to pack up and leave—repeatedly, so that her voice drowned out the band, who had now switched to gospel music. A guard ushered us out of the hall. Diogo, the actors, and the imprisoned audience returned to their cells. I was escorted out of the prison with the other visitors.

When Diogo spoke of himself from the perspective of "two years ago," he was referencing the moment he was first imprisoned. It must have looked something like the experience of Luana, the protagonist in his play. Both had been given a sentence of twenty-three years. Unlike Luana, Diogo had lost his father to police violence at age ten; soon after, he found himself estranged from the rest of his family and living on the streets. A sister had come to see him once or twice when he was first imprisoned, but he hadn't received any visitors for a while. Diogo was also illiterate when he entered prison, although he quickly became an avid reader and writer. The counterpoint between past and present allowed Diogo to position himself as living proof of the capacity for change. When I saw him in René Dotti, he would speak to me emphatically and quickly, aware that our time together was limited. Project Overcome was one of a few ongoing plans of his that also included building a small library, putting together a prison band, and a constant fervor for writing. This energy emanated from an increasingly (and, at one point, alarmingly) gaunt body, a result of the food he was forced to eat, as well as a tuberculosis infection that had taken far too long to diagnose and treat. But when he cast a travesti to act out his story, when he asked "who would have thought" that a young Black man from the favelas could become an icon of human potential, he was also responding to a question of legibility: In whose lives, whose families and communities, is the capacity for reform located?

Like Diogo, Brazilian legislation treats the potential for resocialization as universal. Criminal and prison law outline the convicted person as a law-abiding citizen in potentia, to be judged and treated according to their future as much as their past. As Colonel Gilson and many others noted, the country has had no legislated death penalty and no life sentence since 1890.[37] Prison staff and administrators would often recite these facts as evidence of the progressive virtues of Brazil's legal system and as signs of the nation's commitment to redemption. And yet Brazil is also extraordinarily violent toward those marked as criminal. Most Brazilians endorse the popular phrase "A good criminal is a dead criminal."[38] Television channels broadcast live footage of people being gunned down by police, while reports of these killings routinely identify which victims had a *passagem*, a record of "passage" through the criminal justice system. *Passagem* circumvents the need for any other information about the victim; it communicates that these killings were not only comprehensible but legitimate, regardless of their legality. Popular discourse and "talk of crime" treat criminality as malignant, a force that must be excised from the social body and destroyed.[39]

To affirm resocialization is to counter the assertion that the only possible redemption for those marked as criminal is in death. Resocialization workers and volunteers in Rio's prisons inverted the Brazilian adage by claiming in conversations and public engagements that "a good criminal is a *resocialized* criminal." They understood that they were pushing against a tide of popular hostility against their clients, students, or congregants. So did imprisoned people like Diogo, who carried the added awareness that this tide could very well kill them. The promise of Diogo's potential, and of that held by those inside Rio's prisons generally, turned upon a "future anterior" mode of ethical engagement—a judgment of the present from the perspective of some future point when suffering and struggle might be seen, in retrospect, as having been worth it.[40] But it seemed particularly difficult for the "little Black kid from the favela" to be reconciled with this horizon, and the burden of proving otherwise fell on them most heavily.

"To be human within developmentalist frames," as anthropologist Deborah Thomas observes, means "to be perfectible, and therefore always measured against the ideals of Western liberalism."[41] In Rio's prisons, this perfectibility took the form of a reorientation of one's life toward the acquisition of a set of markers of social respectability. But it was also framed in contradistinction to Blackness, and specifically to Black families and territories like Rio's favelas— sites that the prison and court systems still both saw as causes or vectors of crime. The Black majority within prisons were therefore caught between the expectation of reform and an institutionalized association between Blackness and crime in which they were "simply not imaginable as perfectible."[42] The impasse had immediate, material consequences for their sentences, restricting the possibility for house arrest or parole. The result was a routinized deferral, a "not yet" that permeated these institutions and that often took the form of the denial or postponement of early release.

The legal and moral impulse to resocialize thereby carries and recapitulates another unfulfilled promise: that of Black emancipation. In the wake of the formal abolition of slavery, it delays the possibility of Black freedom to some point on the horizon, and continually extends the juridical imposition of "terms and conditions" for Black life after the abolition of slavery, as well as the interdiction of those who might attempt to move beyond them.[43] Rinaldo Walcott identifies this condition as part of an ongoing historical era: the "long emancipation," a period characterized not by freedom but by the continual experience of its limit. The law reinscribes its own authority, as well as its domain over Black life and death, through the breach between freedom's assurance and its constant deferral. My argument is that prisons, in all their violence and their hope, are one institutional form that this breach takes.

Across the book, I follow people caught up in this breach, as well as some of those responsible for cultivating and enforcing it. But I also argue that this it is open to disruptions and reconfigurations, to being projected upon and appropriated toward different ends. People found ways to live both within and against it, forms of life that are not easily parsed as accommodation or resistance. Many, like Diogo, were invested in following through on resocialization's narrative arc, and saw their reform as a triumph of the will. This did not blunt their critiques of imprisonment. Instead, it became the vehicle through which they demanded recognition from the state and claimed authorship over their own futures. Others refused to be drawn into a redemptive vision that was stacked against them. Divine time, prophecy, and rebirth also crept into the breach, as Christian salvation reworked and, in some cases, eclipsed the conditional promises of reform. Finally, those who studied the progressive structure of imprisonment would occasionally find in its crevices a foothold to escape.

Marking Time

For the early modern social sciences at the turn of the twentieth century, crime posed a problem, one that was difficult to metabolize within budding theories of social order. The response was to reframe the figure of the criminal as something of a time traveler, out of sync with the present. For Cesare Lombroso's criminal anthropology, in particular, this figure was white Europe's internal "primitive," a vestige of its own atavistic origins.[44] Lombroso had an outsized impact on the development of Brazilian jurisprudence over the twentieth century. The elites of the early republic, propelled by theories of criminal anthropology and social Darwinism, were also concerned that a significant portion of Portuguese settlers had been exiled from their home country for their crimes, that these heritable criminal tendencies had polluted the Brazil's genetic "stock" and stifled any attempts at modernization.[45] Legislation framed the criminal as a subject in conflict with civilization's march of progress. It was only in the 1930s that society began to replace civilization as the object wounded by crime, and as the entity in whose name punishment was authorized.

This treatment of crime as an anachronism endures, both within and outside the social sciences. Rising crime rates in Brazil are portrayed by politicians and the media alike as signs of social regression. Brazilians often speak of specific crimes—most often robberies, drug commerce and corruption—as both root causes and symptoms of the nation's underdevelopment. Resocialization workers never openly referred to their clients as primitive or vestigial, but they explicitly spoke of and to them as children caught in a state of arrested development. In fact, many of these workers argued that resocialization was a misnomer, since most imprisoned people had "never been socialized to begin with." Within this reformative telos, the incarcerated person was an untimely, asocial (rather than antisocial) figure, someone who needed to be brought back into the contemporary moment.

There is an uncanny similarity between the cross-temporal encounter of the resocialization worker with the incarcerated person, and the ways my discipline, anthropology, has constructed its objects of study. Johannes Fabian famously describes the anthropological version of this encounter as the *denial of coevalness*: "a persistent and systematic tendency to place the referent(s) of anthropology in a Time other than the present of the producer of anthropological discourse."[46] For Fabian, anthropology framed social and cultural difference as a form of distance by conceiving its own knowledge through a "temporal slope," denying the possibility of coexistence within the same present. The same kind of temporal slope emerged in the psychologist's or social worker's written evaluations of clients, or in a penal judge's written justification for a denied application for parole.

This isn't the only affinity that anthropology shares with the methods and forms of knowledge that circulated through Rio's prisons. Many resocialization workers used the same scholarship that I read as a graduate student to reflect on their own positions, and they quoted it back to me during our conversations. Their suspicions of both the institution that employed them and the imprisoned people assigned to them mirrored the kind of "critical" stance I had been encouraged to take up as a scholar in training. Like the ethnographer's traditional toolkit, prisons and courts relied on semistructured interviews and life histories as methods of evidence-gathering. Currently and formerly incarcerated people met me only after passing through a string of interrogations from lawyers, judges, psychologists, and social workers, all of whom demanded that they trace out their pasts and futures so they could be known and judged. Their experiences with these representatives of criminal justice, and with the interview form itself, shaped how we could relate to one another. These are more than superficial resemblances. Brazil's prisons are social scientific institutions, drawing on its tools of analysis, shaped by various strands of social thought and expertise, and driven, in part, by a similar will to knowledge. The points of contact and the overlaps between these two disciplinary projects shed light on their overlapping histories and objectives; they are also an opportunity for anthropology to rethink the place of each within the other.

On Methods

I started my fieldwork for this project in May 2014 and finished it in December 2017. My focus was on three specific prisons designated for men, all of which were administered by SEAP, the state prison administration. While I visited another twelve prisons in the state (nine designated for men, three for women) and one juvenile detention facility, most of my fieldwork relates to these three. I also spent much of my time with formerly incarcerated people in their first months following release—in their homes, their churches, on the street, or at the parole office. Finally, I conducted research in SEAP's administrative departments; in the main offices of the Public Defense Office's Penitentiary System Nucleus (NUSPEN); in Rio's state and federal archives; and in the enormous, modernist structure in the city center known as the Justice Tribunal, which held the state's penal court (Vara de Execuções Penais, or VEP).

Although this is an ethnography of men's prisons, it is not an ethnography of men. For the most part, it centers the relationships between those imprisoned in Rio and resocialization workers, who were mostly white cisgender women.[47] I also worked with travestis and trans women who were held in men's prisons. Across these groups, questions of gender, femininity, kinship, and family constantly surfaced. But the experiences of those imprisoned in units designated for women are largely absent from this account, and the perspectives of family members of imprisoned people are limited. Families of those in prison are painfully aware that their actions on either side of the walls can result in reprisals for themselves or their loved ones, including having their visiting cards revoked. While a few of them appear in this book, many others were unwilling or uninterested in taking part in the project.

Most prisons in Brazil are named after prominent judges or legal scholars. Many of those figures sought drastic reforms to prisons over the last century and a half but ultimately found themselves memorialized by its expansion, with their names now adorning the hundreds of prisons built across the country in the last thirty years. In keeping with this tradition, I have named two of the prisons in which I conducted my fieldwork René Dotti and Tobias Barreto. The first is a "closed" unit and the site of Diogo's captivity during my fieldwork; the second is one among roughly a dozen "semi-open" penitentiaries in the state. These differing designations of closed and semi-open mean that the people imprisoned in René Dotti were generally held under longer sentences, while those in Tobias Barreto were often close to the date marking their eligibility to apply for parole or house arrest.

I first visited Tobias Barreto in 2014, after receiving authorization from SEAP for a series of one-day visits to different penitentiaries. I was given a tour by the deputy warden and was later left with the prison's social workers to pass the day. Two years later, I returned to spend twelve months working as an intern for the two public defenders responsible for the unit, Lívia and Ângela. Each spent one or two days a week working directly in the prison. I entered with them, alongside either their paralegal assistant or another intern. I spent most of my time in their office and in the surrounding administrative rooms, including the "classification" office, the offices of the warden and deputy warden, and those of the prison psychologists and social workers.[48] On other occasions, I visited the prison school, the soccer field outside, and one of the prison's two temples. I also spent time in Lívia and Ângela's shared office in the city center, where they filed petitions and met with family members of their clients.

By contrast, I accompanied two different groups in René Dotti. The first were members of Pastor Bruno's evangelical church, whom I joined during the services and events they ran within the prison. While I was with them, I spent most of my time in the evangelical temple located at the back of the prison. Second, I obtained preauthorization in late 2016 to work as a volunteer within a program known as Project Life. This status allowed me to quickly organize and receive permission to run activities as part of the project. Chapter 2 includes more detail on the structure of the project and the role of volunteers. While Project Life operated in many prisons across the state, and while I visited a dozen other prisons at least once as a volunteer, most of my work as part of this project was in René Dotti. After organizing a few events, the prison psychologist invited me to participate in what she called the LGBT Group, described in Chapter 5, which arranged regular meetings for incarcerated trans women, travestis, and cis gay men in the prison. Both groups met in the same large yellow hall with the stage and the bad acoustics.

I have chosen to keep the real name of the third prison discussed in the book, Crispim Ventino. During my fieldwork, it was the only "open" unit operating in the state of Rio de Janeiro, which makes it easily identifiable regardless of any pseudonym. I also never entered this prison. The unit was reserved for those who had been granted day release; I spent my time with them in the surrounding neighborhoods, or else traveling with them through the city. As the names of these security regimes suggest, each prison sits at a different point along the progressive scale of imprisonment, part of this process of "opening" up to the outside world. But none of them is any more or less of a prison than the other. Instead, each one spotlights different aspects of resocialization, and of the project of incarceration more broadly.

My letter correspondence with Diogo was one among a variety of documentary forms of research. As I explore in the following chapter, prisons operate through a constant production and circulation of files: case records, sentencing certificates, federal and state laws, writs of habeas corpus, reports, *catuques* (messages requesting assistance scribbled on scraps of paper or cardboard), documents stuffed in cabinets or stored in electronic databases. Through my work with the Public Defense Office, I followed the production and circulation of these files, particularly those that crossed the threshold between the prison administration and the court system. My own presence and movement through Rio's prisons is also now written into this archive: My applications for research authorization were filed by both the prison administration and the VEP, while the logbooks I signed at the front gates for every prison visit are now sitting in storage.

I never asked for, nor was I offered, entrance into the cells of any prison. More broadly, the ways I moved through each institution were shaped by who I was with. On the days I worked as an intern for the two public defenders, my presence was never questioned by guards, and I was rarely searched upon entry (and never when leaving). Working for Project Life, by contrast, I kept authorizing documents with me at all times but was still forced to wait for up to an hour outside prison gates and repeatedly explain the basic premise of the project to a series of skeptical correctional officers. On more than one occasion, despite showing all my authorizing documents, guards barred my entry. Similar limits are placed not just on researchers but on certain prison staff and volunteers. Still, it is important to recognize that my movements were less restricted than those of imprisoned people and visiting family members, at least in the prisons where I conducted research.

While I worked with both resocialization workers and those held in the prison system, my focus on one or the other, in both my fieldwork and my writing, depends on the context. Given the limits to maintaining ethical working relationships with incarcerated people, the bulk of research that I conducted inside prisons concentrated on resocialization workers. Many of these workers were trained in the social science or adjacent fields. They tended to see me as an ally, someone who shared their perspectives on punishment. That affinity was also underwritten by a form of class and racial solidarity, the assumption of a common purpose and shared benevolence between me and other white, university-educated actors within the prison system, one that I interrogate across the book.

The experience of imprisoned people emerges largely from my fieldwork with formerly incarcerated people or those held under an "open" (day-release) regime of punishment. They also come through in artifacts like Diogo's letters—which, as far as either of us knew, were never opened or interfered with during our correspondence—as well as diaries, letters, and photos that people shared with me from their time in prison. Theater performances like the one described earlier, as well as Project Life workshops and music performances, offered another avenue to engage with the aspirations of incarcerated people and their relationships with resocialization workers. Many of those whom I met during their imprisonment were also released in the following months and years. In a few cases, I gained their permission to discuss our earlier interactions in prison at this point.

Brazil's prisons are sites of routinized physical violence, beatings, and torture against both incarcerated people and visitors. That mode of violence rarely pulls into focus in this book; instead, it sits along the edges, its traces running through many of the moments that I describe throughout. As an ethnographer, I was never a witness to it. I am also wary of the repeated and often sensationalized emphasis on violence that dominates accounts of imprisonment in Brazil and Latin America, one that leaves little room for understanding other dynamics of power and governance at play.[49] These narratives so often linger on the spectacle of Black suffering; in doing so, they tend to reinscribe its supposed inevitability, even in the attempt to denounce it.[50] One source of counternarratives can be found in the published works of currently and formerly incarcerated people in Rio de Janeiro, who reckon with torture while refusing to be subsumed by its logic.[51] Here, by contrast, I remain with another set of questions—including how the idea and the threat of physical violence is never far the work of resocialization.

This is not a systematic framework or blueprint for how, or whether, to conduct prison research. Instead, it was the product of an ongoing, uncomfortable negotiation of what was possible and what I saw as ethical within an overlapping array of regulatory frameworks and in the context of an institutional politics that was itself constantly shifting. Those tensions, and my provisional responses, cannot be quarantined here, since they are constitutive of the entire research project. Instead, they continually resurface across different chapters, and in different guises.

Outline of the Book

This book follows resocialization across different domains of imprisonment, in conversation with workers, volunteers, and incarcerated people. Each chapter examines a different permutation of resocialization's promise. The first three focus on a specific process or project that emerges out of the injunction to reform. **Chapter 1: The Promise of Paper**, explores the work of public defenders as they labor, through documents, to secure parole for their clients. It focuses on three files—the sentencing certificate, the Disciplinary Record Transcript, and the criminological exam—that collectively made the future of the imprisoned client available as evidence. I argue that these files channeled a mode of paranoid reasoning, one that emerged over the twentieth century alongside the gradual consolidation of resocialization as a legal ideal. The production and circulation of these documents also rested on a racialized shorthand in which markers of Black life signified an apparent unwillingness to reform. For those confined in Tobias Barreto, paper constituted both a material assurance of imminent "progress" through their sentences and the tool by which their futures were scrutinized and deferred.

Chapter 2: Prison Psychology's Praxis turns to the work of psychologists through Project Life, an educational program in which I participated as a volunteer. This program envisioned participants as empty vessels waiting to be filled, as part of a broader pedagogy of tutelage. Whereas Project Life offered space for psychologists to elaborate and enact a criticism of incarceration, these same workers suppressed imprisoned people's own critiques, marking them as potentially violent "hate speech." But those confined in Rio's prisons were still able to use Project Life to produce another kind of intervention, one that presented resocialization as a triumph of survival.

Chapter 3: Faith and the Weight of the World considers how evangelical life and labor support resocialization, even as they reshape its horizons. Evangelicals overturned the juridical precepts of criminal responsibility and personhood, even promising those who converted that their case files would literally combust. This is, I argue, a spiritual geography anchored in three coordinate points of prison, church, and world. But unlike secular resocialization workers, evangelical volunteers and imprisoned people saw the world as a fallen landscape rather than a space of belonging. The chapter also considers how missionaries came to understand and articulate the hope of salvation through discourses of whiteness.

Chapter 4: If I Were His Mother asks why both resocialization workers and imprisoned men articulated the relationships between themselves through the figures of mother and son. Motherhood provided a metaphor and a paradigm of resocialization, a domain marked by care, violence, and infantilization. I survey these invocations of motherhood and consider the paradoxical centrality of maternity within men's prisons, arguing that both are grounded in Brazilian anxieties surrounding the family, including the ability of Black women to act as caregivers. The chapter also underlines the role that social science played in buttressing and giving form to these concerns since the early twentieth century.

Chapter 5: Evasion follows the path of travestis through men's prisons—a path that demonstrates how resocialization's vision of social life holds no space for trans futures. Travestis became rendered by resocialization's plot as incorrigible, a classification that often trapped them within the system, yet they also demonstrated how the nominally progressive structure of confinement could provide footholds for escape. In particular, I consider evasion, the practice by which travestis and others routinely fled captivity, often only for a few days or weeks, before returning to prison of their own accord. This cycle of escapes and returns brings the incomplete nature of Black emancipation into focus. While evasions offered no definitive escape from Brazil's project of incarceration, they produced an alternative model of inhabiting its predicament.

Finally, the **Epilogue: Resocialize to Conquer the Future** examines how resocialization took new forms, and often unraveled, after release from prison. Whereas imprisonment was driven by various forms of speculative labor, these kinds of anticipation encountered other temporal horizons outside prison and directly collided with an atmosphere of crisis that seemed to evaporate individual and collective futures. The epilogue, and the book, ends with a reflection on the narrative impulse toward redemption in both prisons and ethnography and asks what other conclusions we might reach for instead.

The Promise of Paper

Depending on the day, it was either Lívia or Ângela who picked me up in their car from the subway station, but otherwise the routine was the same. Together with one of these public defenders, I made my way in the early morning down Avenida Brasil, the arterial road that leads from the city center into Rio's sprawling North and West Zones. On both sides, we were flanked by a stream of graffiti that advertised various fortune-telling services, interspersed with promotions for local evangelical churches and reminders that *only Jesus can remove your chains*. After about forty minutes, we would veer off down a side street, heading toward the gates of a prison complex popularly known as Bangu.[1] The complex was inaugurated in 1988, an act that consolidated a few penitentiaries already existing in the area. It grew rapidly in the 1990s with the construction of new units to compensate for the deactivation of prisons in Rio's city center and the remote island of Ilha Grande, and again in the 2000s, with the abolition of police lockups and the transfer of those still waiting for their trial into units operated by the prison administration. These expansions chipped away at the neighboring environmental conservation area to make way for new prisons. By the time I began my fieldwork, the sprawling complex had become one of the most infamous sites among Brazil's growing network of prisons.

We checked in with the guards at these front gates, passing a giant line of visitors that had, at that point, been waiting for hours to enter, and drove into the compound that held half of all the prisons in Rio de Janeiro, and almost two-thirds of its imprisoned population. Inside this carceral city was our destination: the semi-open penitentiary that I call Tobias Barreto. Sitting in the trunk of our car was a carry-on suitcase, weighed down by about five hundred pages of documents that Lívia or Ângela had printed at home the night before. It was my job to pull the suitcase out and wheel it into the prison. Our first stop after signing in was a room called the classification office. A large table covered with papers dominated the center of the room, while two walls were lined with filing cabinets and a pair of computers sat in a corner. After swinging the suitcase up onto the table, the public defenders would open it and distribute a bundle of files to the correctional officers on duty. We received another stack in exchange before heading down the hall to our assigned office, where an anxious line of imprisoned clients had already started forming.

Two years earlier, on my first visit to Tobias Barreto, the deputy warden had led me around the prison, starting with this classification office. One of the guards working on a computer looked up to explain to me that this was the "heart of the prison." But it was only later, when I established my routine with the public defenders, that I began to understand the weight of the guard's metaphor. The room was certainly important within an institution that dedicated an enormous amount of energy to a constant process of documentation. But if it was the heart, it also lay at the center of a vast circulatory system, pumping files both within the prison and into the offices of lawyers, administrators, and courts— and the suitcase was one of its vessels.

This chapter is about paperwork: the labor that is invested in documents and files, as well as the work that paper accomplishes in its travels. Incarceration is an intensely bureaucratic enterprise; as Sora Han argues, punishment "bears a certain materiality of writing through which social identification, political imagination, and both mundane and spectacular statecraft are performed."[2] Rio's prisons and courts held their captives in place not just with concrete walls and iron bars but with an interlinked set of filing systems. These included the one used by the prison administration itself, as well as a separate database employed by defenders, public prosecutors, and Rio's penal court. Progress through a prison sentence and toward release depended on movement within and across these systems.

Since 1984, Brazilian legislation has maintained a "progressive" system of punishment in which sentences are divided into distinct stages. Passage through them ostensibly represents a gradual relaxation of confinement, culminating in early release under conditions of parole or house arrest. But progressive incarceration also demands an evaluation of the imprisoned person, including an account of their past and potential future. In countries like the United States, this demand is partially met by summoning the imprisoned person to account for themself in the form of a parole hearing.[3] In Brazil, the decision rests entirely at the hands of a judge within a Court of Penal Execution (Vara de Execuções Penais, or VEP), and is based on an evaluation of documents. Here I follow those documents as they enact the progressive mandate of the law. Along this path, I also consider how incarcerated people are transformed into evidence and chart the forms of belief and disbelief that files enable.

Lívia and Ângela both worked for the Penitentiary System Nucleus (Núcleo do Sistema Penitenciário, or NUSPEN), the branch of Rio's Public Defense Office that represented those who had received a conviction (as opposed to those still awaiting trial). Collectively, the pair worked with all those in Tobias Barreto who did not have private legal representation, about 90 percent of the prison's population. I began to work with them in late 2016, after receiving the authorization of the prison administration, the VEP, and NUSPEN itself. Each defender visited the prison at least one day a week. I followed them on these visits, and in the central NUSPEN office where they spent the remainder of the working week, over the course of a year.

As legal representatives for those in prison, and as the only agents of the judiciary with a continuous physical presence inside the system itself, public defenders were the main point of contact between prisons and the Court of Penal Execution. They were also the primary channel of communication between these two bureaucratic institutions. The carry-on suitcase held an array of files, ranging from requests for medical attention to logs of recorded work hours and writs of habeas corpus. But three documents made up the vast bulk of its contents: sentencing certificates, Disciplinary Record Transcripts (Transcrições de Ficha Disciplinar, or TFDs), and criminological exams.[4] The form, production, and circulation of these documents made the promise of eventual release tangible within an institution of confinement. They also determined how incarcerated people were made available to a legal gaze as objects of knowledge, evaluation, and intervention. This chapter examines each of the three documents in turn, in order to understand the work they accomplished within the prison. But first, I turn to the historical development of a progressive model of imprisonment itself, and to the evidence-making processes that it has come to demand.

The Progress of Progress

For those held in Rio's prisons, and for those who work in them, *progress* has a very clear definition. Whether as a noun (*progresso*) or a verb (*progredir*), the term refers to the forward momentum through confinement. Each stage of a prison sentence corresponds to a "regime" of punishment—what in English would generally be called a security level. These range from "closed" prisons, characterized by strict security protocols, to "open" imprisonment, which in Rio corresponded to either day release or house arrest, to parole. Movement along this path also corresponds to the reacquisition of various rights. Tobias Barreto was designated as semi-open, something of an intermediary phase. Most of those confined in the unit had progressed there from a closed unit, and most were waiting for their opportunity to progress again.

Today, the organization of individual sentences—and, by extension, entire prison systems—through different regimes or phases is common worldwide. Historians of incarceration often refer to it as the British model, although it arguably has two origins—one in the colonies, the other in the metropole. In 1840, the British captain Alexander Maconochie implemented the first formally gradated model of punishment through what he termed the *mark system* in the penal colony of Norfolk Island. The system established five stages for a sentence, beginning with strict imprisonment and culminating with a "ticket of leave on parole," which effectively amounted to a conditional pardon.[5] Back in England, Pentonville Prison first opened in 1842 as the site of a similar experiment, one that broke up prison sentences into differential regimes. While drawing on the model of absolute silence and collective labor first trialed in Auburn, New York, Pentonville also departed from it by splitting sentences into two phases, the first to be completed in solitary confinement, and the second in shared cells.[6]

These two experiments may appear as relatively insignificant, technical modifications to the brute fact of confinement. But they represented a significant rupture in how states, empires, and prison reformists understood the experience of imprisonment itself. Before this moment, a prison sentence represented a single, solid block of time. Moreover, it rested on a conception of time as both a universal possession and a fungible quantity.[7] This meant that three years in prison for one person could be considered equally harsh as three years for another but half as severe as a six-year sentence. By experimenting with progression, one month in prison was no longer the same as any other. Instead, time began to bend toward the moment of release with the promise of gradual movement through different stages. This movement was rarely automatic; instead, it transformed the single act of conviction into a series of judgments, each of which required some analysis of the imprisoned person themselves.

At this point, such shifts were still distant from Brazil, which had only recently embarked on its own project of prison construction. The House of Correction (Casa de Correção), the first penitentiary built in Latin America, was proposed by the Society for the Defense of Liberty and National Independence of Rio de Janeiro soon after the establishment of Brazil's first criminal code in 1830.[8] The Society's goal was to consolidate houses of detention across the city that variously held indebted people, homeless people, and enslaved and recaptured Africans and their descendants within a new penitentiary model. In a city with a large Black majority at the time, the Society also promoted the House of Correction as a solution to the "insolence" of the enslaved and "free Africans" (*africanos livres*),[9] including their apparent disrespect for the police, and to the uprisings that, it was feared, could result from public gatherings on the city streets.[10] It was planned as a continuation of state and slaveholding dominion, and as a new tool to limit Black mobility within the city. As implied in the name, the House of Correction was also proposed as a site of moral improvement. But the reformative impulse was, at this point, centered on the supposedly ennobling effects of prison labor rather than sculpting the time of a sentence through progression.

Following the formal abolition of slavery and the end of the Empire of Brazil soon after, a new criminal code was introduced in 1890. This code substituted the authority of police for that of slaveholders by directly criminalizing Afro-Brazilian cultural practices, including the martial art of capoeira and religious movements such as Candomblé, summarized as the "practice of spiritism, magic, and sorcery."[11] Listed within the same category of crime was idleness (*vadiagem*), which was now punishable by up to fifteen days' imprisonment. But the code also drew heavily on examples from the United States and Europe. One of its imports was the first outline of a progressive system; Article 50 stated that "those condemned to prison for a period exceeding six years and who have completed half the sentence, demonstrating good behavior, may be transferred to an agricultural penitentiary to complete the remainder of their punishment."[12]

The decree was followed by a series of laws that gradually shifted the structure of prison sentences. Brazil introduced parole for the first time in 1924, with a new decree proclaiming its stated objective to "stimulate the convicted to live honestly in liberty, reintegrating gradually into the society of free men, maintained by the fear of returning to prison."[13] Here, too, eligibility for parole was pegged to an assessment of good behavior. But this was the first time that the requirements of such an assessment were formalized by law. A report was required, which would be written by the prison warden and include the following details:

1. The particular circumstances leading to the penal infraction that may be of importance for the appreciation of the nature of the inmate.

2. The character of the parolee, revealed through their history, as well as criminal practice, oriented by both the psychic and anthropological nature of the inmate (tendency to crime, brutal instincts, influence of their surroundings, customs, level of emotion, etc.).

3. The behavior of the convicted person in prison, their docility or rebellion in the face of discipline, aptitude for work, and relations with companions and workers of the establishment.

4. The affective relations of the convicted (family, friends, etc.).

5. The economic, professional, and intellectual situation of the inmate.

6. Plans for after parole, particularly future vocation.[14]

Most of these criteria have remained remarkably stable from 1924 to the present. This includes behavior—defined primarily through interactions with prison authorities—and the tethering of progress to the incarcerated person's plans for release. Wardens and judges used these reports to discriminate between incarcerated people, including those convicted for the same crime. One clear result was a deepening in the divide between Black and white pathways through their prison sentences. Release records demonstrate that white men were disproportionately classified as well-behaved and therefore eligible for parole, while incarcerated Black men were far more likely to spend the entirety of their sentence—or, in some cases, even longer—in prison.[15]

There was, however, one crucial change over the next three decades. Whereas responsibility for producing the report initially fell onto the warden, the midtwentieth century brought in new professionals and new forms of expertise to accomplish the task. The first was psychiatry. The physician Heitor Carrilho was an instrumental figure in establishing the branch of medicine as a necessary tool for understanding the "personality" of the criminal. He saw the incarcerated person as an individual in conflict with society—a term largely understood along Durkheimian lines as a moral-institutional order.[16] Beginning in the 1940s, the psychiatrist's report began to supplement, and eventually supplant, that of the warden as a tool for determining eligibility for progression. This shift was consolidated in 1957 with the first comprehensive federal law governing the administration of prisons across the country. For the first time, legislation mandated the presence of "psychotechnicians" within the administration of a penitentiary; their primary responsibility was generating evaluations of those held under its custody.

Brazil's punitive landscape shifted dramatically during the years of the military dictatorship, most notably through the criminalization of activists and any unregulated political dissent. Yet the legislation governing prisons remained largely unchanged. It was only during the transition to democracy that legislative reform resulted in the Law of Penal Execution (Lei de Execução Penal), more commonly referred to as the LEP. This law is still in force today, albeit with some alterations. As part of a transition to Brazil's new democratic project, and echoing reforms in other institutions, the LEP made progress a central aspect of imprisonment. In its first article, it identifies two objectives for punishment: "the implementation of the terms of the sentence or criminal decision, and the provision of conditions for the harmonious social integration of the convicted and the interned."[17] Implementation is a technical duty, the execution of the terms of a sentence. The second objective, however, aims for a reconciliation between the individual and society. The LEP thereby brought treatment to the forefront of prison administration, at least in the letter of the law. In practical terms, this meant codifying new gradients and regimes of punishment, including parameters for closed, semi-open, and open forms of confinement. For example, according to the LEP, those held in a semi-open prison like Tobias Barreto are legally guaranteed the opportunity to work and study outside prison, and to move more freely through the unit during the day. The LEP also prescribed a series of evaluations to be conducted by correctional officers, *técnicos* ("technicians," an umbrella term that replaced *psychotechnicians* to designate psychiatrists, psychologists, and social workers) and penal judges, a group of actors who now collectively determined eligibility to progress through a sentence.

The history of legal reform is not a history of how punishment has been experienced or governed. Guarantees written into legislation regarding education, treatment, and work were, and still are, largely unavailable for most. For instance, regardless of what had been set out in the law, nobody in Tobias Barreto was able to leave the prison for work or study during my fieldwork. Furthermore, the LEP established no penalties for officials or administrators who did not carry out its mandate. For the prison workers and activists I met during my fieldwork, the LEP was a story of failed or incomplete implementation, one whose proper functioning might one day resolve many of the problems of the present. But while the breach between law and its application was obvious to virtually anyone who has encountered Rio de Janeiro's prisons, both workers and incarcerated people were still, in many ways, held accountable to the LEP's vision of progress.

Paper as a Sedative

The hour-long commute to Tobias Barreto with Lívia was always filled with conversation. While she drove, Lívia would ask about my family and the state of my research, share news from her colleagues or updates about her partner and two young children, and chat with any other passengers—her paralegal or the occasional law student intern. My trips with Ângela were quieter, although she was happy to answer any questions I had about her work. Both were white, middle-class women in their forties who had spent most of their careers as public defenders. They worked hard for their clients, although they also made a conscious effort to maintain cordial relationships with the prison guards and the warden. This meant, for example, that when we entered the prison, they would hand their bags over for inspection with a smile, despite a court ruling that lawyers should not be subject to these searches.

After leaving one bundle of documents at the classification office, we would head down the hall to the small room designated for public defenders, where an assistant was waiting for us, having already set up some tables and chairs while also keeping the line of clients in check. He was an imprisoned man who had been selected by the prison's faction, the collective of incarcerated people that established internal systems of governance and conduct. Lívia would always spend a few minutes chatting with him in the morning, asking after his family or any new issues within the prison. Ângela was always courteous as well, but she was also eager to get on with work, and I was never sure whether she knew this assistant's name. The two public defenders regularly called on him to fetch documents, speak with administrative staff, or make photocopies. But first, they would give him the largest stack of files from the suitcase: about two hundred pages, arranged alphabetically by the first names of the roughly forty clients who were scheduled to appear in the office that day.

These were the sentencing certificates (*atestados de pena*), and he was responsible for distributing them to clients as they waited in line. They ranged from two to eight pages long and included the same set of fields,[18] beginning with a series of identifiers:

INFORMATION
Code:
Name:

RG:[19]	Sex:

Mother's Name:
Father's Name:

Date of Birth:	Place of Birth:

Place of Internment:

The second section listed the current conviction(s) by both name and article number underneath each heading. It also included a history of all movements within the prison system, from the date of arrest and internment to the date of conviction, as well as any previous transfers or progressions between prisons:

CONVICTIONS

Penal Action/Articles:	Original Punishment:	Court:	Conviction Date:

PENDING CHARGES

Type of Charge:	Police Station:	Charge Nº:	Charge Date:

INTERNMENTS

Date of Interment: Type of Event: Additional Information:

Unless a client was waiting for the results of a pending criminal charge, this information was not particularly new, interesting, or relevant to them. Instead, they would turn to the final sections of the document: the sentence summary and regime progression. The act of pronouncing a criminal sentence involves a series of mathematical operations, beginning with the length of punishment determined by a judge, which falls within a range defined by criminal legislation. This initial number is then multiplied by a coefficient based on any aggravating or attenuating circumstances, such as the use or threat of violence. The product of this legal-mathematical operation is a number that establishes the "base date" of the sentence. But that date then forms the basis of a second operation, known as the *cálculo* (calculation), which partitions it to produce specific dates after which benefits, including eligibility for progression, become available. The calculation also brings two new factors into consideration: whether the person being sentenced is identified as a recidivist (that is, having completed another criminal punishment within the last five years), and whether the crime is categorized as "heinous."[20] In the case of a first-offense, nonheinous crime, one would be eligible to apply for transfer from a closed to a semi-open prison after serving one-sixth of a sentence, and for parole after one-third. Those convicted of a heinous crime, on the other hand, must serve at least three-fifths of a sentence to become eligible for parole. The calculation is only modified to correct for human error or when an incarcerated person is approved for sentence commutation or remission. The most important date appears at the end of the document, marking the projected eligibility for progression:

SUMMARY OF SENTENCE IMPLEMENTATION
Total Sentence:
Sentence Completed:
Sentence Remaining:
Total Days Detracted:
Total Interruptions:
Total Days Remitted:
Current Regime:

Harmonization:[21]

Interruption of Sentence:

Maximum Security Measures:

REGIME PROGRESSION:

Base Date:

Common Calculation:

Heinous, Typical:[22]

Heinous, Recidivist:

Projected Eligibility:

This was the information clients were looking for, and this is what they most often wanted to discuss with their legal representatives. Calculation partitioned and tabulated the future, producing a schedule for liberation. The physical presence of a sentencing certificate confirmed this fact. Public defenders had no legal obligation to bring the document into prison. It was generated automatically by the VEP, it attested to information that had already been established, and it initiated no particular action on its own. All the information present in the sentencing certificate was also available in the electronic database that Lívia and Ângela brought with them on their laptops, one that included much more detail regarding each case. But every public defender working for NUSPEN took part in this practice of printing hundreds of pages and distributing them to clients when visiting their designated prisons. The policy was an attempt to shape the terms of encounter between defenders and their clients, and to mitigate some of the tensions that arose between the two.

Lívia and Ângela each had a caseload of roughly nine hundred clients. This was a direct consequence of the exponential growth in Rio de Janeiro's prison population in the years leading up to my fieldwork, particularly between 2013 and 2016. Lawyers who had worked in prisons before that time, such as Lívia, constantly lamented the loss of their previous work routine. While prisons were crowded beyond their official capacities even then, Lívia felt that she still had the opportunity to develop closer relations with some of her clients. By 2017, defenders had developed a different kind of workflow, one that resembled an industrial production line for handling cases. The two defenders assigned to Tobias Barreto aimed to see each of their clients at least once every four months. Reaching this goal meant that they needed to speak to somewhere between forty and fifty clients every time they visited the prison. Even with the assistance of paralegals and interns, the result was that most incarcerated people had about five minutes, three times a year, to speak with their legal representatives.

For the public defenders, each meeting with a client was one short moment in a long day's work. For clients, this was the only opportunity they would have for months to speak with an agent of the judiciary. Incarcerated people were often nervous as they waited in line for their scheduled meeting. Many clients showed this anxiety in their faces and in their bodies, sitting nervously in their seats or moving restlessly as they waited. Lívia and Ângela saw it as the result of the inflated image many clients had of the power of public defenders within the judiciary. But it was also based on a well-founded mistrust of a system that produced errors and delays at every point in the process, compounded by the brief window they had to speak about their case with the only people who could act on their behalf. Applications for progress must be initiated by a lawyer. While the defense team adopted various measures to deal with the logistics of a constant flow of cases, many still fell through the cracks. As a result, they often did not catch when a client became eligible for parole, regime progression, or a "benefit" like Periodic Family Visitation. Criminal courts also regularly failed to send documents relating to a conviction over to the penal system, without which nothing could be done in terms of progression. Case files routinely contained significant errors that took weeks or even months to correct.

But the main risk was that a case would simply sit still (*parado*) in a desk or a desktop somewhere between NUSPEN, the public prosecutor's office, and the VEP. If the case stagnated, the person inside prison would also be stuck. A case had to move (*andar*) to get anything done. So a client had five minutes, three times a year, to look at their case file, check whether it was moving, and, if possible, jolt it back into circulation. Lívia and Ângela developed an array of strategies to minimize this tension and to assure clients that their cases were still moving, that they had not become lost in the system. Ângela deliberately cultivated a style of presentation and speech that was meant to exude professional authority. She worked quickly through the details of each client's case, noting upcoming dates and highlighting what the defense team had already accomplished. This allowed her to manage her time while still conveying competency and assurance, all wrapped up in language that was understandable but forceful. Lívia, by contrast, gave a little more time to each person. She generally asked clients if they understood the terms she was using, and would rotate her screen to give them a better view of the file she was working with, pointing with a pen to any instances of applications or petitions that had already been filed. As a result, her working day inside Tobias Barreto was consistently longer than Ângela's by about an hour.

The distribution of sentencing certificates was a key part of this work to manage tension. As a physical object that the client could keep after the meeting, the certificate offered a material assurance that went beyond the words of the defender herself. "Paper is the one thing that calms a prisoner," Lívia told me one morning as she drove us out to Tobias Barreto for the weekly visit. "Prisoners just like to go to their cell after seeing us to read their papers and see what's happening. It's the kind of information we should be giving." Most lawyers and paralegals within NUSPEN believed that many clients were unable to read or understand the details of these documents.[23] But by offering paper, by giving the file to a client, they also presented a sign that the case was moving, that they were not forgotten within the bureaucracy. As a prop for these encounters, the sentencing certificate would constantly draw their attention back to the calculation, highlighting the legal assurance of their impending release. The piece of paper continually focused clients' attention away from the present and toward this future date.

Good Behavior

The sentencing certificate offers a schedule of advancement through a sentence, but meeting the "objective" criteria is not enough to guarantee progress. The VEP also requires "subjective" evidence, an evaluation of the character of the incarcerated person. Despite several legislative reforms, there is little difference between the evidentiary demands of contemporary penal courts and those laid out by the 1924 decree described earlier. Both center on concepts of character, behavior, social relations, and plans for the future, none of which are defined by law.

The stack of papers that Lívia and Ângela left in the classification office each morning contained a series of requests for these documents. When they had run through their list of clients for the day, they would pass by the office again, pick up the requested files, and wheel them out of prison in the suitcase.

One of these was the Disciplinary Record Transcript (*Transcrição de Ficha Disciplinar* or TFD). Unlike the sentencing certificate, which is produced by the courts, this file is generated by the prison administration itself. Public defenders and private lawyers are responsible for bringing them out of prison and into the court system. The file begins, like the sentencing certificate, with the name of the incarcerated person, names of parents, and the same slew of government and prison identification numbers. Unlike the sentencing certificate, it includes a mug shot and identifies the imprisoned person's "color" (*cor*)—one of five official categories that map imperfectly onto racial identities in Brazil—and level of education:

Information Certified by the SEI[24]
ID: Name:

GRP Data[25]
RG: Registration: Date of Birth:
Name:
Parents' Names:
Nickname(s):
Other Name(s):
Place of Birth: Nationality:
Color: Profession:
Level of Instruction: Civil Status:

Internment Data
Prison Unit:
Situation:[26]

Its main purpose, however, is to measure and explain a person's behavior while in the prison system. In a single sentence, the TFD classifies each imprisoned person according to a regimented scale, using one of five categories—bad, neutral, good, excellent, and optimal. Underneath this classification, the document lists all recorded infractions that have determined this evaluation.

Behavioral Index
Classified on [dd/mm/yyyy] in [SEAPXX][27] with the behavioral index of [bad/neutral/etc.]

Disciplinary Infractions

Unit: Process Nº: Infraction Type:

Infraction Date: Description:

Punishment Date: Description:

Observations:

Infraction Type refers to one of three grades—minor, moderate, or serious—established by federal and state law. The *Description* fields cite relevant laws that define these specific infractions and outline the corresponding punishments (for example, "Law 7210, Article 52, Section III"). The fields of this section repeat for each successive infraction, listing them in reverse chronological order.

Work, study, or involvement in any therapeutic programs have no impact on the behavioral index. The only way to climb this ladder is to avoid incurring an infraction. For every six months that pass without incident, the person would move one rung higher on the scale. Inside prison, there was no concrete benefit for a rating higher than "good," which qualified the incarcerated person for work or study benefits. However, when the transcript passed through the hands of the judiciary as part of an application for progression, it became an important element in the prosecutor's opinion and the judge's final decision. The only movement that someone in prison could actively initiate along this scale was downward, by incurring a serious infraction that resulted in an automatic reclassification to "bad" behavior. In practice, infractions were most often listed as serious. "You can cough loudly during the count,"[28] Ângela once told me, "and they'll write you up for a serious infraction." This wasn't a hypothetical example, but a reference to a client she had seen earlier that day.

Correctional officers are not judicial actors and have no direct input on decisions relating to an incarcerated person's progress through their sentence. But infractions were a tool for them to influence the sentences of those under their custody. They could, and often did, prejudice a judge against the applicant. To issue an infraction, to mark someone as "badly behaved," set up a narrative of indiscipline that was extremely difficult to counter and almost impossible to formally appeal, and that was often cited by judges as justification for denying parole. The TFD thereby provided an opportunity for coughs, logistical errors, and personal grievances to become documented as qualities of the incarcerated person.

The Criminological Exam

The Disciplinary Record Transcript is a retrospective tool, one that attests only to past behavior. But the LEP also demands that the future be transformed into evidence. The criminological exam ostensibly fulfills this requirement. During my fieldwork, each application for parole or house arrest required three of these exams, one from each profession among the technicians. Judges also occasionally requested them during applications to progress from a closed to a semi-open prison regime, most often for those who had been convicted of a sexual offense. The term *criminological exam* refers both to the set of interviews and to the written reports that were produced as a result. One of the main proponents of the exam during the formulation of the LEP was Álvaro Mayrink da Costa, a magistrate who had previously worked as both a criminal lawyer and a prison warden in Rio de Janeiro. In his doctoral dissertation, Costa argued that the exam would allow for the proper individualization of punishment by identifying and treating criminal or antisocial tendencies. He argued that through the exam, the penal judge might

> take responsibility, within the judicial functioning, for the investigation of the biological constitution of the delinquent, their psychological reality, and their social conditioning [...] which will allow for the application of appropriate measures concerning their personality, thereby recovering the principle of the legality and the dignity of the human being.[29]

Drawing inspiration from the Italian school of criminal anthropology, Costa divided criminal law into the "scientific" study of criminality and the "legal" study of the crime, concluding that only the former would result in any prevention of criminal behavior or recidivism. Part diagnosis, part prognosis, the exam was meant to provide a forecast of one's future "evolution within the social grouping."[30]

A 2003 reform to the LEP,[31] reinforced by a ruling (*súmula*) from Brazil's Supreme Court in 2010,[32] removed the criminological exam as a requirement for progression or parole, although it could still be requested by a judge. During my fieldwork, it had fallen out of routine use in most Brazilian states.[33] But Rio de Janeiro's VEP had refused the Supreme Court's interpretation and maintained the use of the exam as standard practice. Rather than waiting for a judge's formal request, which could delay an application by several weeks, public defenders would often initiate the process themselves. Like virtually all prisons in Rio, Tobias Barreto had a significant backlog of pending interviews. The state's prison administration had not hired any new technicians on a permanent basis since 1999. As a result, in 2017 the entire system relied on fifty-seven psychologists, seventy social workers, and fifteen psychiatrists for the fifty-two thousand or so people who were imprisoned in the state.

The structure of the exam had evolved to reconcile this growing demand with the shrinking number of professionals qualified to undertake it. With the fewest number of staff employed by the prison administration, psychiatrists had the greatest burden of cases to work through. Like all other prisons in the state, Tobias Barreto had no dedicated psychiatrist. On my first day working with Lívia, one appeared late in the morning, proclaiming that he had three hundred pending exams to work through that day, which would have given him a little over one minute to complete each exam. With the personal details of each interviewee prefilled on the forms, his exam was reduced to ticking one of two boxes: one confirming that the applicant demonstrated an "ability to live within society," the other testifying that they had symptoms of some "psychiatric trouble" that might be an impediment to this conviviality.

Interviews by psychologists and social workers were generally longer. Most reported to me that their exams lasted for around twenty to thirty minutes, and the few that I witnessed firsthand fell within this time frame. Both professions followed a life-story approach, constructing a biography that might explain both the crime and any personal growth or development that occurred afterward. The nature of each question and their sequence guided the interviewee through a specific narrative about themselves. *Who raised you as a child? What was your motive? Then what happened? Have you been going to school in here? What about when you get out? And where will you live?* This line of questioning funneled the lives of the imprisoned people into a restricted set of biographical referents, shoehorning them into the familiar story of a dysfunctional childhood leading to insertion into criminal life, imprisonment, and finally a commitment made after the point of arrest to pursuing a different, reformed future.

Most interviewers aimed to write reports that would be favorable to the incarcerated person. While there were notable exceptions, including one that I explore shortly, those who worked in the technical professions understood themselves as allies of imprisoned people, as bound by an ethics of care, and as working in opposition to the custodial imperatives of the institution. They generally saw their own labor as acting *against* incarceration or as an attempt to address its harms, rather than as a part of it. Their aim was to provide a sympathetic portrait of clients by producing an exam that could allay any suspicion of danger, at least within the constraints of time and form. But this defense also reproduced standardized tropes of "unstable" family life and childhood neglect, along with repentance and an aptitude for future work, as the only possible counternarrative.

I chose, both during and after my fieldwork, to focus on interviewers' questions and techniques, rather than interviewee responses, and to avoid reproducing the content of individual reports. As a result, a full accounting for the textures of the encounter between parole applicant and interviewer falls outside the scope of this book, and my understanding of the dynamic between the two emerges out of my conversations with the latter.[34] Variations in the wording of reports, and their effects along the path that these documents take from the prison into the judicial system, lie beyond the grasp of what I can adequately outline here.

Still, what I have described is reinforced in the scholarship of a former prison psychologist, Cristina Rauter.[35] After leaving her position in Rio's prisons and entering academia, Rauter compared the language used across 120 reports. Here, she argued that the format of the exam rested on a deterministic class-based logic in which a troubled childhood and the impacts of a defective "subculture" emanating from poor territories—including both Rio's favelas and the Northeast Region of Brazil—provided sufficient evidence for a criminal trajectory. Even as the exam produced this narration, it also reproduced a vision of justice as an "apolitical regulator of social order," depoliticizing the roles of the penal judge and the courts.[36] Although Rauter understood this discourse as a product of class distinctions, the same terms identified in her analysis also clearly function as ciphers for Blackness. Brazil's Northeast Region and the favelas of Rio de Janeiro are Black spaces, both in demographic terms and within a broader Brazilian racial imaginary. Neither public defenders nor technical staff spoke explicitly about race when discussing the criminological exam with me. Of the few completed exams I read, none mentioned the interviewee's race or racism in the report. But geography nevertheless offered a convenient shorthand in which the favela and the Northeast came to both represent and explain criminal behavior.

The repetition of these tropes across reports reflects what João Costa Vargas has identified as a dialectic of "hyper-consciousness/negation" of race.[37] This is the condition under which many Brazilians are keenly aware of the structuring effects of race and racism, even as they continue to outwardly deny their importance. A wealth of euphemisms surrounding both whiteness and Blackness allow Brazilians to produce a racialized, and specifically anti-Black, discourse without naming it as such.[38] Their use in the exam in place of any direct reference to race obviated the need for any account of, or even reference to, Brazil's racial hierarchy.[39] Of course, this silence was still accompanied by the racial categorization and mug shot carried in the TFD, as the two documents traveled together. Alongside geography, another figure that accomplished this task is the absent father. The exam would draw it out through a single question—*Who raised you as a child?*—that psychologists and social workers asked at the beginning of every interview. The fact that this was often the only question asked about an interviewee's childhood reflects an understanding of the "Brazilian family," understood here as the nuclear and heteronormative unit, as the basis of national security.[40]

Reports would always note when an incarcerated person was raised by a single mother or other family member. This is not to say that all Black interviewees were raised only by their mothers, nor that all imprisoned white people grew up in a nuclear family unit. But when interviewers portrayed the childhood and upbringing of interviewees exclusively in terms of who raised them, they produced reports that measured the imprisoned people in terms of their proximity to or distance from this narrative of Black familial dysfunction. Whether due to time constraints or simply disinterest, this left no space for explaining any other aspect of an interviewee's childhood. I never saw a psychologist or social worker ask about an interviewee's exposure to violence during childhood, about access to health and education, or about previous encounters with police. Nor did any criminological exam ever delve into the causes and circumstances that produced "absent fathers" in the first place, an investigation that might have indicted the prison system itself.

The flip side to these racist tropes, and the elisions that they rely upon, is that they attenuate criminal responsibility. First, they displace it onto family or geography. Second, they relegate the root cause of crime to the past. The interviewee's task was to demonstrate the extent to which they had disentangled themselves from that former life in preparation for a new, resocialized one. This is what many psychologists and social workers understood as their sympathetic portrait, one that gave interviewees the chance to make a case for themselves and their futures. But its redemptive arc often took the shape of the interviewee's struggle to "overcome" the markers of Blackness—by moving out of the community they were raised in, for instance, or by a newfound commitment to maintain a nuclear family with themselves at the helm as father and provider. This shorthand allowed the exam to simplify and communicate a complex set of social relationships through a limited set of figures whose meaning and import were assumed as already known to its audience—including, most importantly, to the judge who would decide the applicant's fate.

On the Uses of (sic)
Prison Unit:
Name:
RG:
Place of Birth: **Nationality:**
Civil State:
Age:
Education:
Name of the Solicitation: Progression
Familiar/Affective Aspects: Was raised by mother and father. Has five siblings. Stable family relationships. Receives visits from his mother and sister.
Perception and Motivation for the Crime: Convicted under Articles 57 and 123. First offense. He has already served two years and eight months. The inmate reports that he committed those crimes as a result of his getting involved with "bad company" (sic). He denies the use of drugs.
Carceral Comportment: Good. The inmate says that he spends his free time playing football. He does not work or study in prison.
Perspective for the Future: He aims to "try" to change his life (sic). He will return to the house of his mother. The inmate has still not thought of what he will do when he leaves prison.

This is a criminological exam. I have left the identifying information blank; the rest is a composite, pieced together from the reports I was given permission to access during my fieldwork, all of which were conducted by one of the two psychologists who worked in Tobias Barreto. It took up one side of a single sheet of paper, with the lines ruled on the other side left unfilled. Its evaluation is mixed, which is to say that it is not favorable to the applicant. Much of the information presented here, including the conviction, length of sentence, and behavioral classification, repeats what appears on other documents. The rest is a speed run through the life of the interviewee, moving quickly from childhood to plans for the future in a handful of sentences. Unfilled report forms come divided into subheadings that already assume which aspects of this biography are critical to the interviewee's development as a moral subject. The result is the formulaic construction of a life history that runs along the grain of a criminal archetype, and that repeats itself with only minor variations across reports.

A specific turn of phrase, or even a single word, often constitutes a deciding factor in authorizing or denying parole. Sometimes these effects took the interviewers by surprise. One psychologist stated in an interview that a few years prior, she had learned from colleagues that public prosecutors and judges were paying close attention to any description of interviewees as *ansioso*. In most contexts, the word means *anxious* or *eager*. But public prosecutors had begun to pick up on this language, using it in their reports to suggest that the applicant was passive and had not taken personal responsibility for their own future, and judges took that interpretation as sufficient justification to deny parole. In response, the psychologist began to fastidiously avoid any use of the word in her reports.

Following a similar pattern, Lívia would often advise her clients to never use the word *tentar (try)*. This was because one of the psychologists stationed in the prison consistently picked up on the word and drew attention to it in her reports. The result can be seen in the preceding exam, where the word is hygienically sealed in quotation marks, as part of a broader strategy in which the author alternates between quotes and indirect reported speech. As argued by Mikhail Bakhtin, any act of reported speech—in which one references the speech of another—sits on a spectrum between verbatim quotation and a looser or "pictorial" description of what was said.[41] The anthropologist Matthew Hull develops his insight further in the context of another state bureaucracy, where officials manipulated the level of direct or indirect reported speech in documents to alter the author's relationship with what was being cited in order to position it as more or less connected with the author's intent.[42] Direct quotations use punctuation to draw a clear line between the voice of the person who first spoke the phrase and that of the author who reports it. An indirect style, by contrast, results in a greater mixture between the two voices.

In the composite exam quoted here, the psychologist alternates between these two poles of reported speech throughout the report to both maintain her technocratic position and incriminate the parole applicant. A sentence like "He will return to the house of his mother" casts no suspicion on the veracity of the interviewee's response. At other moments, doubt creeps in simply by using second-order description: when the interviewee "says," "denies," or "reports," the question of the truth of his response remains open. Direct quotation carries this doubt a step further, pushing the interviewee's words away from the psychologist's authority, a distance that is doubly stressed by the use of "(sic)." The symbol allows the interviewer to cast doubt on responses that would otherwise speak in the interviewee's favor by refusing to invest her professional authority in their truth value.

In this exam, the composite interviewee has partially redistributed responsibility for the crime to his broader social network and announced that he would attempt to change his life after release. But the (sic) in the report condemns him in both cases, trapping those words inside the voice of a convicted criminal. This is how the interviewer can conclude the report with "the inmate has still not thought of what he will do when he leaves prison," even though it directly contradicts the previous two sentences. Her reporting strategy both draws on and perpetuates the assumption that someone in prison is inherently untrustworthy, that any positive self-presentation is an instrumental strategy for leaving prison rather than a sincere description. Reported speech authorizes this suspicious reading, opening space for an interpretation that runs against, and often directly counter to, the actual content of the responses given by the interviewee. This is how " 'try' to change his life (sic)" comes to mean the opposite of *trying to change his life.*

This is also why Lívia advised her clients to never try. She knew the prison psychologist's reporting style, and she had seen judges deny parole based on these reports. In her office, just down the hall from the psychologist herself, she briefly strategized with clients to avoid the language that might earn them a (sic). One result was that interviewees were trained to speak proleptically, to talk about the future as if it were already present rather than something that had yet to be attained. This was particularly important when discussing employment. Trying to find work is a basic but fairly accurate description of what most people leaving prison actually did, particularly in the context of an economic recession, spiking unemployment, and a widespread reluctance among employers to hire formerly incarcerated people. That reality was suspended at the moment of the criminological exam. The interviews, and the reports that follow, demanded a particular biography, one that left no space for even entertaining the idea that someone who was truly reformed might try (and therefore potentially fail, or not try hard enough) to find work. Instead, the interviewee needed to prove that they already had a job waiting for them. And yet these demands provoked the very insincerity that interviewers remained vigilant against. Both Lívia and the psychologist reinforced an approach to the exam as a performance that followed strict conventions. They thus reproduced this impulse to read against the grain of interviewees' responses to expose the underlying criminal intentions that their speech was ostensibly trying to mask.

This was a form of evaluation fixated on the task of understanding whether the incarcerated person had "truly" reformed or had simply mastered resocialization's scripts. Resocialization asked for the truth of the incarcerated person to be discovered, while insisting that it would only be revealed and confirmed in the future. Together, the TFD and the criminological exam produced a biography of the criminal subject. They also established a trajectory that might be extrapolated toward that future moment, the vantage point from which imprisoned people might be judged. The ultimate proof of a transformation lay in this anticipated subject. Underneath this reformative impulse was a fear of the potential "bad surprise" of recidivism that had to be identified in advance so it could be avoided. The result was the paradoxical demand that the incarcerated person confess to their future, even when their confession was never entirely believable precisely because it was forced.

This was a game of bad faith that imprisoned people never won, since they could only be read as sincere when they acted against their assumed interest—that is, when they incriminated themselves. It was a game that I was constantly invited to play, as correctional officers warned me that my project on resocialization was both hopelessly naïve and a dead end, since I could never believe anything an imprisoned person told me. At the same time, these dynamics also crept into my conversations with currently or formerly incarcerated people. Although I deliberately avoided any questions during my research that mimicked those found in the exam, many participants still saw our encounters as an opportunity or provocation to prove how much they had changed.

There is more than a superficial parallel between the exam and the work of ethnography. My own discipline, anthropology, asserted its influence within Brazil's criminal justice system in the early twentieth century. Rio's Laboratory of Criminal Anthropology was created in 1932 to aid in the research and development of criminal identification techniques, including anthropometry.[43] Although its direct influence on juridical forms of veridiction waned from midcentury onward, the resonance between the methods of the exam and those of my own ethnography point back to this familial relation. Prisons also constitute another site where the equation of critical inquiry with reading "against the grain" has become operationalized in the attempt to extract the supposed truth of the incarcerated person from the lie or delusion of positive self-presentation. An interviewee who said they would return to a life of crime during a criminological exam was always understood as sincere; one who claimed they would change their life was always subject to doubt. This form of reasoning circulated throughout the justice system—including in the few therapeutic spaces that still operated, as I demonstrate in the following chapter. Agents of the law demanded a string of confessions before, during, and after the moment of conviction. But those confessions were never entirely believable because of the assumption that the sole aim of the incarcerated person was to leave prison, and that any statement that person made was driven by a desire to achieve this end rather than by the sincerity that the law demanded.

Many of these critiques were shared by those who carried out the exam. Psychologists and social workers were often painfully aware of the conflicts that the interview and subsequent report created in terms of their professional practice and their standing within the prison administration's hierarchy. In 2010, Brazil's Federal Board of Psychology (Conselho Federal de Psicologia) published a resolution stating (1) that the aims of the criminological exam contradicted professional ethics; (2) that the exam itself was not only unconstitutional but had been abolished by legislation introduced in 2003; (3) that psychology did not provide the expertise to judge any individual's risk of recidivism or capacity for resocialization; and (4) therefore, that psychologists should refuse to conduct the criminological exam within the prison system.[44] As a response, Rio's prison administration issued its own notice, distributed to every psychologist working within the system and stating that, based on the advice from the VEP, psychologists who refused to conduct the exam could face criminal charges for failing to carry out their responsibilities as public servants.[45]

The notice succeeded in compelling psychologists to resume conducting the exam. But it did not shift their opinion regarding its use. As a result, during my fieldwork many psychologists and social workers finished every single report with the same statement: "This report was produced from a twenty-minute interview. I have no means of evaluating the inmate's risk to society or the probability of their recidivism." It offered a direct protest against their obligation to undertake the exam. But it also hijacked penal bureaucracy itself by articulating a critique through a document that would then circulate through the VEP, with the hope that the repeated message might sway the opinion of the judge on whose desk it would finally land.

Those two sentences also served another function: to remove any liability on the part of the interviewer. In cases where someone on parole or house arrest committed a high-profile crime, journalists would often speak to the specific judge who had authorized the early release. Judges would then refer to the criminological exam and to the supposed expertise of the technicians as the basis for their decisions, occasionally sharing the text of the report with media. In these cases, the criminological exam produced an extended chain of second-, third- and fourth-order reported speech acts, moving from the imprisoned person to the technician, to the judge, and finally to the journalist. Each person along the chain shifted responsibility for this piece of evidence, one that was ostensibly proven faulty by the subsequent criminal act. The only one unable to perform the shift was the incarcerated person. In the context of the interview, they had no one to quote, paraphrase, or cast suspicion upon, since to do so would be seen as avoiding responsibility. Everything was interpreted as self-referential, since there was no other object being produced as evidence.

Reasonable Duration

For a few months at the beginning of my fieldwork, I conducted short interviews with people who had arrived for their first scheduled visit to the parole office, generally within the first ten days of their release from prison. One common thread among them was the experience of losing documents between arrest and imprisonment. In some cases, police would literally tear up their files—particularly government-issued IDs, but also occasionally worker's cards or voter registration cards—at the moment of arrest. This ritualized destruction, which was apparently established during Brazil's most recent dictatorship, marked the symbolic death of legal personhood upon entry into the criminal justice system. More commonly, police would apprehend documents at the moment of arrest and they would simply become "lost." In some rare cases, those who entered the prison system had no documents, including no birth certificate, to begin with.

In this context, the files that circulated through prisons and courts often served as the most concrete testament to a person's existence. To have a file lost, or to have it sit still, was not just a logistical issue. Instead, it represented a paralysis of juridical personhood, as the subject represented on paper ceased to exist in any meaningful way as both an object of the law and a subject of rights. Prison workers and incarcerated people both knew from experience how common this stalling of the progressive machine was. As a result, Lívia and Ângela could not answer the most common questions asked by their clients: when will a decision be made, when will I get out, when will my criminological exams be scheduled? The best response they could offer was a vague gesture at "soon," which generally signified a few months, or more, or less.

One reason that defenders resisted giving a time frame was that they were concerned that any prognosis might come back to bite them should it not come to pass. The vague promises of *soon* were a means of safeguarding the unforeseeability of the incarcerated person's future. They provided a productive buffer for prison workers who sat between the expectations of the judiciary and the frustrations of imprisoned people. Likewise, we might return momentarily to the phrase written at the end of so many criminological exams: "This report was produced from a twenty-minute interview. I have no means of evaluating this inmate's risk to society or the probability of their recidivism." As one psychologist explained to me, "We aren't clairvoyant, we have no crystal ball that will say if someone is going to commit a crime or not." The phrase mitigated the demand for a prognosis by speaking directly against it: The interviewer simply could do what was asked of them.

For every application for parole or house arrest, a VEP judge would analyze the documents at their disposal to produce another file, one that furnished and justified a decision. These files were written in the opaque language of the law and ostensibly outlined the factors that justified the choice to approve or deny progression. Most of the language in these documents was pro forma, copied and pasted across thousands of rulings. They began with an homage to the law itself, as seen in this decision, produced in late 2016:

> Wisely, the penal sentence has as its preciput objective, beyond the character of general prevention and repression of the practice of crimes, the resocialization of the individual, aiming to make them apt for conviviality within society, dissuading them of the practice of pernicious conduct [. . .] There is no other reason why the Law of Penal Execution has adopted the system of progression, which shows favor to the convicted who demonstrates good carceral behavior, inserting them in a less rigorous regime.

Parole was eventually authorized for most on the first or second attempt. But rejections, including one that began with the preceding phrase, were still commonplace. And the most common justification for denial was not evidence of poor character, but rather the lack of any evidence whatsoever, phrased in these decisions as "the absence of the authorizing subjective requirements for the concession of benefits, from article 83, number III, of the penal code." Here, the TFD and criminological exam simply did not provide enough information to demonstrate resocialization. The evidence was too thin; the subject on file was not enough of a person.

But despite the precarity of this documentation, it still offered the only pathway to legal release. When pending applications pile up, thousands of people in Rio's prisons are left caught in the system, their cases stagnating. In 2016, at the start of my fieldwork, the judiciary was in the middle of a digitization process that replaced paper records with an electronic system known as the Processo Judicial Digital (Digital Judicial Proceedings), or PROJUDI. The shift promised to revolutionize the work of all legal actors, speeding up and automating applications and deliberations. Files would never become lost, documents would move between offices instantaneously, and lawyers would no longer be able to shift their cases to the top of the pile with a bribe. Instead, PROJUDI promised swift, efficient justice.

The transitional period was a disaster. In the middle of digitizing efforts, thousands of documents became lost or unavailable. It was impossible for public defenders and prosecutors to access critical files, including TFDs. Applications stagnated, and when physical files were removed to be digitized it was difficult to determine where and how to recover them. Rather than waiting for these files to reappear, prosecutors often simply recommended against parole given the absence of evidence, and judges generally concurred. The yearlong transition resulted in a massive buildup of unresolved applications, while those that made it through were largely denied. The prison population swelled.

This process was largely complete by the end of the year, and public defenders were relieved to see that cases were moving again. But PROJUDI did not actually bridge the air gap between the courts and the separate file system used by the prison administration. Lívia and Ângela still needed to bring their suitcases to work to receive printed files, take them into their offices, scan them, and upload them into the new system. At the same time, the case backlog remained. One of the measures taken by NUSPEN to address this was to issue what they called a "collective habeas corpus" to Brasília. This measure required all public defenders to identify those in their respective prisons who had been waiting for a decision on progression for months. The office aimed to gather one thousand cases to send to the federal Ministry of Justice as a tool to force Rio's VEP to speed up their work on these pending applications. Each lawyer was given a stack of forms and a request to find at least forty cases of unreasonable delays within their caseloads. The forms were identical, with blank spaces only for the name of the incarcerated person, their signature, and the date. Based on a requirement within a constitutional amendment for reasonable duration of process,[46] the aim was to amass proof of a systemic breach of this right. On the front page of each form was a quote from Psalm 40: "I waited patiently for the Lord / He turned to me and heard my cry."

Over the following weeks, these files made their way into NUSPEN suitcases as Lívia, Ângela, and their team worked through them. In doing so, they grappled with the necessary threshold to qualify a case for the project. Which cases warranted the complaint? One man had begun his application for house arrest eight months before. Ângela sat down with him and looked over his sentencing certificate, cross-checking the data with her own personal file on his case. At first she told him, "we're going to send your case to Brasília." But then she discovered that his family had only handed over the necessary documents a little over a month prior, making the delay less egregious. The man, however, became extremely agitated. Again and again he asked Ângela, "When am I going to leave? When can I get out?" Ângela deflected. But the man insisted, so she responded, "I don't know how to predict the future. Nobody knows!" Eventually she seemed to relent, giving her client the form and asking him to write his name, then sign and date it. He wanted to know how the document would arrive in Brasília. "Is it going by car or by the mail?" She responded, "It's traveling by air." Once the man left the room, Ângela passed the file to her intern and asked him to tear it up. "I just did it to calm him down," she explained to me, as he ripped down the middle of the page.

Ângela gave her client what amounted to a legal placebo to regulate his emotional state, to offer the sensation of movement (*andamento*) and to avoid conflict. In doing so, she also repeated the act of police ripping an identification card at the moment of arrest. Both events reiterated the powerlessness that someone who was being held in the criminal justice system had over their juridical identity. It was the same powerlessness that emerged when case files and parole applications sat for months waiting to be dealt with. The client's anxiety stemmed at least partly from a recognition of his own lack of control, but it also reflected his expectation that Ângela was perhaps the only person who could do anything about it. Ângela assuaged his fears with the document, only to confirm them once he had left.

Files, Futures, and the Unforeseeable

The carry-on suitcase trafficked files in and out of prison, a ritual that allowed the prison administration, NUSPEN, and the VEP to communicate with one another. In the morning, it arrived in Tobias Barreto filled with the "objective" facts laid out in the sentencing certificate, waiting to be distributed among clients. Come afternoon, it would leave with the "subjective" evidence about the incarcerated person in TFDs and criminological exams, documents that might set the gears of a progressive penal machine in motion. Both the presence of these papers and their movement represented a promise. They were a concrete assurance that the incarcerated person was still recognized, even if minimally, as a juridical person. In an institution where people routinely became lost to their families, to the administration, or to their legal representatives, this recognition was critical. At the same time, documents made the prospect of progress material, transforming an abstract ideal into a tangible pathway. The movement of files anticipated and propelled the movement of people. For anyone to advance through their sentence, paper had to first pave the way. Alongside this promise was a current of suspicion that shaped the relationships between defenders, technicians, and imprisoned people. Documents held these two forces together as they both pointed toward and obscured release. This is the effect of a progressive institution, one that has gradually taken shape since the founding of Brazil's carceral project. The forms of violence and incapacitation that emerge alongside this model of progress do not equate to a failure of the mission itself but rather point to its perverse effects.

Early in my fieldwork, during my second visit to a prison in Rio de Janeiro, I was struck by the proliferation of calendars inside the institution. I spent the morning with two social workers in an office with barely enough room for the three of us, with origami flowers adorning the desk and a Garfield sticker on the filing cabinet. I was constantly searching for a clock to give me a sense of how much time I had left in the unit, but I found none on the walls or in any of the offices that I passed. And yet inside this small room were seven calendars, some hanging next to the window, some propped up on the desks, facing away from the social worker and toward whoever they were speaking to that day. As my research progressed, I saw this repeated in all the prisons I visited, particularly in the offices of social workers, psychologists, and public defense officers. There were never any clocks, but calendars were always present in groups of two, three, four, or more.

The scene reminded me of an image of duplicated time analyzed by another anthropologist, Lisa Stevenson, who discusses an archival photo of the interior of an Indigenous household in the Canadian Arctic.[47] There, two alarm clocks appear in the image, a doubling that the photo's original captioner draws attention to with the suggestion that the family may have fetishized these objects. Here, calendars spoke of another time, measured in days, stretching out into the future. This is the time of the *cálculo*, a tabulation that pointed toward a supposedly inevitable moment of release. I came to see these calendars as pointing to the same promise as the one held out by files. When people in prison spoke of the future, they meant a future after prison. Every day until that was part of a long, drawn-out present. But every day was also one day less, as that future gradually drew closer. Sometimes this progress seemed solid and measurable, grounding how time was understood and experienced. It represented one way to talk about prison and afterward, one way to make sense of confinement. Someone sitting in that cramped social worker's office would find a reminder of that kind of time literally everywhere they looked.

But even as time counted down, what was it counting toward? So much of the violence of prison takes place as a deferral. The apparently concrete assurance of release was constantly blurred; dates for progression passed by, and it took weeks or months for anything to happen. Waiting lists for the criminological exam extended outward, files sat on desks, and judges decided that a person did not yet exhibit the criteria necessary for parole. It was this unspecified *soon* that characterized so much of punishment. The promise of progress was tangible, but the future continually seemed to move back out of reach.

Prison Psychology's Praxis

On a Wednesday afternoon, I sat in a local university classroom with Reinaldo, a psychologist employed by the prison administration; three students; and one recent graduate. We were there to plan a workshop that we would run in a few months across various prisons as part of Project Life—the statewide program that aimed to promote "health and citizenship" among incarcerated people. All of us were white. Reinaldo was urging us to consider the potential hazard of assuming we knew the perspectives of our imprisoned participants. Pedro, the graduate in psychology, agreed, and said that we should discard the "traditional" objective in psychology to "catch the other's point of view" (*pegar o olhar do outro*), an approach that he understood as intrinsically harmful. Our work should not be driven by curiosity, nor by denying the social distance between ourselves and imprisoned people. Instead, we were there to facilitate a conversation along the workshop's theme of "mutual aid," which we hoped might allow participants to reflect on different forms of solidarity within the institution. This was, as Reinaldo repeatedly stressed, an experiment, one whose outcome we could not control.

When the meeting drew to a close, I said goodbye to the others and left with Reinaldo. We continued our discussion as we walked down a busy street to the nearest bus stop. Reinaldo was a forceful, and sometimes brash, professor in his late forties, with a graying mustache, a booming voice, and caustic memories of the years he had spent working as a prison psychologist. He had continued volunteering for Project Life after he moved into teaching, although he remained extremely critical of its objectives and its pedagogy, including what he called the "communicative fantasy" of a lecture-style presentation. But as we waited to cross the road, he explained that Project Life was like "a hole in the wall" (*um buraco no muro*), a small opening that we could use to do something different.

These weekly meetings were an opportunity for us to think through what might be possible and ethical in a context of confinement. For the psychologists at the table, they were also a chance to evaluate the nature and potential of their own discipline, to ask what might make a "good" psychologist, whether inside or out of prison. For me, they revealed the close intimacy between the training that had made me an anthropologist and the forms of knowledge that were already circulating in the space that I had marked out as my field. To catch the other's point of view . . . when Pedro said that, I wondered if he was quoting Malinowski.[1] While we might have different "others" in mind, the psychologists and I were both grappling with questions of ethics, representation, mediation, and the value of critique.

This chapter traces our search for answers as we traversed this hole in the wall. Project Life—the Project, for short—was where psychologists struggled with themselves and the prison administration to produce a transformative relationship with incarcerated people. Unlike the criminological exam discussed in the previous chapter, the Project was not tethered to any legal system of evaluation or classification. Instead, its mission was pedagogical and therapeutic, something more aligned with what psychologists understood as their real mission within prisons. As they facilitated discussions, sporting events, poetry workshops, theater performances, or painting classes, volunteers elaborated various theories of subjecthood and development that they hoped imprisoned participants might take up and pursue as their own. But they also reconstituted a form of tutelary governance that positioned participants as wards in need of some intervention to become self-governing.

A little over two decades before our classroom meeting, another recent psychology graduate, Fernanda, was assigned to her first job within the prison system, inside a maximum-security unit in the Bangu complex. She was, by her own admission, an accidental psychologist, having stumbled into the profession after an earlier attempt to study medicine fell apart. She initially felt no particular calling to work inside the prison system; it was just her first successful job application. But by the time I met her in 2014, she had acquired a clear passion and sense of purpose for her work. As she recounted in an interview, at the time she was hired, she was assigned to a prison that held just over one thousand people and had two other full-time psychologists.[2] When she arrived, she felt completely unprepared: "People brought so many situations, so many questions, and they were concrete problems that we had no solutions for, we don't have any way to help, [things like] family problems, institutional problems that have no solution. I said, 'My God, what am I going to do?'" She decided to create something that she could invest herself in, so she formed a group "where people would come together just to share something good, anything good. It was like a cup of dirty water, this is how I visualized it, and we started to pour clean water into it, and little by little we would renew that water." Participants brought recipes, letters from girlfriends or wives, Bible verses, and passages from Spiritist[3] texts: "I accepted anything as long as it was legal." She started with a small group, but each week a few more would arrive, bringing scraps of paper, music, memories, and aspirations to share.

As the meetings grew, Fernanda enlisted the help of a colleague, Luan. After a year of this work, the two applied for federal funding for the program, but this support was tied to a set of restrictions that reduced the scope of their activities to facilitating presentations on sexually transmitted infections and drug use. Fernanda wanted to maintain her focus on the positive, so workshops were always framed in a way that she understood as empowering, such as referring to bodily autonomy rather than addiction. Then, with a grant from the United Nations Development Programme, the two psychologists began to spread the Project to other prisons throughout the state. The UNDP support was temporary; when it ceased after three years, so did Project Life. Since the state's prison administration had no interest in continuing to support the Project financially, it was formally suspended, although Fernanda and Luan continued with smaller discussion groups and activities in various prisons over the following years. The Project was officially revived in 2012, thanks to Fernanda's lobbying and a newly receptive secretary of the prison administration. It was reborn as a program that would operate across most of Rio's penitentiaries, with its new, expanded focus on health and citizenship.

When I began my fieldwork, the Project was officially housed within the psychology department of Rio's prison administration. Most of its volunteers were either former or current employees within one of the state's prisons, but it also attracted students or recent graduates like Pedro, who were searching for ways to use their training in the pursuit of social justice. There were a few others, like doctors and lawyers, who gave lectures on the rights of incarcerated people or addiction recovery. The current coordinator was always looking for more volunteers—she was enthusiastic at the prospect of my participation from our first meeting. But the language, mission, and structure of Project Life were all driven by psychologists as its founders, its primary volunteer base, and its source of institutional support within the prison system. The Project operated across almost all prisons that were designated for post-trial detainees, although some penitentiaries saw far more activities and events than others.

At the start of each year, those held in these prisons had the opportunity to apply for the Project through their unit's psychologist. Interest always outstripped the limited number of places available. As a result, psychologists tended to select one or two people from each cell, with the hope that these participants could share what they had learned with the rest of the unit. For those selected, the program lasted an entire year. Participants who attended most activities would "graduate" at the year's end with a formal ceremony, where they received a certificate and were given the title of *multipliers (multiplicadores)*. The certificate and the title did not reduce a sentence, nor did they improve the graduate's behavioral classification. Once granted, multipliers were also barred from applying for the Project in the future. Occasionally, however, their participation was noted in the criminological exam as evidence of their commitment to improving themselves.

As I examine Project Life, I shift focus from Tobias Barreto, the semi-open prison discussed in the previous chapter, to René Dotti, a closed unit where I participated in various Project Life activities. I also move into spaces like the university classroom, where volunteers reproduced and reimagined the Project. By tacking between these sites, the chapter marks out three key aspects of prison psychology's praxis. The first is the relationship between individual development and security. Like Fernanda's striking metaphor of the "cup of dirty water," the Project framed its own intervention by imagining participants as vessels awaiting the education, norms, or compassion offered to them. This pedagogy was optimistic because it understood those in prison through their promise and potential—but it also defined them by an apparent *lack*. As I argue here, through this approach Project Life joined an ecology of "soft security" programs in Rio, supported by a broader logic of *pacification*.

Second, Project Life demonstrated an ongoing concern with how to cultivate a particular relationship between the psychologist and the incarcerated person. Volunteers meticulously designed activities to engineer their level of emotional proximity to or distance from participants. In doing so, they shared an unease around what I call *improper intimacies*: forms of communication or empathy that breached the loosely defined boundary between professional care and something more intense, more personal, and potentially more dangerous. The final issue is one of critique—what was recognized as a valid critique in the context of the Project, and who was authorized to speak it. Although volunteers debated the harms of incarceration and the role of their profession within it, and saw the Project as a space for this critique, I also demonstrate that we restricted imprisoned participants' right to do the same. This treatment of the incarcerated person's critical voice as a form of violence demonstrates the uneven distribution of the "right to critique" that the Project continually reproduced. But when incarcerated people were given the opportunity to organize their own events through the Project, they used it for different ends, articulating a radically different vision of selfhood, reform, and resocialization than those forms of critique we had carried in with us.

Peace, Peaceball, and Pacification

This is how to play peaceball (*pazbol*):

1. The game is played on whatever field is available.

2. There are two teams. Each team has between four and ten players.

3. Each team is divided evenly between attack and defense; these sides are restricted to one half of the entire field.

4. The ball is thrown between the players. Whoever is in possession of the ball cannot move.

5. Each goal—when the ball is thrown through a hoop, or, in the more likely event that a hoop is unavailable, a plastic container—is worth one point for the scoring team.

6. Immediately after a goal, whoever scored switches with a member of the opposing team.

7. After two goals are scored from either team, those in attack switch with their teammates in defense.

8. There is no physical contact between players.

9. At any point in the game, when conflicts arise, or if there is confusion about the guidelines, any player can come to a mediator to look for a resolution. But the mediator is not a referee and has no final say. Instead, their role is to call players together in search of a common solution.

When Camila invited me to mediate the game with her inside René Dotti, I had never seen it in action, but she promised she would guide me through it. She was a young Black woman and, like Pedro, a recent graduate of a psychology program who had begun volunteering for Project Life as a student, and who kept up this work because she saw it as part of her professional mission. On our first day, we walked together through the front gates of the prison and made our way toward the concrete field that was generally reserved for soccer. Turnout was low today because of a special church event scheduled for the same time. After a dozen participants arrived, Camila ran through the guidelines. "We trust that you can resolve any conflicts between yourselves. If you want us to step in, just raise your hand, but we won't intervene in the game. We can only help you resolve the conflict yourselves," she explained. I struggled, along with the players, to understand how these guidelines would work in practice. But thankfully, an imprisoned graduate of the Project gave a demonstration, showing how to pass the ball, how to stop once the ball was caught, and so on.

The first few minutes were confusing. But soon the players picked up on the rhythm and structure of play, while a few spectators began cheering them on and calling out for intervention when someone seemed to break a guideline. One participant was irritating everyone by dramatically collapsing to the ground from even the suspicion of contact. As soon as he fell, hands would go up and Camila and I would enter the fray to guide the dispute. Each time, the players pushed back, demanding a judgment from Camila or me, and asking for the player to be suspended from the field. We refused. It was difficult to keep track of the scores, especially as the game progressed and teams constantly switched and reassembled themselves. Since nobody ended up on the team they started on, they quickly lost interest in the tally anyway.

Every game of peaceball ends in a circle. At the blow of Camila's whistle, she called us all into the center of the field. Holding the ball in her hands, she explained that she would pass it around; the person holding it would share their impressions of the game, then hand it on to the next player. Most responded that they enjoyed peaceball, and that it was nice to have some variety from the soccer games that dominated the field day after day. Many asked us to return more often to run the game again; each time, Camila stressed that participants could organize it on their own. Then the ball passed to one player who thanked us but was clearly unhappy, saying, "There needs to be some kind of punishment" for those who acted out. As he said this, he cast his eyes at the participant who had faked his injuries. Camila asked why that was necessary, when players could sort out their differences between themselves. The man replied that at least in soccer, players would be sent off when they broke the rules. When the ball finally returned to Camila, she thanked everyone for participating and told players that peaceball was something they could teach their children or play with mixed-gender teams, since it was a noncontact sport. She also took the chance to explain some of the ideas behind the game: to remove the focus on competition and emphasize collaboration instead, and to give players the responsibility for resolving disputes rather than referring to an external authority. Then the two of us said our goodbyes and walked back to the prison's front gates.

Peaceball was based on the Dutch sport *korfball*. But the game was also constructed as a counterpoint to soccer, Brazil's reigning sport and by far the game most played across men's prisons. Camila and I took over the field from that other sport—a move that, we only learned afterward, had taken the space away from the "veterans," a group of older imprisoned men who were scheduled to play at the same time. The structure of peaceball also deconstructed, and in some cases inverted, many of soccer's basic principles. First, the constant cycle of players between teams, and between attack and defense, undercut any straightforward sense of competition. By transforming the referees into mediators, the game also redistributed authority among the players themselves. Most importantly, peaceball had no rules. Instead, its eight "guidelines" were available for players to enforce, debate, or even alter as they saw fit. The intended result was to transform the soccer field from a space of punishment and competition to one of collaboration and collective resolution.

This was the vision set out by Luan, the sport's creator and one of the Project's founders, who was still employed as a psychologist by the prison administration during my fieldwork. But peaceball began not in the prison system, but in the favela complex of Maré. In 2012, Luan volunteered for a project within PRONA-SCI, the National Program of Security with Citizenship, which targeted youths described in policy briefs as "on the edge of criminality." Maré was a unique case within this program since, unlike other areas that had been targeted by PRONA-SCI and designated as "territories of peace," no Police Pacifying Unit had been set up within the complex. Still, both PRONASCI and the pacification programs were part of a broader discourse of "soft security" that aimed to combat violence through investment in the social and moral well-being of residents, with an explicit focus on youth.[4] PRONASCI organized a slate of activities and programs across Rio de Janeiro. As I outline in Chapter 4, the program also included an explicit focus on mothers as an intermediary and a point of contact between the state and the children it identified as potential criminals.

Luan was employed by PRONASCI to run conflict resolution workshops with young women in Maré, outside and unrelated to his work in prison. There he met Paulo, a sports instructor who was running what he then called "social *korfball.*" Paulo had modified the rules of *korfball* when he brought the sport into the city's favelas. When Luan saw the game in action, he could identify in its rules something very close to group therapy. "But," he explained during an interview, "as it was, it didn't make anyone more *social*, more collaborative." He wanted something transformative, something that would produce a different kind of sociality. So he modified it again, this time by transforming the rules into guidelines and by stressing the role of mediation. In his words, the game's form would force players "to learn and think collectively" and to resolve disputes between themselves without resorting to violence.

Part sport, part conflict resolution exercise, part group therapy, peaceball combined its therapeutic aspirations with the principles of mediation and non-violence. Through Project Life, Luan exported the game from Maré into Rio's prisons, acting as a mediator and training others like Camila to do the same. The combination of a shifting constellation of teammates with the removal of the referee created a field where players became responsible for producing and reproducing the game. Neither Camila nor Luan saw the sport as something that would suddenly transform players into more responsible and mutually supportive subjects. Instead, it was a provocation to think differently about teamwork, discipline, and rules and their enforcement; in short, it presented to players a

model of relating to one another. And the psychologists hoped that such a provocation might spread out from the game, in whatever small way, into the lives of
players.

In Maré, peaceball formed part of an intervention that aimed to strengthen
social ties. It contributed to a broader effort to provide an alternative to crime
for the area's poor and largely Black youth. It was, in other words, what anthropologist Benjamin Fogarty-Valenzuela describes as a "pedagogy of prohibition"
that tied educational programs for youth to the country's War on Drugs and
prescribed modes of "proper" citizenship and labor.[5] Project Life worked with a
demographic that was only a few years older than these youth. PRONASCI was a
preventive intervention, one that aimed to put youth on the "right path" before
they became ensnared in either the "world of crime" or the criminal justice
system. In René Dotti, by contrast, this supposedly critical moment had passed,
and players had already been marked by a criminal conviction. What the game
offered instead was a second chance. It attempted to restage this earlier decision
point by offering the possibility of a different kind of social life.

These "soft" security interventions formed part of a broader strategy of development and governance known in Brazil as pacification. Pacification was the
name given to a colonial pedagogy that accompanied projects of settlement and
genocide in Brazil.[6] Initially, it referred to the dispossession of indigenous territories and communities through a civilizing mission that largely centered on
conversion to Catholicism and instruction in manual labor. Under the tutelary
vision of Brazil's colonizers, the pacified subject would take on the values of the
colony (or empire, or republic, depending on the era), while the usurpation of
land was recast as a benevolent or even paternal gesture.[7] This discourse was
revived in the twenty-first century through Rio's Police Pacifying Units, which
transformed the periodic police incursions within the city's favelas into permanent occupations, marketed as a "reclaiming" of these territories. Alongside the
occupation came promises of upgrades to infrastructure and increased investments in social programs, healthcare, and education. In its latest iteration, pacification suggested that "inhabitants of favelas, in contrast to other citizens, are
seen as collaborators with their own oppressors, carriers of a permissiveness or
moral insufficiency that does not distinguish them sufficiently from organized
crime."[8] Separated by over a century, the "unruly" indigenous subject and the
"criminal" Black favela resident were nevertheless interpellated by pacification

as analogous figures in need of salvation, both for their own good and for that of Brazil.

These programs diagnosed favelas, and the youth who lived there, as suffering from a lack of discipline and social ties that might ensure order and integrate them into the broader city. Youths became vessels, waiting to be filled with the skills needed to form these supportive relationships. Individual development and urban security were bound together, and the "problem" of crime was cast as a social maladaptation born out of ignorance. Peaceball bore the marks of this broader pedagogical mission; it was resocialization in the most literal sense of the word, explicitly instructing players into a mode of sociality that it assumed they had not encountered before. Whereas anthropologists have long understood sport as an arena for cultivating, enforcing, and dramatizing morality— and moral masculinity, in particular—Project Life explicitly instrumentalized this approach, asking players to act out who they might be and how they could relate to one another.[9] And like these other soft security programs, it was offered as a complement, rather than an alternative, to the "hard" security of policing and punishment. As Denise Ferreira da Silva notes, while sport and educational activities became the public face of PRONASCI, most programs and resources were directed toward police and other law enforcement agencies.[10] While Luan was teaching peaceball in Maré, the military police were still killing the community's youth and arresting many more. Some of those would eventually encounter peaceball again on the soccer fields of Rio de Janeiro's prisons.

Peaceball was certainly fun, as both a game and a way to puncture the boredom and immobility that characterized imprisonment in "closed" units like René Dotti. When mediators like Camila explained the principles behind the sport's guidelines, players seemed receptive to the idea, although they were less optimistic about the possibility of continuing to play outside the auspices of Project Life. I doubt that, on its own, the game was successful in achieving its aims. But as a story that volunteers offered to incarcerated people, it spoke to the kind of pedagogy that placed participants on that field with the promise of change and the fantasy that their well-being and that of the security state were one and the same.

Improper Intimacy

For three months, I met every Wednesday afternoon with Reinaldo, Pedro, and the three psychology students to develop our workshop. As the two with previous experience with Project Life, Janaína and Pedro took the lead. Both were idealistic, first-generation students in their early twenties, eager to transform their training into firsthand experience and to expand their discipline's work for social justice. But the topic of "mutual aid" was chosen for us by Reinaldo, who was inspired by Russian anarchist Peter Kropotkin's book of the same name that the rest of us had not read.[11] The aim was to promote a discussion of everyday practices of survival among imprisoned people and their families, and to offer the concept of mutual aid as a frame for them. In addition, we hoped that participants could reflect on some differences, like enforcement mechanisms, between the networks of reciprocal obligation that operated among imprisoned people and those that existed outside.

Reinaldo and the psychology students spoke of themselves as facilitators rather than teachers, and they understood this distinction to be critically important. This meant that they aimed to offer an opportunity for participants to reflect on what already existed among themselves and a language to aid in that reflection. The idea was that by explicitly recognizing the potential of different forms of aid, participants might then amplify and build on them. Building on Janaína's and Pedro's past experiences, we decided to organize the workshop around a series of core questions. Each one was designed to be open-ended, while still following a line of development. The bulk of each meeting was dedicated to crafting and refining these questions, and we spent hours debating the choice of a particular word, the use of active or passive voice, or the position of one question before or after another. Reinaldo pushed us to think of these questions as having one of three functions—to open, to "trigger," and to close. "What do these questions *provoke*?" he constantly asked. We ended up with six:

1. How did you arrive here? How was that experience?[12]

2. What does the state provide for you?

3. How do you support one another?

4. Can you give an example of receiving help (*ajuda*) while in prison?

5. And if you hadn't been helped, what would have happened then?

6. Do these same kinds of support exist outside prison?

From this list, questions four and five took the longest to develop. In both cases, we debated the limits of the term *ajuda*, meaning *aid* or *help*, for weeks. Would the participants necessarily understand this work as part of the framework of mutual aid we were using? Should we specify the meaning of *ajuda* beforehand? Would it be clearer to ask instead about instances of "depending" on another person? Which choice would be the most open-ended? Which would give participants the most freedom to speak?

Question five was the prickliest. It was originally my suggestion, and was accepted without much discussion when I put it forward in our second meeting. But a few weeks later, Janaína and another student began to worry about the value of a counterhistorical approach. The problem they saw was that it was framed in the negative, which could encourage speculation about conflict and lead away from identifying what already existed in the present. In addition, they were concerned that this would set the tone for the remainder of the conversation. In the end, the question stayed, but Janaína remained concerned about how it would play out.

The amount of effort that went into each question and the weight that each word seemed to hold were at odds with the group's claim that the workshop would be a free-flowing, open conversation. But these discussions were a way for the students to make a praxis out of their education, to grapple with questions of professional ethics, and to cultivate a specific kind of relationship with our imagined participants. Our work stood in the shadow of two previous events that Reinaldo, Pedro, and Janaína all brought up as clear examples of bad psychological practice. The first had occurred recently, in another set of Project Life workshops that Janaína participated in. In her version of the story, the group had mapped out each stage of the workshop carefully over a few months, just like we were doing. But when it came time to run the activity inside a prison, one member veered away from the agreed structure and began something that he had prepared on his own. Standing in front of participants, he conducted this final exercise. Janaína recalled him saying: "Close your eyes. I want you to think of the person you have left outside, the one you have abandoned. Think about what you would say to this person, how you might explain what you've done to them." Apparently, several participants cried. Reinaldo suspended the student and barred him from any future Project Life activities; he later explained to me that this student was a "manipulator" who "thought he was the shit because he'd read Nietzsche."

The second had occurred about a year before with a young volunteer, a psychology student who had just ended a relationship. According to Reinaldo, in one workshop she also began crying when the discussion reminded her of her recent heartbreak. Wiping tears from her eyes, she told the story of the breakup to participants and added that she was struck by how young they were, how they too must be suffering from the distance from those they loved. As Reinaldo recounted the event, he called the student a "seductress" and began imitating feminine gestures that he saw as flirtatious, before running his hands down the curves of an imaginary woman's body.

Prison workers and administrators were always concerned with inappropriate relationships and forms of intimacy between incarcerated people and staff or volunteers. This anxiety is a common feature across prison systems, many of which codify norms of conduct to discourage "informal" relationships from developing. As a volunteer teacher in a California penitentiary in 2019, for example, I received instructions to avoid becoming overly familiar with my students and to refuse all gifts. I was also emphatically warned to never, *ever* cry while inside the institution. In Rio, staff cautioned me to never promise anything to an incarcerated person, who could take even an offhand comment as a binding commitment. What motivated this concern was an institutional suspicion that intimacy and compassion might evolve into favors, that incarcerated people could weaponize them for personal gain. As Reinaldo's flirtatious parody suggests, improper intimacy was also entangled with a broader paranoia surrounding femininity and the presence of women in men's prisons. While Chapter 4 examines these gendered dynamics in more detail, it is important to stress here that in Rio, staff and volunteers disciplined themselves and each other to maintain emotional distance from imprisoned people, so that they might avoid entering this dangerous field of intimacy.

Improper intimacy could derail our planned workshop. If a correctional officer or warden noted such behavior and reported it to the administration, it might also jeopardize the broader work of Project Life. But for Reinaldo and the students, improper intimacy was about more than this institutional gaze, or even professional ethics. It was also a performance of closeness or concern that smoothed over and thereby ignored the chasm that existed between the lives of volunteers and those of participants. Some empathy was necessary; too much was poison. "What do we see when we go into prison?" Reinaldo once asked us rhetorically during a planning session. "Tragedy. But the streets are also tragic. These are tragic lives; we have to support these people and provide a structure for understanding their pain. You can't take the dignity of their lives from them." The tears that appeared in both stories were clear markers that some boundary had been breached, that the students had risked derailing the entire workshop. As they circulated, these narratives embedded themselves as an institutional memory within Project Life; by discussing them, newer volunteers like me could consider how to relate to participants and to identify dangerous zones of conversation. But this vigilance also set clear limits on which kinds of critique could be cultivated within the Project, and which must be avoided at all costs.

Hate Speech and the Right to Critique

First there's the name, Project Life. I hate the name. It sounds like one
of those churches where they go to do some volunteer work in the prison
system. And I think that that says a lot about what the actual goal of the
Project is. The fact that it's a project that works with health and citizenship,
you know, I think that there's also an intention to talk about certain kinds
of health, certain kinds of citizenship, that end up being instruments to
maintain the status quo that reproduces the system.

Stefanie, recorded interview

Project Life's harshest critics were its own volunteers. Stefanie, who had worked in the Project for over three years by the time I began my fieldwork, was direct in laying out its limitations. In our interview, she began with the preceding criticism of the name, before suggesting that the Project represented a "*dispositif* that forces people into certain positions" through ideas of delinquency and reform. But despite these critiques, she had in fact increased her involvement with the Project over successive years. She conceded that it "opens doors for the possibility of working with a different perspective, you know?"

Psychology in Brazil is a diverse tradition that encompasses heterodox approaches. Alongside clinical psychology and cognitive behavioral therapy, students train in social psychology and various strands of psychotherapy. Their education often includes a heavy dose of French philosophy and critical social theory. Foucault was translated into Portuguese before English; he visited Rio de Janeiro a few times over the 1970s, including for a series of talks that would later be published in English as "Truth and Juridical Forms."[13] Most practicing psychologists today have some fluency in French poststructuralism. Luan, for example, would repeatedly cite Deleuze's "Postscript on the Societies of Control" during our conversations to explain the contemporary nature of punishment.[14] When I asked him why Brazil's prison population was rising, in contrast to Deleuze's argument that prisons were becoming obsolete, he explained that the country was simply *atrasado* (behind the times). Another psychologist described reading *Discipline and Punish* as an epiphany.[15]

All of this is to say that the field of prison psychology was heavily shaped by many of the same forms of critique that I brought to my fieldwork. This extended to Project Life, which seemed sustained by a kind of self-critique that was inherent to its very form.[16] The Project offered an escape valve, a way to pursue goals or ideals that psychologists saw as meaningful against the backdrop of bureaucratic classification work that made up the bulk of their professional responsibilities in prison. Volunteers like Stefanie would describe it less as a coherent program and more as a vehicle that they might hijack for other ends. They often took great care in planning activities to either mitigate or subvert the constraining influence of both the prison environment and the Project itself. But this right to critique was not evenly distributed—and it rarely, if ever, extended to participants themselves.

The concern with hate speech was indicative of this division of critical labor. It began in our planning sessions for the mutual aid workshop. Reinaldo, who acted as the group's coordinator, demanded that we take great care in defining the purpose of the activity, even as he stressed that we should expect it to be taken in different directions by participants. This was one of many groups that he had organized over several years, generally in collaboration with psychology departments at Rio's universities, where he had found eager volunteers who could often gain extra credit for their involvement. Reinaldo had supervised mutual aid workshops in the past; he assured us that it would be "light, beautiful even. A celebration of life." Janaína, Pedro, and I had worked with Project Life before, while the other two volunteers were joining for the first time. We planned to run the workshop across six prisons—five units designated for men, and one for women.

The Brazilian Portuguese term *discurso de ódio* is a direct translation from the English *hate speech* and is generally used in the same way to refer to racist, homophobic, ableist, or sexist language or communication. So when Janaína began expressing concern during a meeting that some of our questions—particularly question two, *What does the state provide for you?*—might provoke hate speech from participants, I didn't understand what she meant. We were expecting participants to discuss the lack of state support and poor living conditions inside these prisons. But she thought that this could easily slide into a conversation where participants amplified one another's frustrations, producing a trap of resentment that we could not control, let alone resolve. Apparently, this was also hate speech.

Our six scheduled workshops were divided into three consecutive days, with two prison visits each day. These prisons were all located inside, or close to, the Bangu prison complex, although none were held in Tobias Barreto, the unit I was most familiar with and the one described in the previous chapter. On the first morning, we took a bus out from the city center, then boarded one of the vans lining the street that ferried visitors to the front gates of the complex. On the way, we met a missionary who handed us a pamphlet and told us she would be praying for us. As always, there was a long line of visitors waiting to enter the complex, but we passed quickly through a separate line, and walked down the central avenue until we arrived at the first penitentiary. Project Life volunteers did not enter prison with the same ease as public defenders. We often waited for up to an hour while guards searched for documents or dealt with some protocol, even as we watched others pass through. The Project was not seen by most guards as legitimate or worthwhile, and many claimed they had never heard of it, despite its presence in the prison system for many years. On this first day, our entry was relatively straightforward, but we still waited in the reception area for half an hour while the head of security confirmed with the psychologist assigned to that unit that she was expecting us.

Then we were led to an empty classroom. When participants arrived, Janaína began with the opening script, proposing "a conversation about relationships within prison" and assuring those present that "although some of these questions may sound like curiosity, everything that we have brought here was shaped with a specific purpose." Like tears, curiosity was an improper intimacy to be avoided. From that starting point, each of the six workshops held over those three days developed into a group conversation oriented by our list of questions. We had expected large differences across different prisons—between those assigned to different factions, for example, or between units designated for men and women. But our discussions largely converged on both the necessity of mutual aid and the sense of camaraderie that existed among incarcerated people.

The first two questions inevitably provoked an extended conversation about poor conditions within the prison system, including lack of facilities, clothing, healthcare, and other resources. Question two was met a few times with derisive laughter. Participants discussed holding their noses and closing their eyes to eat prison food, the rationing of water in cells, and the lack of medical attention. During the first workshop, Janaína stepped in quickly to stop this conversation and direct the group to the following one. The same thing happened with each subsequent group; Janaína allowed the conversation to go on for a few minutes but then interrupted to shift the topic. It was after we had finished the second workshop that she explained that she could see the conversation veering toward "hate speech," and she wanted to cut it off before it began.

What was the danger that she saw? The anger of incarcerated people is almost universally perceived by those who work in prison as volatile and potentially fatal. It could fly out into an act of physical violence against guards or others confined in the unit; it might result in a transfer to the *castigo*, a segregated cell described in Chapter 5; or else it ran the risk of blocking supposedly "constructive" dialogue. This is why psychologists and other resocialization workers spoke of the need to "calm" (*acalmar*), or occasionally "pacify" (*pacificar*), the frustrations and the rage of imprisoned people. Janaína saw participants' denunciations of the penal system as self-destructive. For her, they corroded the positive mood that she was striving for, and they apparently shut down any potential discussion of solidarity. At the same time, this frustration was baked into the structure of our workshop, acting as a foil against which mutual aid could be revealed. Janaína tried to treat it like a switch, allowing participants to recognize a reality that, in her view, was already known, before attempting to sublimate that frustration into some form of solidarity. She might have been the person most eager to flip that switch, but we had collectively built it into our list of questions weeks before we stepped into any prison.

In doing so, we had also fed into a broader preoccupation with, and aversion toward, violence. Violence was not just a central issue within Project Life; it was also an ever-present concern for prison psychologists and other resocialization workers in Rio's prison system. Public defenders, social workers, and missionaries rarely directly witnessed the forms of assault used by correctional officers and imprisoned people as methods of discipline or torture. But they perceived its effects: rumors, long sleeves that covered bruises, abrupt silences in a conversation, or people moving awkwardly through pain. Even then, they were far more likely to treat incarcerated people as potential perpetrators of violence than as its victims. Peaceball, for example, aimed to demonstrate the viability of nonviolent modes of conflict resolution. Whether in the Maré favela complex or the prison system, the game took place in the shadow of Rio's factions, the organized crime collectives that maintained their own codified systems of punishment, including the routinized use of beatings. "Nonviolence" was an attempt to undercut the legitimacy of factional codes of discipline, even as it framed the economies of violence operating in both contexts as the product of a lack of skills or training. For Luan, peaceball did this with a stress on mediation and guidelines against contact. These principles hardly distinguish peaceball from most other sports, including soccer, which are nonviolent, noncontact team activities. But the game was built around this assumption that, with the proper education, players could resolve conflicts without violence—and potentially, without the factions themselves.[17]

The concern with violence extended across Project Life activities. When Renata, one of two psychologists working part time at René Dotti, suggested that I run a workshop on violence, I took up her idea with enthusiasm and, thinking out loud, began to imagine how a discussion on institutional violence could play out. She immediately pushed back and warned me that such a discussion could excuse the immediate physical violence present in prison or suggest it was inevitable. In her conversations with me, Renata was critical of the penal system and the forms of violence that it produced. But opening up a conversation on systemic or institutional violence seemed to threaten the premise and the pedagogy of Project Life itself. An affirmation of nonviolence between incarcerated people was far more actionable in this context, something to build a discussion or a game around. Within the terms set forth by the Project, violence could be reduced through conscious reflection, education, and proper training, by giving incarcerated people tools to use on themselves.

This approach was built into the Project from the outset. Here we can return to Fernanda's account of the group's formation that I gave at the start of this chapter, where she explained that the Project emerged from her initial encounters with "concrete problems that we had no solutions for [. . .] institutional problems that have no solution." As this quote suggests, the Project was born out of what it foreclosed; it was an attempt to shift the focus and mindset of incarcerated people from the institutional, and therefore intractable, to the individual and interpersonal, which Fernanda felt far more capable of addressing. Two decades later, Janaína invoked hate speech for the same effect—to limit the denunciation of the conditions of confinement and move toward a recognition of, and reflection on, solidarity and mutual aid.

At the same time, her use of *hate speech* inverted the term's former meaning, transforming it from an indictment of racist or sexist speech into a euphemism for Black rage. It was a label that lent credibility to Janaína's feeling threatened by the frustrations and critiques our group was hearing from the predominantly Black participants. It attached hostile intent, or anticipated some violent impact, to these forms of critical commentary that were forged from the visceral experience of imprisonment. The actual content of this "hate speech"—concerns about health, hygiene, physical assaults, and crowding—was not significantly different than some of our conversations a few weeks prior in a university classroom. But what counted as critique in the university classroom had transformed into something hazardous when articulated by Black people in prison. Janaína did not want to give airtime to this discussion, fearing that we would not be able to leave this space of negativity.

In his analysis of New York's Attica prison rebellion and its aftermath, Orisanmi Burton demonstrates that the state promoted therapeutic and educational volunteer-based programs as a tool to surveil, divert, and defuse radical organizing among incarcerated people.[18] In contrast to the incentivization he describes, Rio de Janeiro's prison administration seemed alternately indifferent and hostile to the continued functioning of Project Life. But the case of "hate speech" nevertheless demonstrates how the imperative to contain and redirect the frustrations of imprisoned people still permeated our workshop—because of, not despite, the careful planning of a group of volunteers, including myself, who saw ourselves as deeply critical of the prison system and sympathetic to the imprisoned participants. This was an attempt to manage the workshop's atmosphere, insisting on a sense of optimism and sucking the air out of denunciations. The intended result was to leave no space for participants' "right to hostility," sentiments that could not be sublimated.[19]

At the same time, it is important to note that our attempts to engineer positivity failed. In all six workshops, participants continued to circle back to the crowding, violence, and corruption that shaped their confinement. Although the questions were designed to distinguish these conditions from the networks of mutual aid, and to guide our conversation from the former to the latter, participants understood the two to be inseparable. We discussed the pooling of money to help those who had just entered the prison system and who had no family support; the internal codes of conduct set out by the prison's faction; and incarcerated people's financing of renovations for the visiting room. But these forms of solidarity were all directly tied to institutional negligence and a lack of basic support from the prison administration. Almost every thread of conversation brought us back to question two.

In part, this dynamic reflected how participants interpellated our group as a particular kind of actor within the prison system. Within the Project, and in some other areas of my research, I was often identified by incarcerated people as "human rights" (*direitos humanos*). In this context, *direitos humanos* was not a juridical or moral precept. Instead, it referred to those within in the system who entered prisons to examine and report on their conditions; who were autonomous of the prison administration itself; and who could therefore act as channels for *denúncias* (denunciations, or formal complaints) to the appropriate authorities. Civil society groups, journalists, independent government oversight bodies like the State Mechanism for the Prevention and Combat of Torture, and Project Life volunteers were all wrapped up in this label. To *be* "human rights" meant being a listener and a channel, recording *denúncias* and carry them to the courts, the press, or the state legislature outside. What Janaína deemed as hate speech was perhaps better seen as an audit of the system's failings that needed to be exposed. But it was also a challenge to Project Life's division between the individual and the institutional, and its assumption that the latter was simply outside the scope of intervention.

In Janaína's assessment, our inability to move beyond frustrations with the prison system and the state itself meant that the workshop had fallen apart. But to suggest that it had been either a success or a failure would be to judge it solely based on volunteers' expectations. Project Life activities were often valued by participants for reasons completely unrelated to the structure and content of the events themselves. Our workshop allowed participants to move around the prison—a kind of movement that is often severely restricted, particularly in closed penitentiaries. This circulation allowed people to see friends from other cells and communicate between them. It also provided the chance for contact with "human rights" and with the prison psychologist who would generally be present for some of the activity. Participants passed on queries and messages on behalf of cellmates to prison staff, including requests for urgent medical care, written on scraps of paper or cardboard. They also took the opportunity to ask volunteers questions regarding legal procedures. The conversations themselves were valued as an opportunity to exchange experiences and learn something; in one of the women's prisons, participants expressed their gratitude to us for being able to *desabafar* (vent) and express these pent-up frustrations.

Our aim was to take up the space of Project Life to produce something that was neither paternalistic nor didactic but rather a recognition of the potential of solidarity and mutual aid. The result, despite being based on a critical approach to incarceration and to the Project itself, nevertheless did not overcome the tensions that marked Project Life as a whole. Our vision of collaboration functioned only up to a point, one marked by the limits between supposedly "productive" dialogue and "hate speech." But it was precisely when participants crossed this boundary that they found the space to express their own forms of critique.

All the World's a Stage

Stefanie and I were running late. We had arrived at the front gates of René Dotti on time, but the guards couldn't seem to find the document that authorized our entry, so we spent a while outside, clinging to the shade as we waited for it to emerge. Once it finally appeared, we signed in and passed through the metal detector, before a guard led us to the large warehouse structure that held the prison's wings. This time, we were headed back to the yellow education hall, the space described in the Introduction and the room most used for Project Life activities. Enough plastic chairs had been left out for a hundred people, although in the end only about half were used. As usual, the seats near the front had been reserved for visitors, so we sat down next to Renata. Diogo was sitting at a nearby table. He crouched down as he came over to greet us so he wouldn't obstruct the audience's view of a performance that had just begun.

Leo, an incarcerated white man in his midforties, had worked as an actor before his arrest. He and Diogo both participated in Project Life the previous year, and both had graduated. As I mention at the start of this chapter, those who completed the program earned the title of "multipliers," a term that reflected the expectation that they share what they had learned with others, whether inside the prison or out. Multipliers often continued to assist Project Life by setting up chairs and tables, calling participants to the hall, and assisting volunteers. But in 2017, the statewide coordinator of Project Life began a new initiative where multipliers could propose their own activities. Diogo and Leo both took up this opportunity. I wasn't able to participate in Diogo's event, but he told me in a letter that he had organized a discussion on the theme of "accepting my imperfections and respecting our differences [. . .] I spoke about my ideas and tried to plant them in the minds of others, that we aren't trash, we aren't garbage, we're citizens and we need to understand this, fight for this."

Leo had planned his show months in advance, together with the Freedom Theater Group, a collective of eight cisgender men and five travestis. This gave Stefanie and me time to request authorization to attend as part of the audience. The presentation was divided into two acts. The first gave a condensed, five-minute version of a landmark play over history, with Leo explaining the context and importance of the work over the microphone as he stood in front and to the side of the stage. We arrived right before *Oedipus Rex*, with Diogo in the titular role. Beginning with a visit to the Delphic Oracle, the play moved quickly through its major plot points. Leo narrated the story, while a guitarist provided soft background music that did not always match the tone of the play. The group took some liberties with the plot: Rather than blinding himself at the conclusion, Diogo/Oedipus pushed a knife into his chest and collapsed over the body of Jocasta.

With a fast-forward through two millennia, Leo began to narrate a story about the life and times of Shakespeare, introduced as the "greatest playwright the world has ever known," from his first job, slaughtering oxen, to his years caring for the horses of the owner of the Globe Theatre until his big break came. There was a lesson in Shakespeare's life for us, Leo reminded the audience: The playwright never gave up, and achieved his dream after years of struggle.[20] While

Leo talked, Diogo snuck across the hall to greet Stefanie and me. She gave him a set of news articles she thought he might be interested in; I handed over a stack of academic journal articles and book chapters I had printed earlier, and whispered that I still hadn't received the letter he had sent through the mail about a month ago. By the time my attention returned to the stage, the performance of *Hamlet* had begun. One of the actors was a short, charismatic man who had once worked as an extra for TV Globo, Brazil's largest broadcasting company. He had no trouble making himself heard over the whir of the fans—even through the white sheet he wore as the ghost of Hamlet's father—and he also played his parts with an exaggerated, slapstick physicality. This, combined with the breakneck speed at which the performance covered the plot points of Shakespeare's longest play (Rosencrantz and Guildenstern died before ever stepping onto the stage) transformed the tragedy into a comedy that had the audience continuously laughing. The performance concluded with a comic pileup of bodies and a huge round of applause.

Next up was Gogol's *Inspector General*. With no props aside from some chairs and a table, Leo asked us to place ourselves inside Hotel 171. That name, a riff on the play's nameless inn, was a reference both to Article 171 in the Brazilian criminal code, referring to fraud and embezzlement, and to the popular phrase that arose from it: "one-seven-one" (*um-sete-um*), meaning deceitful, manipulative, or untrustworthy. This play, Leo explained, was about corruption in public institutions, "which should resonate in today's Brazil." The talented extra was absent for this piece, and the actors onstage were less successful in making themselves heard. I saw some furtive bribes passed between hands and understood that I was watching a representation of banal forms of corruption, but still found it difficult to follow along, even sitting in the front row. Diogo snuck over to me a second time toward the end of the performance and handed me a *catuque*, a scrap of paper with the information on an imprisoned person needing medical attention, asking me to hand it to Renata afterward.

The final performance was from the Brazilian playwright Oswaldo de Andrade, titled *The Candle King* (*O Rei da Vela*). In the original version, the owner of a candle factory attempts to resolve his financial woes by marrying his daughter off to a wealthy foreigner. But Leo explained that they had decided to give a gender-flipped version of the work, replacing the daughter with a son and Mr. Jones with Mrs. Jones. Once again, the extra stole the show as the son and prospective husband; for the other actors, the performance became a struggle to speak their lines through their own fits of laughter. The plot quickly fell apart and the actors improvised a quick conclusion, but this performance received a standing ovation from the audience.

Now we moved to the second act, what Leo described as the "motivational speech" element of his presentation: four short pieces that had been developed by the group, each one with a specific message, and aimed as "us, prisoners, to grow and advance." In what followed, the relationship between the narration and the action flipped. Before, Leo had introduced the work, its context, and its significance, then let the story and its message play out onstage. Now, he only announced the title, and each scene was a brief one- or two-minute prelude to his lengthier discussion on specific virtues as he explained the moral lesson behind each vignette, like a Greek chorus. The first: "You are Unique." Two men sat silently, center stage, side by side. As the one toward our left mimed opening a newspaper, the other did the same. The first man noticed and turned to the second; every movement was reflected back at him by this other man. He told him to quit it, and got the same reply. Shouting in frustration, he stood up and rushed off stage left, while his double did the same off to the right. "So many people try to be someone else," Leo explained over the microphone, "but out of all the billions in the world, you are the one who is best qualified to be you. What is God's plan for you?"

The second scene was titled "Live in the Moment." Diogo walks onto the stage, clearly exhausted. His wife asks him to go out with his son—played by the extra—for his birthday, but Diogo shouts in response that he is tired and just wants to rest, collapsing into a chair. The son's clownish face of disappointment makes his mother break character, but after stifling the laugh, she takes him by the hand and they leave together. Diogo finally wakes up, stretching out to show that he is finally rested. Still sitting, he mimes receiving a telephone call and repeats, in horror, the news being given from the other side: His family was in a terrible accident, and his son has died. The scene ends in a scream of despair. Leo's voice returns over the sound system: "This man gave no value to those who he loved the most. Remember, today is the future that you were waiting for. Start living now; each day brings its own gifts."

Then we move to the third scene: "Be Faithful to Small Steps." A father, sitting onstage, stands up to greet his son, who explains that he has just returned from his graduation at Harvard and hopes to take over the family business. The father welcomes him back but tells him that if he wants to manage the business, he has to start by cleaning the toilets. The son, now infuriated, refuses, shouts at his father, and announces to the audience that he will abandon not just the business but the family itself, before storming off behind the orange curtain. Leo's voice intercedes: "Nothing is gained in kilometers, and everything in centimeters. Small acts that are carried out are better than large acts that remain as plans. The most important thing is to begin." The final, and shortest, scene was called "The School of Life." A woman tries to raise her son, slumped over on a chair, out of sleep, and warns him that he will be late for school. At first he tries to invent excuses to stay home; when he finally asks "Why do I even need to go?" she responds "Because you are the principal!"

The audience responded to the final punch line with a murmur of laughs, which then transformed into loud applause as Leo stepped up onto the stage. Rather than exploring the meaning of this final vignette, he thanked every member of the Freedom Theater Group for participating, and reminded the audience to "do whatever you can, with whatever you have, wherever you are. It all depends on you." Drawing on figures across history, he spoke of the Book of Romans' message "for us to never give up"; of Beethoven, producing his most beautiful music after he became deaf; and of Martin Luther King, a man who, for Leo, "pursued that which he believed, who had a dream." Already on the verge of tears, he began to speak about Abraham Lincoln, who he claimed ended slavery in the United States but was assassinated "by an actor like myself." At this point, he seemed overwhelmed by remorse, and paused to wipe the tears from his eyes. Once he had steadied himself, he wrapped up the event by stating that everyone had talents, that it was our job to discover and use them, even while in prison. With that conclusion, Leo stepped off the front of the stage and was immediately swamped by fans and friends in the audience. Stefanie and I found Diogo at the edge of this crowd, gave him a hug, and congratulated him on his performance.

This is the second of three theater performances that I describe in this book, all of which took place inside René Dotti. The presence of a stage—far from a typical feature of Rio's prisons—facilitated these kinds of events. About a month beforehand, Luan had run his own Project Life activity here, using techniques from Augusto Boal's Theater of the Oppressed to build and work through scenes of conflict with incarcerated participants. Rio's Prison Theater Group, run by volunteers from a local university, also organized theater workshops drawing on Boal's methods across the state's prisons, using whatever space was available, although these were much less frequent. Today, Boal's dramaturgy was nowhere to be seen—this was not an explicit "rehearsal for the revolution," and the division between spectator and actor was firmly in place.[21] The second half of the event seemed to share more with the conventions of a fable or Christian morality play. This was a contrast to the pedagogies and forms of participation imagined by other Project Life activities. Peaceball was a sport that aimed to demonstrate the viability of a particular kind of sociality. The mutual aid workshop was envisioned as a horizontal, open-ended process of bringing a latent form of solidarity into focus. These performances, by contrast, were unidirectional and explicitly didactic (*live in the moment, be faithful to small steps*), two qualities that psychologists tried to avoid in their work with the Project.

The lessons also had little to do with social ties. Instead, they were affirmations of the individual will; each motivational message was framed around self-worth and perseverance. But the performance itself was a deeply communal act. It drew the crowd into shared moments of both pathos and comedy, experiences that were otherwise inaccessible within conditions of imprisonment. Even the point of apparent breakdown, when one actor's scene-stealing talents caused the others to completely break character and derail the performance, offered a moment of collective catharsis. Leo's tears were another, a public demonstration of sorrow that many in the audience could identify with.

The final two plays from Leo's history of theater—*The Inspector General* and *The King of Candles*—each offered an examination of the theatrics of Brazilian social and political life. There was no direct representation of, or commentary on, incarceration itself. But in occupying the stage, these actors also stepped out of the bodily restrictions of confinement itself. As Christen Smith observes, if state violence individuates and cuts at social ties, theater brings together new forms of community and "wrests the black body away from the spiritual domain of the state."[22] To be on that stage was to present oneself as something other than an object of punishment. It offered a different modality of self-presentation, but it also presented a rare opportunity for incarcerated people to narrate something outside themselves. In addition, it allowed the actors to move in ways that were physically impossible elsewhere in the prison. Even the fifteen feet between one side of the stage and the other offered a field of movement that simply did not exist in the severely overcrowded cells where actors and spectators alike spent most of their time.

Perhaps most importantly, the event refused the kind of deferral that saturated both incarceration and resocialization. As discussed in the previous chapter, juridical techniques of sentencing and popular discourse surrounding punishment produce the time of a sentence as something that does not belong to the incarcerated person. Prison staff and Project volunteers put forward an understanding of confinement as a time for reflection and preparation but not for social action. The future was always located after release, and the time between the present and that moment was understood as suspended agency. Leo undid this deferral. His lessons made reference to the future, but they also pointed to his audience's agency in the present, insisting that they need not wait for anything. While the performance showed an optimism that many of the Project's volunteers aspired toward, it was also infused with sentimentality and an emphasis on virtue that Stefanie, Reinaldo, and others carefully avoided. But because of that, it did not aim to manage or temper the audience's expectations. Instead, it gave time back to the audience and affirmed their capacity to do something with it.

Graduation Day

Project Life wrapped up at the end of every calendar year. Participants who attended most of that cycle's activities were invited to a graduation ceremony that was scheduled for December or January, depending on the prison. Most did not make it that far—the Project had a high attrition rate, since sickness, transfers, and regime progression all meant dropping out. Even though the Project ran in most state prisons during my fieldwork, an incarcerated person could not sign up for the Project at the beginning of the year and complete it in another. In the case of René Dotti, the unexpected arrival of a new warden resulted in multiple delays for the ceremony, but it was finally confirmed for the end of February. The Project's administrators, the prison psychologists, and all those who had volunteered in the previous year were invited to join. When I arrived, I found a bottleneck at the prison entrance, since the guards were only allowing two visitors to sign in, present their documents, and pass through the security check at a time. Eventually, we were all sitting in the yellow hall again. Today the new warden was present, as was Colonel Gilson, the Subsecretary of Treatment for Rio's prison administration. Most of the other audience members were new graduates of the Project. The rest were participants in the Project who had not fulfilled the requirements of graduation but wanted to take part and show their support for their friends.

Diogo opened the event, standing in front of the stage with a microphone in hand. He thanked everyone for their presence and reminded us that we had gathered together in the belief that "everyone can be different, it all depends on us." Renata, who had organized the proceedings, took the microphone from him and gave a brief history of Project Life, with a nod to its cofounder, Luan, who was sitting with us in the audience. She was quick—later, she would tell me that she arranged the proceedings to give as much time as possible for participants to talk and perform. Leo was up next; he told the audience that "we are all here for what we've done, but that remains in the past. Today we are here for change; we make the future today."

Then Leo introduced a series of performances. First, there was the Freedom Theater Group, who performed a rap onstage titled "Everyone Wants to Be Loved and Respected." Then a band of four came up to play two self-composed rock songs. The first, titled "Resocialization," had me furiously attempt to write down as many lyrics as possible in my notebook, but I could only pick up a few lines: "The prisoner wants to resocialize"; "We want an upright life"; "There are many innocent people who are condemned." Running with the same theme, the second was called "Resocialize to Conquer the Future" and reminded listeners to "forget the past" and that "Jesus is the way, the truth, and the life." But it ended on a less optimistic note, asking "How much longer will families cry?"

Renata had printed out certificates for all those who would graduate. She invited me to the front along with Colonel Gilson, Stefanie, and a few other volunteers, and gave each of us a stack of them. We passed the microphones between us and read out one name at a time. Each graduate received a huge round of applause from the audience. Some participants were beaming as they stepped to the front and received their certificate. Others were more reluctant. As we read through the names, I noticed that most trans women and travestis were being called out by their registered birth names,[23] and many were clearly offended by having those names announced over a speaker. As soon as the certificates were in the hands of these new multipliers, Renata asked for graduates to return them immediately; the new warden still had not taken the time to sign each of them. She promised that they would be redistributed in the coming weeks.

The warden then gave the last words of the event. He thanked everyone for their patience with the delays, assuring the audience that they were needed to plan the event properly. Then he spoke of his own childhood, including his pride at being born and raised in a *comunidade* (a poor, peripheral community, generally a favela), like many of the graduates. "People say there is no opportunity," he informed us, "but I found my own." He gave his own employment history as an example, laying out a trajectory that supposedly represented a self-made man. He offered this biography as an example for the audience before appealing to them to find a life outside prison: "If there's one thing I want you to hear today it's this—don't come back. Prison is no place for anyone."

That last sentence was a strange admission to hear from someone who had made imprisonment his career. For many members of the audience, with years or even decades left on their sentence, this exhortation to never return was also a little premature. But the Project was an established site for this kind of self-critique, a space where prison staff might work through the contradictions of the institution, reconsider their position within it, and perhaps alleviate some of the resulting tensions. Project Life held these contradictions together, often uncomfortably. It offered space for a demand for rights and recognition alongside pacifying discourses of lack that positioned participants as a void to be filled. The ability to recognize and reconcile these tensions was not extended to imprisoned participants, who instead were pinned down by particular pedagogies and asked to maintain a hopeful attentiveness. But *through* that optimism, people like the Freedom Theater Group still managed to smuggle in other projects, highlight other aspects of violence, and articulate different futures for themselves.

For psychologists and other treatment workers, resocialization was largely understood as a fight against crime. A reformed subject was one who left prison with the capacity and the support to construct a life for themself within the confines of the law, no longer in conflict with the security state. The messages of empowerment that were embedded into Project Life largely served that goal. And many incarcerated people, particularly those who participated in the Project, shared in these concerns. But for imprisoned people, resocialization was also a fight against death. This includes social death—the exclusion from the realm of the human through routinized violence and the severance of kinship.[24] But it was also physical, biological death at the hands of police, militias, factions, tuberculosis, or hypertension. To be incarcerated was to live in close proximity to death, in this institution meant for no one. To be resocialized meant making it out of prison alive.

As the graduation event finished, a new band came to the stage—two men, one on guitar, the other on percussion—and performed a song they had written for the graduation. Renata had printed out the lyrics and passed them to the audience so we could sing along:

> When we see that time is passing
> And the pain of the past doesn't return
> Inside our chests there is a hope
> I will go forward, I will begin again
> I know that life isn't full of flowers
> There are thorns that bring us pain
> But between everything I've lost I find a love
> That time hasn't erased.
>
> I just want to live life
> And show that I am happy
> Erase the scenes that I lived badly
> And that time left in me.
> I know that in life we learn by our mistakes
> And today I learned
> That it is worth it to begin again,
> My story doesn't end here.

I followed along until the end of the song. Then I folded the page in two, slid it into my notebook, and carried it with me through the prison's front gates. The hall would have emptied out soon after as Leo, Diogo, the band, and the rest of the audience returned to their cells.

THREE

Faith and the Weight of the World

Vilma was anxious about her first visit to a prison. She and I had been invited by Pastor Bruno and his mother, a missionary named Magnólia, to a special event inside René Dotti. Vilma was an active member of a wealthy and largely white evangelical church in Rio's West Zone; her congregation provided financial support for Bruno and Magnólia's work inside the system. As we gathered outside the prison walls, we held hands and Bruno led us in a short prayer. Then we signed in at the front gate, had our bags searched, and passed through the metal detector. I walked alongside Vilma across the inner courtyard, past the administration building, and back into the warehouselike structure that contained the prison's wings. Our destination was the temple at the far end of the building. We quickly passed the guards' station and the yellow education hall. Farther along was the first wing of the prison, with the "cells of the impious" (*celas dos ímpios*) lined up along one wall. A few people came up to the grated iron doors to greet Magnólia and Bruno. They waved in response, but we did not stop walking.

Then we entered the second wing, which was entirely reserved for incarcerated evangelicals. I had passed through here before, but like Vilma I was still struck by the contrast between the two spaces. The first wing was painted in the two-tone gray that was standard across the state's prisons; the second was covered in bright murals that depicted biblical scenes in warm colors. Underneath these images were Bible verses written in Portuguese and Greek. The space seemed brighter, cleaner, and the characteristic prison smell was more faint. For me, the path between the cells of the impious and the evangelical wing pointed to an unequal distribution of resources and opportunities within the prison. But for Vilma, our walk demonstrated the power of conversion through a sensorial shift in which colors, smells, clothes, and what she described as the "completely different look" on the faces of the imprisoned people told a very clear before-and-after story. When we reached the vestibule of the temple and began to feel the vibrations of gospel music through the floor, Vilma asked me, "Why would anyone want to live in the cells of the impious?" The question was both a puzzle and an invitation. Soon an incarcerated man invited us to enter the temple, where over one hundred people turned to greet us as they sang in harmony.

Once we were done, there would be at least one more church service that day. Like many other prisons in Rio, René Dotti struggled with the demands of both incarcerated evangelicals and outside missionaries for worship, Bible study groups, and other religious activities. The prison's two social workers were responsible for scheduling the use of the temple. On most days, two or three separate church groups would enter the prison to run a *culto* (church service). Many of those imprisoned in the evangelical cells would participate in all of them; they were also joined by some from the cells of the impious. Outside the prison system, church-run programs and religious nongovernmental organizations (NGOs) dotted the city. They offered services for both families of imprisoned people and those who had recently left prison, including basic food assistance, emergency shelter, psychological counseling, free dental and medical treatment, and employment opportunities. No other community and no other profession matched the scale of this presence. During my fieldwork, fifty-seven psychologists and seventy social workers were employed by the prison administration. But over 1,200 people were authorized to enter Rio's prisons to provide what federal law described as "religious assistance." Evangelicals made up the vast majority. They found "brothers in faith" (*irmãos na fé*) among imprisoned people, correctional officers, administrators, social workers, and psychologists. And the message they brought—of faith, hope, sin, and redemption—spilled out from the temple, reshaping the entire prison system in the process.

By the time I began my fieldwork, evangelical community, labor, and theology had grafted itself onto almost every aspect of Rio de Janeiro's prison system. Missionaries and church groups supported, and occasionally substituted for, many of the basic systems of punishment.[1] Christian discourse saturated talk not only among incarcerated people and missionaries but also social workers, psychologists, and guards, shaping how they understood the nature of punishment, reform, and justice.[2] It was during a Project Life workshop, not a *culto*, that an incarcerated man once asked me if I knew who created prison. Surprised by the question, I was struggling to come up with a response when he opened his Bible and brought my attention to Ezekiel 7:23: "Make a chain [*cadeia*], for the land is full of bloody crimes, and the city is full of violence." For him, the verse demonstrated that prison was a God-given institution. That interpretation is more evident in Portuguese than English, since the term for *chain*, *cadeia*, is also a synonym for *prison*. Both incarcerated people and outside missionaries referenced this verse at least a half-dozen other times throughout my research. In each case, the citation was meant to demonstrate that prisons were made by God, that incarceration was an instrument of divine justice.

Christianity, as anthropologist Kelly Gillespie argues, "provides the frame in which the state's injunctions—morality, family values and rehabilitation—make sense at the level of implementation" inside prisons.[3] Evangelical Christianity, in particular, is a religious movement that frames human life through the choice and the experience of being reborn. Most incarcerated people and staff recognized the resonance between this spiritual transformation and the work of resocialization. But for many, the affinity went beyond resemblance or even shared aims; instead, they saw resocialization and Christian rebirth as fundamentally the same process. Conversion had become the dominant idiom to articulate futures for both incarcerated people and the prison system, and to conceive the possibilities of reform not only for individuals but for Brazilian society as a whole.

These imbrications of Christian redemption and rehabilitation are not new. The penitentiary model was first forged in the United States through the heavy involvement of Protestant churches, most notably through the efforts of Quakers to found Pennsylvania's Eastern State Penitentiary.[4] Before the medicalization of rehabilitation, crime and sin were largely considered synonymous, and imprisonment was explicitly conceived in theological terms as a process of reflection, penance, and the pursuit of virtue.[5] Still, the relationship between incarceration and Christianity was never entirely symbiotic; American Protestants gave up on the project to build a properly "Christian" penitentiary, and governments often worked to limit the influence of missionaries inside the prison system.[6] While some strands of Protestantism offered support for rehabilitation, others—particularly those influenced by Calvinism—were far more pessimistic about the potential for reform.[7] It is arguably the enduring *question* of whether someone labeled as criminal can be resocialized, rather than any particular answer, that marks Christianity's clearest impact on the development of imprisonment.

But for most of the tens of thousands of evangelicals who entered Rio's prisons as staff, missionaries, captives, or visiting family members, the answer was a resounding and unqualified *yes*. The capacity for both individual and collective transformation was the cornerstone of evangelical life within these institutions. It also bled into juridical and "psychotechnical" forms of expertise. Missionaries offered legal assistance and advice to incarcerated people; evangelical psychologists combined therapeutic methods with biblical scripture; and regular church attendance was noted on criminological exam reports as both a marker of one's commitment to resocialization and proof of community support after release. Whereas psychologists, social workers, and public defenders lamented that rising levels of imprisonment had made it impossible to properly "accompany" (*acompanhar*) an individual through their sentence, they saw missionaries and churches as the only groups now capable of providing that continued support.

Despite this surge in evangelical involvement within the prison system, the relationship between the religious movement and punishment was still marked by fundamental contrasts and challenges to the state. Missionaries and incarcerated evangelicals problematized institutional authority and called into question the nature of history, personhood, and social belonging put forward by Brazilian jurisprudence. Christian rebirth, and the distance it places between one's present and past self, eroded the subject envisioned by the law who remained self-same and responsible for past acts. Whereas the Law of Penal Execution outlined resocialization as a process of reintegration with a social order, for evangelicals, society was fundamentally both sick and dangerous. Incarcerated members of the faith were engaged in a constant struggle not to rejoin society but to overturn it, even as they worked to maintain a spiritual, mental, and physical distance from it. It was at these points of friction that evangelical Christianity and incarceration remade one another.

This chapter follows evangelical life and labor within and around the prison system. Here I move back and forth between missionaries like Magnólia and imprisoned, or formerly imprisoned, members of the faith, including one man whom I call Elias. Both groups saw themselves as invested in the work of resocialization, and both dedicated an enormous amount of time and energy into the production and maintenance of hope. But in the process, they also engaged in a continual resignification of not just reform but imprisonment itself. By taking on the mantle of reform, often in open collaboration with the prison administration itself, evangelicals inside and out of prison altered the horizons of punishment.

The Prison's Two Temples

Magnólia told me the story of her first visit to René Dotti, twenty-five years before Vilma's, as I sat with her in an air-conditioned office above her church. Her soft-spoken voice and short stature belied her reputation as a "missionary-sergeant," a leader and a tough-love disciplinarian for her incarcerated congregants. Born in Brazil's Northeast Region, she moved to Rio de Janeiro with her family as a teenager, part of a broader wave of migration to the industrializing city in the 1960s. When she first came to René Dotti as a missionary in the early 1990s, the prison's designated place of worship was permanently adorned with images of the saints and the Virgin Mary. The Catholic chaplain, defying federal law, refused to take them down or cover them for other religious groups. So Magnólia asked to build a new temple. After negotiating with the prison warden over a few months, she was led to an empty space at the back of the prison. She recalled seeing dried blood on the floor, a trace of its former use as a space of torture. But she also understood that the authorization to build *there*, at the point farthest from the guards' station, was a sign of trust in her and her congregants. She pulled together donations from various churches to purchase materials, while incarcerated evangelical men provided the labor. The blood was soon scrubbed away, and six months after construction began, the new temple was complete. Over the next few decades, more and more evangelical church groups came to the prison and into this temple to offer church services, Bible study groups, and adult literacy classes, while the Catholics were left to their own, slightly smaller space.

Brazil's first evangelical churches were established in the early twentieth century, after the arrival of missionaries from the United States and Europe. Many of those that now dominate the religious landscape, such as the Universal Church of the Kingdom of God, were founded in the late 1970s and 1980s. But it was in the 1990s, during the time of redemocratization, that Brazilians, along with many others in Latin America, began to embrace the movement in unprecedented numbers. Black Brazilians, women, and the urban poor led this transformation.[8] It went hand-in-hand with the decline of the Catholic Church, not just in terms of the number of adherents but also in the rising evangelical visibility and influence within public life and institutional politics.[9] This new movement was far from monolithic—Pentecostals made up the vast majority, but a constellation of different churches, teachings, and forms of organization have emerged both from within Brazil and from a continual dialogue with overseas churches. Still, the consolidated visibility and collective power of evangelicals rapidly became a ubiquitous part of everyday life and institutional politics across the country.

This ascension of evangelical Christianity reverberated quickly across Brazil's prisons. Prior to the 1984 Law of Penal Execution, the Catholic Church held a de facto monopoly on missionary work and spiritual guidance in the nation's prisons. In the world's largest Catholic country, this church played a heavy hand in the criminal justice system. For example, Rio de Janeiro's first prison designated for women was formally administered by the state, but day-to-day operations were given over to an order of nuns.[10] Other denominations and other faiths did not hold regular services in prison. It took until the redemocratization of Brazil and the 1984 Law of Penal Execution to loosen the alliance between Catholicism and incarceration. This law listed religion as one of six forms of assistance guaranteed to imprisoned people and prohibited discrimination "of racial, social, religious or political nature."[11] It also established freedom of religious association and the circulation of religious texts inside prisons. Finally, the LEP required that any space for religious services be ecumenical and free of immovable icons.

Magnólia, who was then in her thirties, took part in this first wave of evangelicals to enter Brazil's prisons. Over the 1990s and early 2000s, she would be joined by hundreds of missionaries. Together with their imprisoned congregants, they repeated the story of René Dotti across Rio's entire prison system, building new temples to avoid sharing space with the Catholics and their icons. Today, most penitentiaries in the state have two separate spaces of worship: an older one, left for the Catholics and generally in a state of disrepair, and a newer space, largely occupied by evangelicals but occasionally used by other religious groups like the Spiritists. Of the 121 organizations that were registered to provide "religious assistance" in the prison system during my research, 105 were evangelical. Demand for authorization was so great that in 2016 the administration froze the application process for new evangelical groups in the name of protecting and promoting religious diversity. The Catholic Church was registered as a single group on this list and continued to conduct mass in most of the state's prisons, although by 2017 many of these services had been reduced to once a month. Other groups included the nondenominational Biblical Society of Brazil, one Afro-Brazilian Umbanda congregation, seven Spiritist temples, and a lone rabbi working for the Beit Lubavitch Society.

Inside the prison system, the evangelical movement was represented by a range of denominations. The majority were Pentecostal, a branch that emphasizes the individual's direct access to the gifts of the Holy Spirit, such as speaking in tongues. In a previous ethnographic study of Brazil's prisons, including Rio's now-defunct police lockups, Andrew Johnson spoke of "prison Pentecostalism" to examine the relationships between faith and imprisonment.[12] Here I speak of evangelicalism more broadly. This is because, despite doctrinal or political conflicts between churches, missionary work in prison routinely blurred denominational boundaries. The terms *evangelical* (*evangélico*) and *Christian* (*cristão*)[13] were far more widely used by incarcerated people and prison workers than *pentecostal*. My interlocutors referred the segregated cells, the temple, the collective work of missionaries, and the broader community of the faithful as *evangélico*. Incarcerated people rarely aligned themselves with one church or another, although the Pentecostal influence seeped into the work of missionaries from other traditions. Magnólia and other Baptists, for example, observed that imprisoned congregants would often engage in their *cultos* through the call-and-response dynamic that was characteristic of Pentecostalism during their work in prison, and would often fall to the ground while speaking in tongues.[14] One missionary jokingly referred to herself as "Bapticostal" while in prison, in reference to this elision of doctrinal differences inside the institution.

The creation of René Dotti's two temples and their diverging fates are symptomatic of a profound shift in the religious landscape of punishment. Today, Brazil's Catholic Prison Ministry plays an active role in advocating for prison reform through the National Agenda for Decarceration. Its São Paulo branch has provided the primary vehicle for facilitating ethnographic and other research since the early 2010s.[15] And state governments across Brazil also contracted out the administration of dozens of penitentiaries to a Catholic-founded (although now evangelical-dominated) NGO known as APAC, which advertises itself as a more humane and reformative model of captivity.[16] But the networks, resources, and institutional influence that Catholics have maintained within Brazil's prisons have all shrunk, particularly when compared to those of the evangelical movement. Other religious traditions have felt the effects of a rising evangelical presence. While the Law of Penal Execution opened the possibility for Afro-Brazilian religious traditions to work inside prisons, these groups have encountered enormous resistance among evangelical prison administrators, staff, and incarcerated people themselves. In Rio, only one such group had formal authorization to enter Rio's prison system. Tensions between its leader and the evangelical warden resulted in the suspension of visits several times over the course of my research, while correctional officers made it clear that the volunteer group was not welcome inside the temple.[17]

Most of the people I met during my fieldwork were pulled into the orbit of the criminal justice system at a moment when the temples had already been built, the social and political influence of the evangelical movement had already been established. Beyond the temple itself, incarcerated evangelicals had also established their own form of governance, one that mirrored the structure and disciplinary codes set out by other collectives such as the factions. Such transformations mirrored, and perhaps anticipated, the expanding presence of evangelical Christianity everywhere in the city, particularly in the peripheral communities that were most directly targeted by policing and incarceration. But they also brought a new horizon into the prison system—one that seemed to affirm the possibility of redemption, even when an exploding prison population and a shift toward security funding had made the prospect of a substantial program for resocialization seem distant. At the same time, the religious movement disturbed the temporalities of crime, punishment, and redemption through the experience of rebirth, one that directly brought into question the pasts and futures set out by a criminal sentence.

Testify

Elias began his testimony by describing his first birthday inside a prison, a day that was also marked by an attempt to end his own life. We had first met at Magnólia's church-based group, which provided support for formerly incarcerated people and family members of those still imprisoned. Immediately after she introduced me to the group, Elias approached me, excited by the opportunity to talk, and gave me his number. A few days later, we were sitting on the balcony of a public hospital, where his wife was receiving treatment for a complication in her pregnancy. He started our conversation by recounting his brush with death:

> I was already tripping, taking the drug in my veins, and I really wanted to kill myself. I'd lost my family, I'd lost everything, I'd lost money, I'd lost—and I saw an exit. And a friend had sent me cocaine for my birthday in prison, and I decided that with that cocaine I would commit suicide, I could kill myself quickly, and I started taking it, needle in the vein, needle in the vein, needle in the vein. By the time I had summoned the courage I was already tripping, and now I'm going to give myself the big dose and it's going to be my last one, but I couldn't do it, I couldn't get the needle into my arms, my legs, my feet. I tried to snort it, I couldn't even snort cocaine, it seemed like it wouldn't go in, my body didn't let it enter, and I was despairing in that cell with nothing to do and I turned on the television, and in prison there were only two channels, one was evangelical, and I ended up settling on that one, and when I stopped to watch, in the exact moment that I stopped to watch to pay attention was when the pastor said: "You who are thinking of taking your life, I don't know where you are in this moment, if you are at home or if you're at work, if you're in prison, even. You who are thinking of taking your life now, I am going to tell you this, this, and this." And what she spoke about was *my* life, right? It was me she was talking about, that I couldn't find a solution, but that it wasn't all lost, everything had a solution, and in that moment I started crying and I asked God, I asked God, I asked God, and she was talking and I was crying and asking God, and the funny thing was that in the end—actually, it's not funny—she was speaking the truth, she said, "God in this moment will give you gifts." And I had never touched the guitar, there was a guitar in the cell, and even today I don't know if it was like miming, or a gift, or what it was, but I know that I picked up that guitar and I played it, and in that exact moment I composed my first *louvor* [song of praise to God]. And in that moment of my life I began to transform.

At that point in the conversation, I hadn't asked him anything. Elias was offering me his biography unprompted, with this moment serving as its linchpin. The story was harrowing, but I was also struck by its lyricism, including the brief switch in tense during a moment of existential horror and the repetition of phrases in groups of three, as if the momentum of his testimony had caught itself on the sharp edge of a particular detail (*I'd lost, needle in the vein, I asked God*). The narrative drama contrasted with the relative calm of the hospital balcony. The effect was enhanced by Elias's own presence—he was relatively short but gained a charismatic stature through gestures, even as he leaned in close to talk. He spoke with passion and wide, urgent eyes. I would soon learn that he often talked like this in everyday speech. As he continued, he traced his life outward from the moment of his attempted suicide in both directions. A Black baby found in a pile of trash on the streets of São Paulo, he was taken to a hospital and adopted by a white family. He joined the military as a young man but was discharged a few years later for issues relating to drugs, which he tied to his father's death. It was at this point that he began working for the Primeiro Comando da Capital (PCC; First Capital Command), the dominant criminal faction in the city, before transferring to their then-allies in Rio, the Comando Vermelho (Red Command). "I was the king of the hill [*dono do morro*]," he told me. "They called me Elias the Rottweiler." He married his first wife, had a child, and began to use what he called *macumba*[18] rituals to protect him in his work. He lifted his shirt to show me the scars that bullet wounds had left on his body, alongside the tattoos that warded him against death. But all of this came to an end when he was imprisoned.

During my fieldwork, I did not ask currently or formerly incarcerated people about their life history before the moment of their arrest, except to clarify specific details when they were offered to me. As I describe in in Chapter 1, those in prison were constantly transformed into biographical data that rested on a standard racialized shorthand in which family or community dysfunction served as an ostensible explanation for someone's path into the prison system. Questions about childhood or a life before imprisonment carried the echoes of this previous string of interrogations. Regardless of intent, they also reproduced the same implicit accusation, the demand to explain the path that led someone to crime—a demand that I was not interested in repeating. But regardless of how I presented myself and my research, evangelicals like Elias offered me these biographies freely and repeatedly.

As an act of bearing witness, *testemunho*—meaning both testimony and testament—is embedded in contemporary Christian and juridical traditions of truth-telling and signals the shared history between the two.[19] Elias was intimately familiar with both. Like most people sentenced in Brazil, he was convicted largely based on police testimony.[20] He was also compelled to repeatedly testify during criminological exams as part of his parole applications. But evangelical testimony did not respond to the same narrative demands, and it held out different possibilities for self-constitution and self-representation. Court testimony and criminological exams elicit, extract, and order a history in service of a judgment. Evangelical testimony returns agency to the speaker, while interpellating the listener and intervening on them. When Elias gave me his testimony, he laid bare the transformative power and grace of God to me, a non-Christian—and to you, the reader of this book. He was enthusiastic about joining my research project because he wanted his story to be shared with the world. From the beginning of our relationship, he openly speculated on how readers like you would marvel at what he had endured and overcome. I was a researcher and friend but also an intermediary in this undertaking.[21] Each testimony was a provocation to the audience—*What will you do in the face of God's redeeming grace?*—but it also asked them to witness and verify the speaker's public commitment to a new life, their intention to *be*, rather than simply *give*, a *testemunho*.[22]

This testimony was not about guilt, in either the religious or legal sense. Elias's brief sketches of a career in Brazil's factions provided only background information. In the roughly dozen times that I heard Elias testify,[23] he never mentioned the crime for which he was convicted. Courts and the prison system unspool the truth of the incarcerated person from the moment of a crime and measure resocialization as a distancing from that moment and that subject. But here, Elias pointed to a rupture afterward, in a moment of crisis and unbearable solitude that fell outside the law's interest and gaze. The turning point is the call of a woman through the television, although this is also the moment where Elias seems to run up against the impossibility of communicating God's message, where his narrative loses its detail (*I am going to tell you this, this, and this*). Instead, by telling the story, Elias presented himself as an embodiment of that message, living proof of the triumph of hope over despair. It was miraculous not just because Elias's body seemed to resist the death that he wished upon it, but also because his fingers moved across the guitar strings like he had always known how, like the song was waiting inside for him to sing that night—and again to me, years later.

Every evangelical testimony I heard in Brazil spoke to the individual experiences of the speaker, while drawing on a shared "grammar" of despair and redemption. The subject of each *testemunho* is the individual speaker; still, as other scholars have noted, in their accumulation they sketch out shared histories of violence, poverty, and despair that thread each testimony into a broader landscape of suffering.[24] At the same time, they produce a collective affirmation of the possibility and the impact of rebirth. Almost every evangelical service I took part in, whether in prison or outside, included an opportunity for members of the congregation to "give a testimony" or "give a word." The faithful were also prepared to testify outside, in daily life and casual conversation, or to the foreign anthropologist. On learning of my Catholic upbringing or current lack of faith, evangelicals would inevitably respond with the story of their own experience of accepting God's grace, and promise me that the same day would soon arrive for me. Testimony was both a provocation and an assurance.

Whether inside or out of prison, these testimonies were anchored in similar themes of despair, abandonment, and crisis. But imprisoned people's narratives were also characterized by a proximity to death. My interlocutors would describe an extreme closeness to death, the feeling of its weight bearing down on them. In the case of Elias, it was his own—as he sat in prison, with all the relationships that had formerly sustained him flaking off, death came to him as a potential exit. In that of another incarcerated man, Marco, it was his daughter, who was gravely ill with meningitis. As Marco recalled during an interview, when his mother (the daughter's grandmother) brought him the news during a prison visit, he broke down and immediately walked to the prison's temple, where an evangelical service was taking place, carrying his daughter's photo with him. "I started talking to God, I asked him to take my life but save hers, and I asked everyone to pray for her as well." When his daughter was released from the hospital "without any permanent damage," he returned to the church, where the pastor, whom he did not know, called him out by his full name: "Marco Henrique Silveira, God has sent me to tell you that you achieved what you sought. The cure of your daughter was decreed." Then the pastor asked him, "And now, will you make a decision or not? Will you accept Jesus?" From that day onward, Marco explained, he had remained a practicing Christian.

As we will see shortly, these brushes with death marked the limits of a pre-Christian life and agency, which were released by a divine intervention that both saved the person and called them to service. For both Elias and Marco, conversion was the beginning of a communion and a pact with God, one that opened up possibilities in the world to the extent that the convert himself could become open to a divine will. Both accepted these messages. This moment was the defining point of their lives, but it was also the beginning of a longer process of change that both were still grappling with. They had taken up a lifelong task of cultivating a new way of being in the world. In doing so, they also stepped out of a juridical personhood founded on a self-sovereign and selfsame individual—one where a break in subjectivity or identity often registers as madness.[25]

To many within the prison system, the process of rebirth seemed to be a natural complement to the project of resocialization; to others, they were essentially the same thing. But the ubiquity of testimonies within the prison system nevertheless introduced a friction. It emerged in various guises, including a frustration on the part of psychologists and social workers that clients used the fact of their conversion to refuse reflecting on and taking responsibility for their criminal acts. But perhaps the most vivid example came from an evangelical missionary, who recounted a recent prison visit during a meeting I attended regarding the distribution of Bibles within the prison system. In his telling, the pastor had asked those who were willing to accept Jesus into their lives to raise their hands. When only a few emerged from the crowd, the pastor then promised that those who made a commitment to God that day would have their case files immediately combust. The promise of erasing a sentence by burning the documents that tethered imprisoned people to their sentences demonstrated the dramatic triumph of a divine crack within the law's uninterrupted chronology.

This kind of combustion represented a triumph of the future over the past. At the same time, the convert must take up the cross, assume the burden of navigating a fundamentally fallen society, and commence a never-ending self-examination that requires an astounding level of diligence and discipline. Magnólia's son, Pastor Bruno, spoke about this in terms of a distinction between "accepting Jesus," by which he meant the moment of rebirth in which one commits to living one's life according to Christ, and the *real* conversion, an endless process of opening oneself up to be transformed by God. As a result, the past is always present for the convert, whose identity and future are built in constant conversation with and contradistinction to their former life.[26] Elias carried around a physical token of this past: a receipt for a prepaid funeral, bought by his mother over a decade before in anticipation of her son's imminent death, now stained light blue from age. He would occasionally pull it from his pocket or out of his Bible during testimonies for effect, to demonstrate the miracle of his survival, even if the person this funeral had been purchased for had perished.

The past was a negative image against which Elias and others expressed and understood themselves. That is why he told me about his life before conversion and testified about that fateful birthday in prison—to me, to others, and to you, again, and again, and again.

Prison, Church, World

The increasing presence of evangelicals in Brazil's prisons has transformed the role and status of the imprisoned faithful. In the 2000s, Camila Nunes Dias examined the social and religious life of incarcerated Pentecostal men in São Paulo. She described her research participants as a persecuted minority, arguing that "in their relations with the carceral mass, evangelicals are considered extremely untrustworthy, unworthy of belonging to the world of crime, subjected to all sorts of humiliations."[27] This mistrust apparently spread to the prison administration itself, which understood conversions as attempts to gain some level of unearned respect. Journalists and scholars echoed their suspicion: Drauzio Varella, the physician and journalist who documented his experience in São Paulo's infamous Carandiru prison, argued that conversion was primarily motivated by the desire to shield oneself from violence and avoid retaliation for unpaid debts.[28] The phrase *hiding behind the Bible* was commonly used to both describe and deny the faith of those who used evangelical Christianity as a tool of survival. The collective result, as Dias documents, was a constant torment and ritualized humiliation of believers to test their faith.

But when I began my fieldwork in 2014, the accusation that conversion was a self-serving performance detached from any belief had largely evaporated. In part, this is because evangelical Christianity was no longer a religion of imprisoned people. Now a growing number of correctional officers and staff shared in their faith. Broadly speaking, Brazilian evangelicals remain disproportionately poor, and their presence in Rio de Janeiro is most visible in the city's peripheries. But the movement has grown across all social classes, drawing in wealthy worshippers like Vilma, as well as high-ranking members of the prison administration. One important consequence of this shift was a growing sense among imprisoned people, missionaries, and the administration that the Bible was the most important, or perhaps the *only*, effective tool for resocialization. This claim was championed by Colonel Gilson, the subsecretary referred to in the Introduction and the man responsible for the coordination of all "treatment" efforts within the prison system. Gilson was generally seen as a personable man who worked well with nonreligious initiatives including Project Life and an education project run by the Black activist Nelson Mandela Institute, among others. He was also known by evangelical missionaries and many of the incarcerated faithful as a "man of God" and a "brother in faith." He constantly blurred what I saw as the line between secular and religious forms of treatment, giving churches the opportunity to run programs that fell outside the ordinary scope of religious assistance. For example, he maintained a formal and exclusive contract with one Assemblies of God church to organize and facilitate collective weddings within the prison system.

The focus on the Bible as an instrument and catalyst for transformation also shifted the priorities of resocialization and education programs, including an intense preoccupation with literacy. Given the Protestant emphasis on reading as a form of direct communication with God, missionaries were concerned with the numbers of incarcerated people who were illiterate or semiliterate. Many ran adult literacy classes for imprisoned people; others established small evangelical libraries in various penitentiaries; still others successfully campaigned to include the New Testament in a pilot program that offered a four-day reduction in a prison sentence for each book read from an authorized list. Pastor Bruno regularly arranged for his optometrist wife to visit René Dotti, diagnose vision problems, and provide reading glasses at no cost.

For imprisoned people themselves, this shifting landscape also changed the terms of conversion and brought new challenges to living a Christian life in prison. Rather than facing the suspicion of a false conversion, they encountered a new accusation: that it was *easier* to be a Christian inside prison than outside it. This sense of doubt circulated between incarcerated evangelicals as much as, if not more than, skeptical outsiders. One imprisoned man I met, for example, had converted while in prison but refused to be baptized until after he was released, since he wanted to be sure that he could hold true to that commitment once he was exposed to the world. Doubts about the resilience of faith had replaced those concerning its sincerity. Many suggested that while the life of any Christian was punctured by tests of faith, *real* fortitude would only be revealed against the pressures of the outside world. Prison was no longer a unique site of suffering or tribulation; on the contrary, it had become a fortress against evil.

Prison thus took up a special place within an evangelical spiritual geography that was otherwise dominated by the antagonism between *the church* and *the world*. For Brazilian evangelicals, the world (*o mundo*)—and worldliness, by extension—refers to the space outside the evangelical community and the churches that constitute its center. The loosely defined dualisms of good and evil from Catholic and Afro-Brazilian traditions are reconfigured by the Brazilian evangelical movement as stark opposites engaged in constant war, with each side claiming territory for itself.[29] *World* designates the territory belonging to Catholics, witchcraft, atheists, and the devil, a space dominated by vice and temptation. But while evangelicals must inevitably navigate the world, they are not *of* it. Instead, they belong to the church, a territory that extends from the physical space of a temple and into the homes and lives of the faithful.[30]

Inside prison, the clearest manifestation of this boundary was the division between evangelical wings and the cells of the impious. Segregated cells for incarcerated evangelicals began to emerge in the 1990s at the request of both imprisoned people and outside missionaries. They were justified as a means for evangelicals to distance themselves from what they saw as the "vices" of sex and drug use, and to maintain their own codes of conduct and self-governance. During my fieldwork, those living in the evangelical cells dedicated themselves to a strict timetable and set of obligations. In René Dotti, the day would begin at four in the morning with two hours of prayer. The remaining hours were structured around cleaning the cell, silent time for Bible reading, attending the temple, and assisting with its upkeep. Those housed in these cells did not participate in soccer matches; they were prohibited from using drugs or cell phones; and they were required to attend at least one religious service each day. In some cells, television and radio were also prohibited; in others, their use was strictly limited to religious programming. If newspapers entered a cell, its pastor would first block out any text or images considered obscene before circulating it to others.

Just as the evangelical wing produced a distance from the cells of the impious, many incarcerated people came to see the prison as a refuge from the world and its temptations. The institution was like a church, a space removed from at least some of the dangers of society. This analogy between church and prison was solidified through the figure of the pastor. Within prisons designated for men, every evangelical cell had at least one spiritual and political representative who was given the title. They were generally older than others within the cell—Elias, for example, became a pastor during the final years of his imprisonment while in his late thirties. Pastors provided guidance to their brethren and represented their interests to other pastors, to the leadership of the impious (that is, to the representatives of the prison's faction, known as the *comissão* or "committee"), and to the warden. Imprisoned pastors had no formal link with any evangelical denomination, although they sometimes aligned themselves with one doctrine over another. But they solidified and maintained a community of the faithful living in solidarity with one another and against the world. They did not run *cultos* within the temple—instead, they acted as volunteers to clean the space and organize the congregation.

By 2014, every men's prison in Rio de Janeiro contained either a handful of cells or an entire wing reserved for evangelicals. It was now possible to spend an entire sentence within them, separated from the impious, surrounded by "brothers in faith" and governed by their schedule and code of conduct. But many evangelicals chose to remain in the cells of the impious. They often disagreed with the rules governing these spaces or found them impossible to follow in practice. Two points of contention were the prohibition of cell phones—which for many were the only point of contact with loved ones—and the separation from other incarcerated people. Elias, for example, moved in and out of evangelical cells over the course of his sentence. As he put it, to remain cloistered within the community of the faithful was to preach to the converted. Reaching out to the impious was part of the work of reclaiming the world for God.

By circulating between the cells of the evangelicals and those of the impious, Elias built a religious practice that tied self-transformation with proselytizing. Alongside prayer and Bible study, he continued writing songs of praise; he was a talented songwriter and excelled across different genres, from Brazilian funk to samba and rock. He also began writing regular reflections, where he wove biblical commentaries with insights from his own life and reflected on the process of regaining control over his mind and soul. Although he threw out some of this writing, many works survived, folded in two and slipped into his leather-bound Bible alongside song lyrics and lists of prison rules. As Elias collected this material, his Bible grew fatter, eventually splitting down the spine as his life and words punctuated the testaments:

06/06/14: I try to look beyond disgrace, defeat, otherwise nothing in my life works out since in this moment we enter an infinite abyss by suffering through anticipation. By recognizing this, we begin to move beyond the negativism that stops us from surviving any difficulty.

So, reflecting on this I remember a biblical passage in the Book of Numbers, Chapter 13 that very much describes this pessimistic, negativist act, where Moses sends twelve men to scout and write a detailed report on the promised land so that the people of Israel might continue their journey, and here enters a lack of trust in yourself, in God, since ten of the chosen return running scared saying that it really is the land of manna, milk, and honey, but it is impossible to take it since it was the land of terrible giants and that it would be impossible to overcome them, the negativity of these scouts spread to thousands of people that had fled from Egypt, but in the middle of so many negativists and pessimists there are two people, Joshua and Caleb. These two are able to take Canaan and so they begin to enjoy the blessings of our Lord God who had freed them from slavery in Egypt.

If we prepare to enter into the reality of this biblical passage we see how negativity is contagious and that many times it doesn't simply prejudice the negative person but even those around them.

Although Elias insists on the importance of "looking beyond," these writings also show the double-sided nature of anticipation as a potential source of both suffering and assurance. Since negativity is contagious, the maintenance of hope requires internal and external vigilance. However, unlike his testimony, these reflections provide space for guilt and regret to rise through, even if they are recalled as part of a past that has now been overcome:

26/6/14—The Great Decision Is to Welcome Blessings: It's been twelve years of prison, twenty years lost to drugs, alcohol, an uncontrolled life, and at the bottom of the well, in the abyss, alone, abandoned, with only myself to blame, that's where God showed me that even a mother could abandon her child, but He will never abandon me.

Here Elias offers an accounting of his past life, an audit of lost years. And yet that site of hopelessness was precisely what allowed Elias to receive and accept God. His writings are replete with these lessons, where he speaks at once to himself and to an as-yet-unidentified audience. Part sermon, part diary, this process brought together work on the self and preaching to another:

10/7/14—**To Dive Headfirst into the Path of the Lord:** I know that often inside
prison the questioning of happiness became something very complex, but regarding that question, happiness is the discovery that there is a choice, a very
important choice that we all have to make, that I had to make, I had to put the
direction of my own life in the hands of God. Only he can forgive man, only he
can change our character, so let us free ourselves from the eternal death called
Hell [. . .] Only the true Christian is freed from the power of sin. He is no longer
dominated by carnal desires. That does not mean that he is freed from a constant war against the daily pressures of our world or the traps of the devil. True
freedom will only come when, I mean we will only be free when Jesus Christ
returns to bring his church into heaven. If we remain steadfast and focus on this
logic of living, a logic founded on a new life, we will achieve the blessings of this
spiritual plan, things we could not even imagine. Think about it!!!

Within these reflections there is no self-sovereign subject. One is always
a vessel for something greater, either "dominated" by sin or given over to God.
Autonomy lies in the choice between these two paths—a choice that is ongoing and requires fortitude, but that is nevertheless synonymous with happiness
itself. Each entry is signed at the bottom by *Pastor Elias*. He carried that title
from the evangelical cells and into the cells of the impious. Elias spoke to me
about his work there to convert others, rather than remaining surrounded by
his "brothers." One day, he gathered his cellmates around, handed them each
a piece of paper, and asked them to complete a sentence beginning with the
phrase *society is . . .* (*a sociedade é . . .*). The responses expressed frustration and
disenchantment—society is corrupt, society is cruel, society is unjust, society
is cowardly. Then he asked everyone to cross out *Society is* and replace it with
I am (*eu sou*). Apparently, many in the group became angry and tore up their
paper. "But," Elias recounted to me, "one man stayed to talk, and that one was
important."

The music, the written reflections, and the group exercise all focused on the
power of words to provoke a shift in the person. Each time, they echoed the Word
of God, not only in their message but in Elias's faith in their effectiveness, regardless of the intention or position of the listener. Words established direct communication with God; they were the medium of a divine message. In another
conversation, Elias suggested to me that those leaving prison should be forced
to attend three or four church services every week. When I asked him what good
that would do for a nonbeliever, he responded with the Brazilian maxim "Soft

water on a hard stone strikes until it pierces" (*Agua mole, pedra dura, tanto bate até que fura*). The phrase extols the virtues of patience and persistence, but it also suggests that every word, every conversation, is part of a continuous flow that can run over and reshape even the hardest, most intransigent soul.

School of Prophets

Whereas the segregated cells marked out a frontier where incarcerated people evangelicals negotiated their relationship with the world, the temple was the spiritual base for a community of the faithful that flowed over prison walls. In René Dotti, this room was strangely elongated, with pews stretching out to the sides, rather than directly in front of a raised central pulpit. Over the course of my fieldwork, I attended many religious services in this temple, most often with Magnólia's son, Pastor Bruno. His services began with a series of songs played by the band over a sound system. The instruments and the multiple speakers were donations from visiting church groups; the resulting soundscape could envelop the room, a stark contrast from the education hall's single speaker and microphone, where it was a constant struggle for anyone to be heard. The songs included works composed by imprisoned people themselves, with titles including "René Dotti Is a School of Prophets." Visiting missionaries and pastors would then take turns preaching in the pulpit, building a fervor through scripture and the call-and-response style of worship characteristic of Brazilian Pentecostalism, whereby the speaker and the congregation amplified each other's energy as their cries echoed against the temple walls. Toward the end of the service, pastors would ask if anyone in the audience would like to accept Jesus for the first time, or perhaps return to God's path after being led astray.

Alongside Project Overcome and the Freedom Theater Group, René Dotti had a third troupe, one whose members were all housed in the evangelical cells. The group occasionally performed during or after the *culto* given by Pastor Bruno. I only saw one of these performances, right after Bruno's sermon, in a midafternoon service. Sitting in the front row, I heard the narrator's voice from the loudspeakers behind me. This voice echoed through the temple, bringing us into the play's first scene—the final moments of a *culto* at a church in Rio's periphery. Without curtains, the division between the stage/pulpit and the audience was less marked, and the performance took advantage of that to bring us into a scene as congregants for a fictional service, now superimposed over the one that was already taking place. Pastor Bruno remained in the pulpit but had now slipped into his role as an extra, while an actor stepped up beside him and began to give the last words of this fictional service. With a voice that boomed through the temple without the assistance of a microphone, he asked if anyone who had gathered here desired to accept Jesus into their life. Four men who were dispersed among the pews to either side of me came to the front and stood beneath the pulpit. The pastor asked each one, in turn, if they would give their life to God. One by one, they said yes. The audience, who had witnessed similar scenes play out almost every day in this space, already knew their role; they lent their energy to the moment by shouting "Hallelujah!" and "Glory to God!" in agreement. But as the scene ended, and as the actors began to set up the pulpit for the following scene, the disembodied voice of the narrator came back through the sound system and cautioned us that there were different levels of accepting Christ. Drawing directly on the parable of the sower, he reminded us that a seed planted on barren ground would shrivel and die before it bore fruit.

The rest of the play was a demonstration of this message. Each scene followed one of the four men in the weeks and months after their conversion, and each represented a different "ground" for the sower. To help us follow along, a cardboard sign stuck to the back wall of the pulpit displayed the number of each ground in ascending order, and an actor swapped it out between scenes. The pulpit itself was wide but not deep, so the scenes largely played out along one plane of movement—or else vertically, between the pulpit and the ground below. On "Ground 1," the first convert walks past a bar when a friend asks him to stop in for a drink. When he refuses, the friend begins to laugh, telling him that the only Bible he would ever need is the one in his pocket—and he pulls out a cardboard pistol to demonstrate. After a short debate, he convinces the convert to open a can of beer, and they sit along the edge of the pulpit drinking. The conversation quickly morphs into planning a kidnapping, until the two say their goodbyes and walk off on either side of the pulpit, inebriated and dreaming of riches. The scene was essentially comic, largely thanks to the actor playing the friend (the same one from the Freedom Theater Group who had previously worked as a television extra), who gave a tongue-in-cheek performance that kept the audience laughing. That mood was immediately snuffed out by the narrator's voice, explaining that the two botched the kidnapping, ended up in a shootout with police, and died. Loud sound effects of gunfire and sirens rang out from the speaker and vibrated through the floor, passing over the now-silent congregation.

Ground 2 begins with the second convert receiving a phone call from his friend, telling him that his wife and child have been in an accident. He rushes from his home on one side of the pulpit to the hospital on the other, where he meets a friend who has already arrived, and who tells him to calm down and trust in God. But the convert is too distraught to pay attention to either God or the man in front of him. The doctor, played by Magnólia, walks up the stairs with a stethoscope dangling around her neck and, shaking her head, informs the man that his wife and child have died. The actors clear off the pulpit, leaving the convert alone, back at home, where he pulls out the same prop pistol from Ground 1 and shoots himself. The sound of gunfire rings out from the sound system behind us.

On Ground 3, the pastor from the first scene knocks on the door of a house, stamping his foot for effect. When the third convert opens the door, the pastor asks why he has stopped attending church. The convert explains that he recently received a promotion and is just too busy, but he gestures toward the appliances and furniture he has bought, signs of his new wealth. The pastor manages to convince him to come back to the church and turns to leave, crossing paths on his way with another friend of the convert. This friend, played again by the slapstick actor, comes with a counterproposal: there will be a party tonight, and the "girl" that the convert has had his eye on is sure to be there. At first the convert says no, but then he reasons that while the church will be there every day, this party might be a once-in-a-lifetime experience. The two leave his house and walk away from the pulpit, letting the narrator finish their story: the convert gets drunk at the party and picks up the girl, but on the way to a motel he loses control of the car and crashes. Sounds of broken metal and glass echo through the temple. He dies, and the girl is seriously injured.

Finally, we arrive at Ground 4, with the last convert returning to his favela as a man of God. Here the performance plays with the verticality of the stage as a reflection of the hillside geography of these neighborhoods. The convert steps up and into the *boca de fumo*, the local site for drug commerce.[31] There, he is recognized by men brandishing cardboard weapons—semiautomatic rifles, rather than the pistol of previous scenes. He tells his former "brothers" that he has found happiness as a man of God, and that although he is poor, he can sleep safely at night without worrying that rivals might kill him or his family. The other men laugh him out of the space—but as he walks down the pulpit and toward the audience, one man follows him, explaining that he wants to give up this life and find "real" work, to be present for his children and to see them grow up. He brings out his gun and throws it on the ground. Standing on the stairs between the pulpit and the audience, but above this man, the convert puts his hands on his shoulders and, in a repetition of the play's first scene, asks him if he will accept Jesus into his life. The man says yes, and they embrace.

The superimposition of one church on another at the start of the play blurred the line between the two spaces—one inside prison, the other explicitly described as in Rio's periphery. But each of the following scenes was located out in the world. The weight of the world bore down on each man with an inexorable pull, like gravity. The same point was demonstrated to me a few months prior, in another church where I had been invited by Marco, the man whose daughter almost died of meningitis and who was now serving time in house arrest. There, the pastor called his daughter to the raised pulpit, then stepped off it and took hold of her hand. It was much easier, he showed us, to pull someone down off the pulpit than to pull someone up onto it. This was the task of the faithful: to find the strength and fortitude to bear this burden. The alternative was death. Like the testimony of imprisoned people, death marked the limits and the ultimate fate of a worldly life. Watching the play in René Dotti, I was struck not just by the presence of death but also by its swiftness, arriving as soon as each convert was led astray from God. The sound effect of gunfire, combined with the prop pistols and rifles, evoked the various degrees and manifestations of armed violence that those in prison, like most who had lived in Rio's peripheries, were familiar with.

In this narrative, there is no time to turn around, no possibility of getting back on course after a diversion. But death finds an ally in another worldly figure: the friend. The play shows friendship as a potentially volatile social relation that can either save one or drag one down into the world, and thereby to death. Each "ground" involves a friend, a figure who apparently knew the convert before the moment that they accepted God into their life. In Grounds 1 and 3, the friend recognizes something in the protagonist that they have attempted to cast off through their conversion. Alcohol looms large in both cases, but sex also appears in the "girl" offered as a gift in Ground 3. Each friend refuses to acknowledge the transformation that the two men experienced by giving their lives to God. And this refusal is confirmed when the converts offer only token resistance to their friends' suggestions before ultimately turning back to the world. In Ground 4, former friends and colleagues laugh at the man standing in front of them. But the laughter recognizes, even as it belittles, the new path this man has chosen.

The play does not damn friendship outright. In Ground 2, it is the friend who offers a voice of reason and faith in a moment of profound despair. The convert's error is to not hear this message in the midst of his own suffering. But the play still places this kind of social relationship under scrutiny. In particular, it points to the limits of a conversion that is not accompanied by a broader transformation of social life. Friendship becomes a hazard when it crosses the line between church and world. This performance thus mirrors the kinds of biographies constructed in the criminological exam, discussed in Chapter 1, where life stories converge on the narrative of a dysfunctional family leading one to "fall into the wrong crowd" in adolescence and early adulthood. Whereas resocialization posits a return, it also requires stitching together a new network of friends and kin. During an interview, one prison psychiatrist suggested that Brazil needed to lengthen its prison sentences, because the typical two or four years of incarceration was not enough to dissolve the social ties that led the confined person to commit crime in the first place.

But for evangelicals, the potential scope of pathological relations was far broader—first, because sin is a far more capacious category than crime; and second, because the world is not a space to seek inclusion within, but rather one that must itself be transformed. As Ground 4 demonstrates, the task of the converted is to become an instrument of God, someone who is capable of reaching out to others without being corrupted by them. As I argue in the following chapter, many prison staff posit family, rather than friendship, as the mechanism for reforming imprisoned people. But in this performance, even family must be subsumed to God. Ground 2's protagonist becomes so invested in his family that his grief at losing them blocks him off from hearing God. Within the play, some ties might provide the support needed for the life of a new convert, but no social relations are immune from the danger of distancing someone from God, *unless* those relationships are anchored within the church itself.

Resocialization was one word among many that evangelicals used to refer to a profound moral and spiritual reorientation that incarcerated people underwent as they sought to change themselves. "Recuperation" (*recuperação*) was another, a phrase that was also used for addiction recovery. The distinction between the two, as with crime and addiction, was minimal for most evangelicals, and church-run recuperation centers employed the same strategies of intervention and reform on both groups.[32] But even as they used the language of resocialization, both missionaries and imprisoned evangelicals departed from its juridical meaning as a path to social belonging and "proper" citizenship. For the faithful, the resocialized were not those who reconciled with society; like the man in Ground 4, their own transformation was the first step in a much broader project to transform it, conquering the forces of evil and reclaiming the world.

The Word of the Year Is Hope

Magnólia sometimes joined her son in his visits to René Dotti, but she had mostly scaled back her work inside the prison system. These days, she worked much more closely with family members of imprisoned people and those who had recently been released through an NGO that she founded five years before I met her. That was where I met Elias, during one of the monthly meetings held in the church basement. Outside these meetings, Magnólia spent most working days in a small office above the church, a space filled with photos, files, and donated clothing. A framed notice on the wall declared that the organization could not provide any money for transportation. There, Magnólia received a stream of calls every day with requests for assistance in finding work, medical care, or food. When I came into the office one afternoon in early 2017, I found her sitting at her desk, Bruno at her side, facing a middle-aged white man I vaguely recognized. He introduced himself as Milton and reminded me that we had met briefly inside René Dotti. Bruno had visited the prison in the morning to run a *culto*; while he was leaving, Milton was being released from his sentence. As they both stepped out from the front gates, Milton confided to Bruno that with no family support and no immediate prospects for work, he had nowhere to go. Bruno drove him immediately to Magnólia's office, where a man named Jeferson—a volunteer for the NGO who had also once been imprisoned in René Dotti—offered to put him up for the night. After that, Magnólia had found a shelter where he could stay for at least a week.

Milton was happy at the news, although he was also overwhelmed by the day's events. Release is often abrupt and unexpected. Milton was still waiting for a transfer to another prison, one that he had requested through his public defender months ago; when he received the news of his release, he asked the guard if he could at least wait a few days to figure out what to do. Magnólia instructed me to go through the bags of clothing leaning against the wall and find something in his size. But before I had searched them properly, she brought us out of the office and into the hallway, where a banner stood with the organization's name. She asked Milton and Jeferson to stand in front of the banner. They took their positions, with Jeferson reaching one arm over Milton's shoulder while Milton held a Bible in front of his own chest. Magnólia explained that she wanted a "before and after" photo, with Milton still in his prison uniform—blue jeans, a plain white shirt, and white flip-flops—and Jeferson, now several years after his release, clean-shaven, wearing a shirt stamped with the NGO's logo, and smiling.

People like Milton found their way to Magnólia's office several times a week. Sometimes they had just been released from prison and were directed there by the parole office or a local church. Others heard about the group by word of mouth while held captive, especially if they had passed through René Dotti. The years 2016 and 2017 saw a surge in demand, since an economic crisis had forced similar organizations—especially Catholic and secular ones—to suspend or roll back support programs for those impacted by incarceration. As a result, many would redirect those in need to Magnólia. People often walked for hours from other parts of Rio's periphery, arriving at the office tired, sweating, and without change for the bus fare home, continually testing Magnólia's commitment to her no-money-for-transport rule.

Evangelical churches' role as a community and a social safety net has been recognized by state actors, anthropologists, and evangelicals themselves for decades.[33] The religious movement has produced a capillary network of service provisions that links smaller churches to larger and better-resourced ones; directs those in need to evangelical health providers or social workers; and has minimal barriers to access compared with state-run services. These ties have the capacity to corral resources and services with an efficiency that often surpasses that of Brazil's welfare system. Even in the 1990s, when the evangelical sphere of influence was much smaller, anthropologist Alba Zaluar recognized that Rio's state institutions had largely failed in the "socialization" of youths from the periphery.

As she observed, "Everything indicates that, in fact, it is evangelicals who are able to work constantly for the prevention and reeducation of drug users and criminals."[34] Still, she remained unsure about their ultimate impact: "Regarding their permanence or efficiency, we shall wait and see."[35]

Zaluar's skepticism, and that of social science more broadly, regarding the efficacy of this work is indicative of a broader academic distrust of evangelicals.[36] It is arguably warranted in a city where fluctuations in reported crime rates show little correlation with the steady rise of the evangelical faithful. But to quantify "efficiency" also effaces the models of personhood and sociality that constitute evangelical Christianity's understanding of itself. We can see this in both the temple play and Elias's "Society is/I am" exercise. Both place a focus and valorization on the individual, the single person who stays even as others laugh at them—a figure that is lost in the aggregate. As in Ground 4 of the performance, it is the one who listens and turns to God, not the mass, that both proves and expands the transformative presence of God in the world.

At the same time, rebirth and transformation are everywhere in Rio's peripheries. The ex-criminal (*ex-bandido*), the man[37] who, through God and faith, leaves a criminal career and finds the "right" path, appears in almost every evangelical church. In each of the dozen churches outside prison that I visited during my fieldwork, upon learning of my research project, the pastor or missionary would call for one of these men to see me. They were often, but not always, formerly incarcerated, and they began by giving me their testimony to aid my research. Rio is saturated with these "after" photos, living embodiments—*testemunhos*—of both the transformative power of faith and the capacity of evangelicals to support those who decide to lead a Christian life. Milton left prison as an evangelical, but he had yet to find a place for himself and construct a new life around his faith. Jeferson was the living proof of what was waiting for him. The photo staged a message of hope, both for Milton and for those in similar positions.

A few weeks before Milton's release, Magnólia began her NGO's first monthly meeting for 2017 by greeting the fifty of us who had assembled in the church basement. Microphone in hand, she thanked us for coming and wished us a happy new year. But, she added, "there are still so many problems in Brazil, and people who have lost all credibility. The word [of God] is dying in so many hearts, but we cannot give up. I want you to focus on one word this year: hope." She asked us to repeat this word back to her, then continued. "Even though so many are despairing, God does not let me lose hope." She pointed to the audience as evidence of this hope—this was a "union" of people who, in a former life, had belonged to warring factions within Rio's drug economy but were now sitting together as one. After this welcome, she was joined by another volunteer missionary who brought news of a partnership with a management firm for several condominiums to hire workers as doormen or janitors. "I understand that the job market is difficult," the volunteer said somberly, "but 'despair' is a word that we need to throw out of our vocabulary."

The two poles of hope (*esperança*) and its opposite, despair (*desespero*), oriented how the NGO understood its role in the world. Magnólia's discussion of lost credibility was a reference to the corruption scandal that had engulfed state and national politics over the previous year. But she saw it as running far deeper than a question of economics; instead, it was a crisis of hope, as people increasingly lost faith in their own futures. Over the rest of the 2017 meetings, Magnólia returned to the question of hope. In most cases, hope was intimately linked to the state of the nation itself: "Facing the crisis in our country, the crisis in our state, it seems like we can neither move forward nor backward; it seems like everything is stuck. But we cannot give up hope," she would tell the assembled crowd. After her opening remarks, meetings generally transitioned into singing, before opening up the floor for anyone to give their testimony. Participants would return month after month, even after they stopped receiving material support from the group, to listen, speak, and sing. One notable absence was Milton, who dropped out of contact with the NGO about a month after that first meeting in Magnólia's office. But she never dwelled for long on those who did not return to the group. Instead, she surrounded herself and her work with success stories, victories that she had witnessed both inside prison and outside it. She was building a landscape of hope, one where there was worthiness and redemption to be found at every turn.

This landscape was predicated on the universality of hope, anchored in God's promise to all of humanity. But Magnólia conjured it by recourse to a racialized idiom that both held out the universal possibility of salvation and inferred that whiteness was the embodiment of that promise. And she did so while avoiding direct references to race or racism; in fact, she often chose her words carefully, gesturing toward race while awkwardly contorting her stories to speak around it. My own presence and my foreignness seemed to provide license to transgress these limits. "He doesn't look Brazilian, right?" she asked the audience the first time I attended a meeting, before noting that I came from a prestigious American university to "learn about our lives, our struggles." As I sat in an audience of largely Black adults and children, she would call on me as the *branquinho*. The diminutive form of *branco* (white) was used here for emphasis, a reference to the paleness of my skin that put me out of place not just in this room but in Rio de Janeiro's North Zone more broadly.

These references contrast with a story she offered during the second month in the year of hope, detailing an encounter with another young white man in prison a few months before. After she participated in a *culto*, some members of the congregation asked her to meet a new arrival who had been openly declaring his desire to die. The rest of his cellmates had been taking shifts to watch over him during the night. Magnólia prepared herself with a short prayer, asking God for the strength to help this man, before she was led to the cell to see him. She described him as a "beautiful man," pausing for a second before explaining that he had a "good appearance" and was a student before his arrest in Rio's wealthy South Zone. In her version of the story, she asked him, "How is it that you, such a beautiful young man, how can someone like you be distraught like this?" The man explained that he was in his third year of university, but after his arrest, his family wanted nothing more to do with him. Magnólia reminded him that his family might have left him, that he might even have given up on himself, but "God has not given up on you." Apparently, these words took a hold on him— two weeks later, on her next visit, he had recovered from his depression and was now working as a cleaner inside the prison. Soon afterward, he was released— Magnólia heard that he had recently joined a church in the South Zone.

This story almost gratuitously accumulated references to the incarcerated man's whiteness while refusing to name it directly. These include the phrase "good appearance" (*boa aparência*), which often appears in job listings to signal that Black people, particularly those with darker skin, need not apply.[38] The stress on locating him as a resident of the South Zone placed him in the center of white Rio de Janeiro and, along with his university studies, suggested middle- or upper-class wealth. This mode of speech offers another demonstration of the combined "hyperconsciousness" and outward "negation" of race that also emerge in the criminological exam, discussed in Chapter 1.[39] Magnólia drew on a shared euphemistic language to situate whiteness as the site of potential and possibility.

The fact that the man did not recognize his own potential, a life prophesied in the "beauty" and "good appearance" written on his own body, threatened the coherence of this position. Magnólia's intervention, and her subsequent narrativization of the drama, secured whiteness against the existential threat of despair by making the latter provisional, an ordeal rather than a condition. The young man's story ended where it began—outside prison,[40] in Rio's wealthy South Zone, with his status now affirmed by having survived this moment through the support of God and the church. The imprisoned people who called on Magnólia to help him quickly disappeared from the narrative, presumably remaining in prison. While Magnólia seemed to offer this story as an affirmation of the ubiquity and the transience of despair, it placed the restitution of whiteness as both a model of universal salvation and logically prior to it.

Ambassadors in Chains

Pray also for me, that whenever I speak, words may be given me so that I will fearlessly make known the mystery of the gospel, for which I am an ambassador in chains. Pray that I may declare it fearlessly, as I should.

Ephesians 6:19–20

On my first visit to René Dotti's evangelical temple, I noticed a large mural on the back wall of the pulpit. It depicted a sun peering out of distant clouds, all through a window lined with iron bars. In front of the image, and partially blocking the window, was a book opened to the verse from the Gospel of John: "And you will know the truth, and the truth will set you free." The entire image was framed inside a circle, with the phrases *evangelical church* and *only Jesus Christ frees* written along the outside. Every church service, every performance in the temple, played out in front of this mural. But what initially struck me about it was the presence of bars. Why were they there? I saw many other murals inside Rio's prisons. All of them seemed to have been painted by those who were, or had been, imprisoned. Windows were a common motif, offering an artificial but unobstructed portal to the outside world. So why did this artist, or these artists, decide to reproduce prison architecture in their mural, rather than depict an opening?

I never received authorization to bring a camera or any recording equipment into a prison—these are essentially prohibited for researchers, although in exceptional circumstances some journalists have been given permission to take photos during controlled visits. But on the day of the theater performance described earlier, Pastor Bruno reached an informal agreement with the prison's warden to allow him to bring a camera into the temple and photograph the service. After the play and the service had finished, I asked him to take a photo for the mural. He sent it to me a few weeks later (see Figure 3.1).

I came back to this temple repeatedly during my fieldwork and often found myself trying to decipher what those bars expressed. Now I think that they subvert the idea that freedom is something to be found outside the prison. The sun appearing from behind parting clouds is beautiful but ultimately a far-off echo of the Bible, front and center, propped up to reveal another kind of truth. The same Bible verse was written across the walls of many other prisons I visited during my fieldwork—either at the front entrance or within an internal courtyard. To

FIGURE 3.1. Mural within the evangelical temple at René Dotti. The text surrounding the circle reads "Evangelical Church: Only Jesus Frees," while the Bible in the center is opened to John 8:32, "And you will know the truth, and the truth will set you free." Source: Photograph by Pastor Bruno, reproduced with permission.

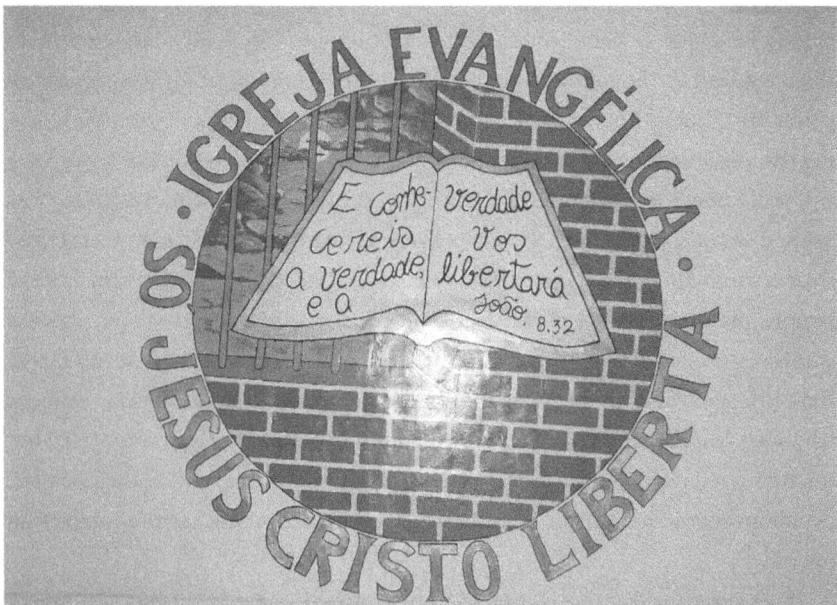

reinforce this point, incarcerated evangelicals would occasionally remind me that they were already free, in fact freer than many outside who were shackled to their own vices. In both René Dotti and Tobias Barreto, a few wore T-shirts with the phrase *imprisoned, but free (preso, porém liberto)* stamped on the front, most likely printed and donated by visiting missionary groups.

Such expressions of faith unsettle the moral geography of incarceration, articulating a different relationship between captivity and freedom. In doing so, they echo Paul's letter to the Ephesians, quoted earlier. I found the verse quoted in a training manual for missionaries, one that specifically offered guidance for working inside the prison system. In it the authors make multiple references to Paul's letters, and particularly to his description of himself as a "prisoner of Christ," a "prisoner of the Lord," and, in this case, an "ambassador in chains."[41] The manual mixes biblical exegesis with social science. One section offers an analysis of Erving Goffman's *Asylums* to highlight the processes of dehumanization at play within the prison system. But then the authors turn to argue that "prison is not always a disaster" and delve into biblical scenes of transformation that took place within confinement.[42] Paul's own repeated imprisonment looms large here as a model for contemporary Christians. The apostle resignifies his own chains; he is a captive not because of his faith but through it. Here again, the Brazilian use of the word *chain (cadeia)* as a synonym for prison lends the image a particular resonance. As the manual declares, "If one does not turn themselves, like Paul, into a prisoner of Jesus in the substance of their character, in their doctrine and in their hope, they cannot be his disciple. Paul's visiting card needs to be your card and my card. We are all happy and blessed prisoners of Christ!"[43] Like Paul himself, the manual deliberately slips between these two senses of confinement, suggesting that imprisonment itself is a reflection, however imperfect, of submission to God's will.

This is the work of evangelical Christianity within Rio's prisons: a continual resignification of incarceration itself. Imprisoned evangelicals suffer from their imprisonment and wait anxiously for the day of release. But they also unsettle the distinctions between confinement and freedom, and in the process they trouble the authority of the warden, the judge, and the state. These shifts are material and palpable. They come out in the mural, asking the viewer to discover God's truth and become free by yielding to it—*within*, rather than in spite of, their captivity. They also emerge in the constellation of sounds, sights, and smells that Vilma noticed with amazement on her first visit to René Dotti, "pieces of grace" that cut through the darkness and the smell.[44] As these resignifications accumulate, they transform the sensory experience of imprisonment and challenge its hold over the souls of imprisoned people.

As a part of this transformation, evangelicals also redefine resocialization itself. Missionaries still saw themselves as allies to the state in the task of reforming those in prison. They asked their congregants to be better people, to reject crime and build law-abiding futures. Incarcerated believers demanded the same of themselves and each other. But this transformation was less about producing security or promoting a reintegration with society than a reorientation toward God. The fact that the Subsecretary of Treatment would publicly claim that the Bible was the only tool for transforming imprisoned people reveals the extent to which this mission, grafted onto a juridical project of reform, has now overgrown it. Beyond the horizons of resocialization, evangelicals live in the shadow of another unfulfilled promise: that of a world redeemed and reclaimed for God. To transform oneself is both to experience this redemption in miniature and to bring it one step closer to realization. In the meantime, those held inside the evangelical wings of René Dotti will continue to wake up at four every morning and pray.

FOUR

If I Were His Mother

I caught Lívia in her office late one afternoon. While this public defender was assigned to the semi-open prison of Tobias Barreto, on most workdays she could be found here, in a cramped, air-conditioned space near the city center. Wednesdays were for speaking with family members of imprisoned clients: generally mothers, wives, and *companheiras* (companions), but with an occasional sister, aunt, father, or grandmother. They all called to arrange this appointment, but since demand was so high, most had to wait two or three months. When they finally arrived, they would come with questions prepared regarding their loved ones—things like upcoming dates for transfer to a lower-security prison, the status of an appeal, or next steps after a denied parole application. Lívia and Ângela's team prepared for these visits with the same kinds of information they would give their imprisoned clients. They printed and distributed sentencing certificates, checked upcoming dates, and noted any process that might require the support of families, such as home visits or transfer to house arrest.

Lívia was between meetings when I arrived, so we had a few minutes to catch up. But she soon asked an intern to call in the next appointment: two Black women, both somewhere in their fifties, and both mothers of men who had been arrested and ultimately convicted for the same event. Since the office was narrow, one of the women had to sit behind the other, her face obscured to Lívia as the defender began running through the basic details of each man's sentence. As a result, it took Lívia a few minutes to recognize the woman sitting at the back. She let out a cry of joy, stood up, and hugged her, before explaining to the rest of us in the room that the woman in her arms was "the cousin of the woman who raised me and worked with my family for forty-five years." Lívia was speaking about her *babá*, the Brazilian term for the maid and nanny who had taken care of her since her birth. Through that relationship, Lívia had grown close with the *babá*'s own family, including this cousin, who now reappeared to her as the mother of her imprisoned client.

If at first the woman in front was speaking on behalf of her friend, now she was mostly silent while Lívia traded stories with the cousin about various members of their respective families. It took a few minutes to return to the situation of the two sons. Having received identical sentences, both men were approaching the date to become eligible for a type of furlough known as Periodic Family Visitation (Visita Periódica à Família).[1] Lívia began by listing the documents that the women needed to submit to assist in these applications. But the cousin of her *babá* stopped her to explain that they were not looking for that kind of advice. Instead, she spoke of her anxiety about whether her son would be able to "follow the right path," or if he would just fall back on worrying old habits. She began crying when she revealed that what hurt her most was neither the crime nor the punishment, but the fact that her son had lied to her before his arrest, swearing to her that he was keeping himself out of trouble.

The question at hand was whether the two mothers should support their sons' applications for home visits. As part of the process, a family member would need to submit proof of residence and sign a document in which they agreed to take responsibility for the incarcerated person while they were outside prison custody. The woman whom Lívia had met as a child, through her nanny, was now explaining to her that she knew her own son was suffering. But she also admitted, "I would be more scared for him out here on the street than I am in there." Lívia affirmed that fear and explained that, in her experience, home visitation was a dangerous option for many of her incarcerated clients. Some would be tempted to "evade" (*evadir*), to remain outside prison and thereby become fugitives. Others might try to return, but struggle to come up with money for the bus fare back, and any delay in their arrival would result in an administrative punishment. "If I were his mother," Lívia reasoned, "I would not sign that document." The men's actual mothers, seeing their concerns validated by the public defender, agreed. They decided not to sign the form, at least for now. As a result, both sons would remain in prison.

Lívia's speculative reasoning—*if I were his mother*—emerged out of a thicket of relations of authority, responsibility, kinship, and care. She offered the phrase to support keeping two men inside a prison she had worked in for years, a place where she knew at least some of the suffering her clients were exposed to. Her position as a public defender meant that she had a professional obligation to act in the best interests of her clients. In most cases, this meant initiating requests for progression, parole, and benefits like Periodic Family Visitation, or submitting appeals when these requests were denied. She rarely even consulted clients before starting these applications on their behalf, since that would produce another bottleneck in a process already prone to severe delays. But here, Lívia's invocation of motherhood shifted the tone of her responsibility toward these men. Speaking in the subjunctive, Lívia built a bridge between her profession, her own experience as a mother, and the anxieties of the two women sitting in front of her. At the same time, the scene indexed a gulf in Black and white Brazilian experiences of family—namely, that some kids are raised by a *babá*, and others are swallowed by the prison system.

This chapter is about what brought that phrase into Lívia's office. It is also about motherhood more broadly. By motherhood, I first mean the kinship position and the forms of relatedness that my interlocutors invoked when they talked about mothers. At the same time, mothering emerged as a theory and a praxis of care, sacrificial love, discipline, and redemption. Lívia's use of motherhood was not isolated; it drew from a repertoire of maternal gestures, metaphors, and postures that resocialization workers took up as they worked with their imprisoned clients, congregants, or patients, and as they explained the importance of that work to others. Motherhood provided a language and a set of subject positions to understand or debate how to construct responsible, moral subjects. It was, in other words, a problem space, one that emerged between incarcerated cisgender men, their families, and the largely white and feminine domain of resocialization workers.

In Brazil as much as elsewhere, crime, punishment, and resocialization are underwritten by narratives, expectations, and anxieties surrounding manhood.[2] Politicians and media depict crime as symptomatic of a generalized crisis of masculinity; resocialization workers within men's prisons often frame their work as facilitating a reconciliation between patriarchal authority and the law. But the longer I spent within and around men's prisons, the more I saw that these concerns were also continually displaced onto the women whom the state held responsible for making men. The mother-son relationship offers a counterpoint to another dyad that looms large within studies of confinement: the imprisoned person and the guard. The latter grounds incarceration in a dialectic of oppression and resistance or a system of panoptic surveillance. Mothers and sons offer another set of reference points, revealing questions of individual development, national progress, the productivity of violence, and the looming concern of what counts as family. By following the discourse and enactment of motherhood across different domains of imprisonment, I tease apart these relationships and examine how maternal compassion is set within and against the violent order of Rio's prisons.

Love and Mass Incarceration

Women were constantly surveilled within men's prisons. Female visitors experienced this most forcefully, through constant body searches, accusations of trafficking drugs or phones, and the superimposed regulations placed on them by guards and imprisoned collectives. But the movements, gestures, styles of speech, and motives of resocialization workers were also objects of continual discussion and scrutiny. This emerged from two somewhat contradictory accusations leveled at them by guards, prison administrators, and their own colleagues. The first was that their mere presence might provoke some inevitable reaction from imprisoned men. Like Reinaldo's imitation of a young Project Life volunteer and his description of her as a naïve "seductress," described in Chapter 2, these assertions pointed to, without explicitly naming, a desire on the part of incarcerated people that was understood as potentially dangerous.[3] Concern was directed less at women's safety than at the maintenance of order. Women were reminded by other workers to police their bodies and to avoid appearing available or desirable. The printed manuals that offered guidance to evangelical missionaries urged them to "never wear low necklines or any form of clothing that 'valorizes' your body! Remember that you are in a masculine environment, in which women appear only through television."[4]

The significance of this "masculine environment," and of men's supposedly uncontrollable (hetero)sexual desires, apparently needed no explanation.[5] Instead, it was the taken-for-granted backdrop to women's work within the system, the assumption that the sexuality of a majority-Black prison population was inherently threatening.[6] Invocations of motherhood helped many women to deflect, endure, or sublimate male desire, as well as to demonstrate their vigilance against it to others. In fact, during their conversations with me, most resocialization workers seemed far more concerned with the suspicion thrown at them by their colleagues and other prison staff than the behavior of their imprisoned clients, patients, or congregants. Most also understood that incarcerated men heavily policed one another's sexual desires, and their behavior toward women generally, through internal statutes of conduct that codified punishment for the "disrespect" of women.[7]

The second accusation was that resocialization workers were agents, rather than catalysts, of illicit desire, that they entered prison motivated by a search for love, a relationship, or simply sex, with an incarcerated man. Many prison staff suggested that this assertion was less prevalent than it had been a decade ago. As the social worker Mariana—a *parda* ("brown" or mixed-race) woman in her early fifties[8]—explained:

> Before, if a technician showed any kind of affection with a prisoner, automatically the response was "Wow, what's going on here?" So, for instance, I used to have this habit of hugging, but I had to stop because it was really common to hear not just that we were being mothers but that we were—that we were flirting. There was always a sexual connotation, and it was hard to resist, so we had to be careful with our appearance, with any contact, so careful with everything, because people were trying to prove we had some "involvement" with the prisoner. I think now the guards know better.

But the shift in attitudes that Mariana had perceived did not extend to the evangelical women who worked inside the prison system as missionaries. It was a running joke among both prison guards and technical staff like social workers that single evangelical women entered prison "looking for love," and stories of these romances, whether real or fabricated, circulated constantly.

These two assertions cast suspicion on the presence of resocialization workers within men's prisons. They also denied the professional acumen and ethical commitments that they brought to their work. Women found a few ways to defend themselves. Some doubled down on their credentials or their spiritual devotion to reassert their authority and the value of their labor. But most also turned to explicit or implicit invocations of motherhood. These set up a frame for the affective labor of resocialization that lay outside the realm of sexual desire. To call an incarcerated man "my son" was to combat the suspicion of inappropriate intimacy by the incest taboo, and by calling him into relation with the female worker as a pre- or protosexual subject. It also became a paradigm that allowed these women to explain and defend that relationship to others. Motherhood served as a shield to protect the small spaces and moments of compassion that resocialization workers had carved out within an institution that policed and pathologized both.

This was reinforced by a glaring demographic reality of the penal system: Brazil's prison population is *young*. According to federal statistics, 55 percent of the imprisoned population is between ages eighteen and twenty-nine, compared to 18 percent of the nation as a whole.[9] Rio de Janeiro's prisons, in particular, skew significantly younger than this national rate—during my fieldwork, 37 percent of those incarcerated in the state were under age twenty-four, compared to 30 percent for the nation. At the same time, the average age of technicians—the term encompassing social workers, psychologists, and psychiatrists—had risen considerably in the decades leading up to my research. I began my fieldwork fifteen years after the last hiring round for permanent employees in these sectors. Since 1999, the administration had only employed new psychologists and social workers under temporary contracts; when the economic crisis began to constrict the prison administration's budget in 2016, these were not renewed, leaving only workers who had been employed within the system for decades. As a result, most technicians were in their fifties during my fieldwork, and the majority had children who were roughly the same age as their imprisoned clients.

Motherhood was a vantage point to both perceive and intervene within this broader landscape. It was not just a model of compassion; it also provided a justification of discipline and punishment as necessary for propelling human development. Mothers could be disciplinarians, but they raised their hands against their sons out of love, and they did so in service of the men they might become. This is how social worker Edilaine once explained it to me: "Now it's illegal for a mother to hit her son, but what is more humane for him? If a mother doesn't hit him, society will when he grows up. That's what prison is, you hit someone so they can grow."

On Being Saved

Prison is like that; as much as you try, there comes a moment where you become unstable. I became depressed, I started to withdraw. But then I met Paloma [the prison psychologist], who pulled me out. She was someone who—I'm going to tell you sincerely—she was my mother. She was my mother inside the system.

Elias, recorded interview

I think of all the prisoners of Rio de Janeiro as my children.

Mariana, recorded interview

While Elias found salvation on his first birthday in prison, he continued to struggle with isolation, depression, and fear. His separation from his first wife and estrangement from his daughter following his initial arrest, combined with the distance from his mother, who lived in São Paulo, left him with little outside support. But he found another savior figure in Paloma. Their encounter occurred during a particularly difficult moment brought on by his transfer to a new prison:

> I got lost in the place and I became depressed again with nobody to talk to. There wasn't anybody left, and I was thinking about suicide again. And this psychologist was like a gift. I have her phone number today. I still talk to her when I need to. It's funny how God always sends the right people when you need them. And when I met her, I hadn't spoken to my real mother for a long time, and she offered to call her and let her know how I was. And then there was this one December, it was almost Christmas, and we were talking, she said she knew I liked to read, and she brought out this bunch of books, [laughing] it was piles and piles of books! And she said, "I know it's Christmas, you'll be thinking about your children, you'll be depressed, but you shouldn't think less of yourself for being depressed, depression is normal." And then she got me to write a letter to my mother for Christmas, and when I wrote the address she realized that she was from the same city [in the neighboring state of São Paulo]! I remember she said to me, "I've been working many years in prison, but I can see that you're different, I want to help you." So I started talking to her, telling her about my life. There comes a moment where you have to trust someone.

This story repeats many of the same elements of Elias's first birthday in prison, as discussed in Chapter 3. Then the voice of a female pastor over the television brought him back from despair and an attempted suicide, giving him a sense of purpose and allowing himself to accept God's love. Now it was the psychologist, who he also recognized as a gift from God, who offered books and a sympathetic ear. By marking out this small space of trust and compassion, Paloma was able to turn Elias back toward life.

Elias's use of motherhood to articulate this relationship suggests that Paloma was a tangible and transformative presence in his life. I heard similar stories in interviews and informal conversations with incarcerated men, or else in public events such as church meetings or activist groups where they spoke about their experiences in prison. These accounts also emerged during my interviews with resocialization workers and formerly imprisoned people. They pointed to a field of intimacy that was difficult for me to witness during my fieldwork inside prisons. But they referenced maternal care as a set of specific skills, gestures, and forms of relatedness, some of which I did observe. For example, the evangelical missionary Magnólia stressed the importance of touch, both in our conversations and during our visits to René Dotti. She would take the hand of anyone who approached her to talk, and frequently stroked their shoulders or embraced them. This tactile work was a marker of recognition and presence; the softness of her hands and her grip were a deliberate contrast to custodial regimes of physical force (body searches, cuffing, arms held behind backs, shoves and beatings). At the same time, it also expressed the limits of her care—Magnólia would converse with travestis and trans women who came up to her, generally asking for her prayers, but she never touched them.

Magnólia was perhaps more able to use touch because of her age; as a woman in her late sixties, she was not subject to the same scrutiny regarding affection that other resocialization workers were. Between Elias and Paloma, by contrast, the key element of care was a dialogue that both recognized his pain and affirmed his worth outside it. Mariana, the social worker, mirrored this observation during an interview, when she explained how she used the criminological exam as an opportunity to build a conversation that could transcend the limitations of the evaluation at hand:

> I talk about my own life too, my own history, sometimes I talk while I'm writing, to recognize something in the story, to start, you know, "My mother was from wherever," "Oh, really? So was mine!" So there you can start a dialogue where they feel they can talk to me, because I'm not a distant person who is just interrogating him, I'm actually relating to him, giving him something of myself. And

through this we are actually able to make a diagnosis. But then again, you don't always need one because we're not there to talk about guilt—*What guilt does he have when he was raised by an alcoholic mother?* When the judge passed down a sentence, he was already judged, I don't need to judge him again. But I can think about the positive things he has done while in prison [. . .] And from that we can reflect together. It's really sad that most don't have plans for when they leave. So as far as I can, I can offer him a plan. [emphasis added]

Mariana shared her own history, using it to draw out and connect with that of the imprisoned person. This required her to step at least partially out of her professional authority in order to be present with her interviewee in the moment. In the context of a criminological exam, the resulting dialogue was meant to enhance rather than interrupt the evidence-gathering function of the interview itself. Mariana talked while she was writing; the two modalities were simultaneous and complementary. She refused the role of the judge, but the product of this dialogue was still a report that would be used for a judgment on the outcome of an application for regime progression or parole. Anthropologists have noted a similar posture in both the United States and South Africa, where prison workers explicitly take up parenting as a model for understanding and explaining their labor.[10] In those cases, the position of the parent legitimated care as an integral part of development. At the same time, "parenting as a central trope opens up a space in which compassion and the gathering up of the truth about inmates share a common ground."[11] In Rio, it was motherhood specifically, rather than parenthood more broadly, that cultivated this space.[12] But it provided a similar discursive ground for workers to gather and record biographical data even as they distanced themselves from the custodial imperatives of the institution.

Both Mariana and Elias had converted to evangelical Christianity a few years before I met them. Still, her symbolic adoption of the entire prison population, and his narrated encounter with Paloma, indexed a broader, Catholic-inflected conception of maternal love as the closest earthly representation of God's love.[13] But while both incarcerated people and resocialization workers called on motherhood to understand and position themselves in relation to one another, these invocations were not identical. First, for men like Elias, motherhood was only ever identified after the fact. Mariana could preemptively claim children for herself, but Elias and others recognized this relationship only after a particular moment of receiving compassion or care. From this latter perspective, motherly love was an unexpected gift, rather than a duty or mode of ethical action. Second, mothers made demands on their incarcerated sons, but they did not expect any reciprocal gesture of compassion in return.

This asymmetry distinguishes the mother-son relationship from another invocation of kinship within men's prisons: brotherhood. Like *my child (meu filho)*, *brother (irmão)* is a commonplace term of affection in Brazil. It also functions similarly as a tactic to preempt or sublimate sexual desire—both between men and by regulating encounters with women. Yet unlike the mother-son relationship, this brotherhood is predicated on reciprocity. Evangelicals—particularly those held in the segregated cells described in the previous chapter—would refer to one another as brothers. In that setting, the term was a marker of solidarity through faith. Many of the collectives linked to organized crime that operate within the men's prison system also enforced the use of the term *brother* among members as a title of respect and camaraderie.[14] In both cases, brotherhood demanded something specific of its members through enforced rules and internal systems of discipline. These included tight restrictions on access to and communication with partners and family members of one's "brothers." At the same time, these bonds consolidated and affirmed the expectation of mutual support.

The fact that imprisoned men cared for one another—*loved* one another, in fact—was rarely recognized by prison administrators or staff. It was certainly never invoked as a potential motor for change or growth. As we have already seen, many considered that successful resocialization required severing all social ties to build new ones upon release. This line of argument was consequential—those who could not prove their intent to leave their neighborhoods or friendship groups were often denied parole. And so, rather than the horizontal and homosocial relationships between brothers, it was the vertical, intergenerational transmission of care from mother to son that came to represent and embody the transformation of a male criminal-object into a responsible and upright citizen-subject.

The third distinction between the uses of motherhood by incarcerated people and resocialization workers was blame. When Elias spoke of Paloma as his mother, or when others described the mothers that they had found during their sentences, these claims did not come at the expense of their actual mothers. In fact, Elias praised Paloma precisely because she helped him to reconnect with his own family. But when I spoke with Paloma, she was extremely critical of

Elias's family and upbringing, suggesting that it had been the root of most of his problems as an adult. For both her and Mariana, maternal posturing might provide a *defense* of imprisoned people against the prison system's zeal for isolation and violence. But wrapped up in this act was the accusation that those men were worthy of care precisely because they had, at some point, been failed by their carers. Motherhood was not just a salve for the wounds of confinement; it was something that had to be intervened upon, a problem in need of a fix.

What Guilt Does He Have When He Was Raised by an Alcoholic Mother?

There was a common structure to many of my conversations with resocialization workers when discussing their work. Almost invariably, women in these roles explained the experiences and life stories of their incarcerated clients with reference to their own children. For example, in the same discussion where Edilaine lamented the prohibition on parents hitting their children, she switched back and forth between describing the childhood experiences of her clients and those of her own son. As she explained, the most indicative symbol of family breakdown in the prison system were the letters *ND, não declarado* (not declared), which often appeared within documents in the space for listing the name of the imprisoned person's father. And beyond this, she continued, "Where are these men's mothers?" As we continued talking, she brought out her wallet and pulled out pictures of her son, telling me that she refused to finance his studies at a private university so that he would instead enroll in the free public system. "Now," she told me proudly, "he has all the money to make the choices that I kept from him when he was younger."

By moving back and forth between their own children's upbringing and the (real or imagined) life histories of the imprisoned men they had worked with, staff like Edilaine produced a theory of deviance anchored in family breakdown. Between the successes of some children and the ostensible failures of others lay an explanation not just of crime but of a broader breakdown within Brazilian society. Motherhood was a vantage point to perceive and act upon this decay, since it provided a model for intervention oriented toward human development. As Mariana explained, at a point in our conversation where I could no longer tell if she was speaking of her own sons, her incarcerated clients, or both:

I am a very harsh mother with my children, imposing limits, holding them responsible, and I think that it doesn't make anyone's life easier for you to place the blame on a system so that you don't recognize the responsibility of the actual person. Obviously, you need to care for them and think about the difficulties that someone has gone through. But at some point you need to take a step forward. I think of myself as strict like this, you have to be strict to stimulate someone to grow. I don't think anyone needs my pity, all that does is bring stigma, the only thing they need is to have their humanity recognized and stimulated.

These theories of human growth and potential returned to the figure of the incarcerated man as a subject in development, or at least capable of development given the right circumstances. As in the criminological exam, the promise of growth rests on the premise of a lack of functioning kinship ties. The mother-son relationship stages that absence, partly by inviting the resocialization worker to step in for the supposedly absent or negligent family, and partly by positioning the incarcerated person as a protosexual subject, someone whose incipient desires could be guided toward producing the kind of family he had never experienced. The return implied in the *re-* of *resocialization* was not to a past moment in the life of the imprisoned person; instead, it was to a model of family life that was assumed to be lost.

Here we need to return to Mariana's discussion in the previous section regarding her approach to the criminological exam, and specifically to her rhetorical question "What guilt does he have when he was raised by an alcoholic mother?" Why did she say this? Brazilian political and media discourse often locates the source of crime and insecurity in the "disaggregation of the family," a phrase that largely functions as a euphemism for Black families that are assumed incapable of socializing children.[15] These narratives trace parental negligence back to absent fathers and irresponsible Black mothers whose fertility is treated as a literal breeding ground of crime.[16] The discourse held steady across the political fluctuations in Brazil between the 1990s and 2010s; it was the center-left president Lula who, during his first term, described conflict in Rio's favelas as domestic terrorism caused by the disintegration of family values.[17] The absent father and the negligent mother served as reference points by which the biographies of imprisoned clients were made legible to prison workers and courts. They functioned as a shorthand for a pathological childhood, and as sufficient explanation for crime itself. The hypothetical man that Mariana conjured in our interview was never truly criminal, whatever that might mean. In fact, she refused to judge him because she saw him, through the eyes of a "real" mother, as a child. That refusal also stripped the interviewee of the chance to use crime or conflict with the state as grounds for any claim to manhood or respect, since it made criminality itself the symptom of a boylike immaturity.

For the criminal anthropology of Cesare Lombroso and his disciples at the turn of the twentieth century, the criminal represented a vestige of underdevelopment, written on the bodies of those marked as criminal, features that were alternately described as "animal" or "primitive."[18] To study the person marked as criminal was to look across time. Where Lombroso saw the vestiges of an uncivilized past within Italy and Europe, his followers in Brazil adapted his theories to their nation's own racial hierarchy. In particular, Nina Rodrigues argued that the new republic's Black, Indigenous, and mixed-race inhabitants held less criminal responsibility than its white citizens, given what he saw as their unequal positions along a linear scale of social and psychic development.[19]

More than a century after Nina Rodrigues's work, the same questions of time and development were now transposed onto the family. The infantilization of imprisoned clients produced its own temporal slope, one in which resocialization workers spoke back to clients caught in a state of arrested development, one that explained exactly when and how their paths diverged from those of their own sons. The alcoholic mother that Mariana conjured in our conversation was a key to this shift. She was the reason that Mariana felt no need to either "diagnose" or "judge" her imprisoned son. That mother absorbed both his pathology and his guilt; in doing so, she also extinguished his claim to adulthood. That apparent failure became the space Mariana could step into, a place for her to make sense of her own professional responsibility and mission. Finally, this abstract, negligent mother imbued the kinds of care and transformation that treatment workers offered with the righteousness of white saviorism.

This chapter, and the book as a whole, do not offer a detailed account of the experiences of actual families of incarcerated people. Still, it is important to note that the repeated insistence on maternal dysfunction was jarring to me because the resocialization workers who relied on it were constantly surrounded by proof of the contrary. Black mothers were a constant presence within the prison system. Every day, thousands upon thousands of them—what one psychologist described as a "river of women"—lined up across the state's prisons with food, medicine, and other necessities in clear plastic bags. This was an enormous and highly visible form of care, a coordinated effort to maintain some basic standard of living in the face of state violence and neglect. The dissonance was even more acute for social workers like Mariana and Edilaine because contact with family members constituted a core responsibility of that profession. Many still recognized and even championed the presence of wives, mothers, and other family members when speaking of specific people and cases. But as they moved toward generalizations and a broader diagnosis of the prison system, these mothers simply dissolved in the assumption of familial breakdown.

That sleight of hand draws on a long-standing tradition in social science, including anthropology, that has defined order through the status of the family. Anthropologist Mariza Corrêa traces the development within social science of a historical narrative in which first the patriarchal rural family and then the modern nuclear family became the basic units of Brazilian society since the beginning of the project of colonization.[20] As Corrêa highlights, those familial forms were never common among most Brazilians, who produced diverse constellations of kinship and community across different times and regions. But the narrative privileges them as the "birthplace" of Brazilian society at the expense of non-elite models of sociality, reducing the latter to negative space, to the realm of the nonfamily: "If there is a family defined as normal, it is only in contrast to the great non-familiar mass that surrounds it, defined as abnormal."[21] Abnormality was alternately marked as peripheral, dangerous, amorphous, or destitute, but always as a threat to social cohesion.

But elite family life never fully embodied the ideal of the nuclear family either—or rather, it could only do so by cutting someone out of the family portrait: the *babá*, the Black maid and nanny. This was the absent figure around which the scene opening this chapter turns, the woman who raised Lívia, who introduced her to her own family, including a cousin that would one day show up in her office, asking for help for her imprisoned son. The *babá* is a fundamentally ambivalent figure that shores up elite and middle-class families but also questions their integrity—both by complicating the relationship between care, affect, and transaction and by implicitly posing the existential threat that a white child might misrecognize their Black caregiver as their mother.[22] Out of this "emotionally explosive area of social relations" between white families and Black domestic workers, Brazilians have built a routinized set of ritualized performances and scripts to contain the implicit challenge that the presence of a *babá* might otherwise force into the open.[23] One example is the ubiquitous phrase "as if she were part of the family" (*como se fosse da família*), which functions simultaneously as an expression of love and as an attempt to keep the prospect of duplicated motherhood at bay. The use of the subjunctive *as if* holds together all the ways a *babá* both is and is not kin. At the same time, it provides a buffer between the Black woman and the family she has helped reproduce, protecting the latter's self-image, including its whiteness.

The encounter between mother, *babá*, and child offers an important counterpoint to those between resocialization workers and imprisoned men, another scene of duplicated motherhood. Livia's use of the subjunctive *if I were his mother* points to a similar ambivalence—not only between the public defender and her incarcerated clients but also in her relationship to the mothers sitting in her office. In this moment, there seemed to be no danger of misrecognizing who was the real mother; in fact, motherhood was the bridge among the three women, a point where legal expertise and lived experience were able to meet. At the same time, white women like Lívia were recruited by the state for the care, discipline, and socialization of Black youth. They were also called to intervene upon, rather than simply support, the production and reproduction of families.

This is not to say that the ideal of a patriarchal, nuclear family has gone undisturbed or unchallenged. Since the 2000s, government programs and welfare policies very explicitly broadened their definitions of the family outside the nuclear unit, with a newfound stress on matrifocality. Brazil's conditional cash transfer program, known as Bolsa Família (Family Payment)[24] defined family as "ties of kinship or affinity which form a domestic group." The program gave mothers and female caretakers priority as the direct recipients of monthly payments, aiming to promote financial autonomy, including independence from male partners, and to provide security in food and household expenditures. The conditions of the payment also pulled women into a network of obligations with the state and formalized their responsibilities to children. In a similar vein, "soft security" projects like PRONASCI, discussed in Chapter 3, emphasized the political agency of women within marginalized communities. Under the original PRONASCI umbrella, the program Women of Peace (Mulheres da Paz)—initially slated as Mothers of Peace—offered training for women to identify and support teenage boys in their community, to divert them away from crime and promote their formation as citizens.[25]

These programs neither replaced nor seriously challenged the violent strategies of policing and security policies that have dominated Brazil since the formation of the republic and the formal abolition of slavery. Instead, family programs, specifically those hailing poor women, were presented as a complement to the expanding scale and scope of policing. The state gained a body, a material presence, in the mother-child relation as both an alternative to and an ally of the police force. Millions of women materially benefited from these programs, gaining some measure of economic autonomy and securing basic household expenditures. But these interventions and those material gains were also justified primarily as a means of making women the solution to boys'—and therefore men's—ungovernability. Women of Peace dramatized this scene in its promotional imagery: a mother and visiting female community worker advising an adolescent son, while his father watches from the couch.[26] For Bolsa Família, money was expected to flow *through* women and toward children, while the conditions attached to the cash transfer asked women to combine the roles of teacher, community health worker, and police officer.[27] This security ideology thereby continued to hold space for understanding every imprisoned man as indexing a woman's failure.

This was not the sole vantage point from which politicians, prison workers, and others approached crime or security. It directly competed with a widespread understanding of crime as a malignant evil, and the criminal as an inherently immoral character with no possible redemption except in death. Resocialization workers generally refused this line, but in its place they attempted some form of triage, building distinctions between a minority of lost causes and the majority who might still be saved. They were less likely to concede that prison itself was a machine that deliberately and systematically tore at the ties of kinship, that the Brazilian myth of the absent Black father became real through imprisonment, while incarceration blurred the lines between boyhood and manhood, criminalized Black gender as a whole, and made the "Black family" an impossible project.[28] As a sphere dominated by white women trained in fields within or adjacent to social sciences, resocialization workers continually returned to a matrix of family and security, which gave the clearest horizon and sense of legitimacy to their own work. Mariana might have invented the alcoholic mother, but this mother gave Mariana a purpose and a method.

How to Make a Man

There was a remarkable consensus among resocialization workers, despite their political differences,[29] that the security of communities, cities, and the Brazilian nation all depended on the family unit. My interlocutors relayed this to me through various metaphors. One prison psychiatrist described society as a human body composed of familial "cells"; any malfunction in the cell would cause a sickness in the entire system. During 2016 and 2017, the main period of my fieldwork, ongoing political and economic turmoil had produced a generalized sense of an eroding social order. For those who worked in the prison system, the rapid rise of the incarcerated population seemed to offer proof of this breakdown. And yet many workers also argued that this was simply the most acute phase of a much longer arc of decay whose root cause was the steady disintegration of family life over the past fifty years.

Within this frame, family emerged as the fulcrum between individual and national development, and motherhood as a resource that might be mobilized in service of both. But motherhood was defined by its own problem: manhood. This is the dialectic of the mother-son dyad. The imprisoned (or formerly imprisoned) cisgender man is seen as proof of his mother's failings. An apparent victim of family dysfunction as much as a perpetrator, he summons the care and compassion of surrogate maternal figures in response. But resocialization workers and volunteers also point back to him, making claims on his gender, and pushing him to redirect his sexuality and his masculinity away from crime and toward something else. The ostensible solution to the letters *ND*, the mark of fatherlessness, was to empower incarcerated men to take their place at the helm of the family, providing for their children and taking responsibility for instilling in them the values that might prevent them from following the same trajectory as their fathers. It was through a mother's care and compassion that currently and formerly incarcerated people were constantly compelled to be men.

Inside Magnólia's evangelical support group, described in the previous chapter, participation was generally split evenly between those who had recently left prison and family members whose loved ones were still being held captive. This division was gendered; I never found anyone in these meetings who had passed through the women's prison system, while the relatives of imprisoned people were all mothers, wives, girlfriends, or children. Magnólia began most meetings with a song called "God's Newness." Beginning low and soft, the lyrics are nevertheless full of hope, and a crescendo gradually builds up to the chorus:

> Family, you can dream
> Mother, your son will come home
> Father, on the table bread will not be lacking
> Promises will be fulfilled
> Blessings will follow you
> What has passed, has passed,
> God's newness has arrived.

This was how it was in August, during a special celebration of what Magnólia called "Father's Month," her extension of Father's Day.[30] After the song ended, she turned the microphone over to Artur, a formerly incarcerated man who had become an evangelical pastor after his release. Artur sang another song before giving his testimony, including how Magnólia met him inside prison and pulled him away from a life of crime: "This woman here was my mother," he exclaimed to the audience, before correcting himself: "No, she *is* my mother." As he spoke, Magnólia stood close behind him and, at one point, ran her hands over his collar to straighten a crease. Next, she called for all "fathers and future fathers" to receive a blessing and a gift. I sat awkwardly while every other man in the room gathered to receive a handshake and a blessing from Magnólia, as well as a gift bag containing a notepad, a pen, disposable razors, and soap.

These meetings always ended with the donation of food to those registered in the organization: the *cesta básica*, a set of staple nonperishable items like rice, dried beans, and powdered milk, all tightly wrapped in plastic. But as the men sat down, Magnólia explained that the organization was facing unprecedented demand. The ongoing economic crisis had tightened funds, so although she "would like to embrace the entire prison system," hard choices had to be made. She had decided to institute a temporary policy where formerly incarcerated men would have priority over family members. This meant that the wives and mothers present would receive whatever was left after the men had taken their share, since "for men it's so difficult to not have any food to bring home." After the final prayer, we moved out of the basement and into an open area outside the church, where Magnólia and her daughter set up plastic tables to hand over the food baskets. The men quickly lined up, while the rest sat off to one side, waiting to see what would be left.

As Magnólia's preferred song for these meetings, "God's Newness" suggests that new life is experienced in and through the family. But here it was the father, rather than any other figure, that became critical to its success. The group's food basket policy directly inverted the logic of the federal Bolsa Família cash transfer program. Instead, Magnólia offered material support and affirmation for men as providers within the family unit. If inside prison, fatherhood was only an indirect concern, here it had returned to the foreground. The distribution of food produced a tableau of "traditional" family values, as women stood aside to ensure that men could bring food to the table, ceding space to a supposed crisis of masculinity.[31] At the same time, these men formed a line in front of two white women to receive the donation—of food but also of masculinity itself. Still, Magnólia's concern with paternal authority did not prevent many men from immediately dividing their share with the women sitting off to the side.

"That men must work is one of the most basic expectations associated with manhood," Nikki Jones writes in her ethnography of reform efforts in San Francisco's Filmore district.[32] In Rio, too, work was paramount to the image of respectable masculinity and citizenship, the centerpiece of a drawn-out renegotiation of masculinity. The polar opposite of the worker was the figure of the criminal *bandido*, and resocialization was widely conceived as a shift from the latter to the former, a redirection of the source and focus of masculinity from the street to the home.[33] The injunction to work was repeated by prison workers, in spaces like this church group, and among both currently and formerly incarcerated men themselves. There was no possible resocialization, no future outside the "world of crime," that did not have work as its cornerstone.

The donations were an attempt to bridge the gap between this expectation of work and the material possibilities for it, particularly in the midst of an economic crisis. The church group tried to smooth over the troubles of the first months of release, shoring up men's position as patriarchs until such a point where they could do so for themselves. What happened more often was that men were simply phased out of the group. Magnólia and other volunteers brought news of job opportunities to each meeting, but these were precarious or short-lived gigs that generally did not pay a livable wage. At the same time, volunteers often oversold rumors or vague talk of work as a concrete promise. So most of the time, after eighteen months with the organization and one or two stints in bad jobs, men were cut off from receiving support. This was necessary, as Magnólia argued, to free up space for new members. Thus, these donations anticipated a future man, one who could bring bread to the table on his own. But they also situated masculinity as an interminable waiting for such a future to cohere. In lieu of a job, manliness could be demonstrated by sticking it out, resisting the clear economic opportunities of theft or the drug trade and enduring through the predicament of the present.

As discussed in Chapter 3, I first met Elias in these monthly meetings. He knew Magnólia briefly during his time in René Dotti but lost contact with her after his transfer to another prison. With nowhere to stay after his release, he first found a Christian homeless shelter, where a volunteer referred him to Mag-nólia's church group. This reencounter was closely followed by Elias meeting his future wife, Rosa. Although the pair moved farther from the church soon after-ward, Elias kept coming back to these meetings. Even after eighteen months, when Magnólia advised him that he could no longer receive food donations, he still showed up, grateful for the emotional support and affirmation that he found in this community.

By this time, he had married Rosa,[34] and the couple were expecting a child. One afternoon, when Rosa began to feel a strange pain in her abdomen, he drove her in their van straight to the city center, where they had received treatment before and knew they would get at least a basic standard of care. But they were denied admission at the hospital, with the reception nurse declaring that there was currently no room in the maternity ward. Without money to buy fuel for the journey back home, they were left sitting in their parked van a block away. That was when Elias called me, asking if I knew someone who could help him out with a connection to the hospital, or another clinic. The first person who came to my mind was Magnólia, but he quickly dismissed that option, saying that he had already tried to call, but she wasn't answering the phone.

The next day, I came to meet the couple in the hospital, and Elias brought me to the balcony where he first gave me his testimony. Thankfully, Rosa was fine—their son, Elias Junior, would be born without further complications two days later. For now, though, we sat together on a bench while Elias went through the previous night's ordeal. He explained that while Rosa slept in the van during the night, he came back to the reception desk every hour and pestered the nurse until she finally relented. Now that Rosa had a bed, she would stay in the hospital until the birth of their son; Elias would go back to the van every evening to sleep. He had an almost uncanny cheer and ability to stay positive through the struggles that he dealt with. But a sense of bitterness and disappointment showed through that afternoon, as he explained to me what had happened the previous day. Magnólia had, in fact, answered the phone the first time he called last night. She offered to pray for him and his wife but told him that there was nothing else she could do for him. He tried her son, Pastor Bruno, who responded with an audio message explaining that he would call Elias as soon as he was free. The call never came. When he tried Magnólia again, he received no answer. It seemed clear to him that she was blocking his calls.

Elias never spoke to her again. For her part, Magnólia mentioned him once to me in the next monthly meeting, only to note his strange absence. She was accustomed to attrition in participation. Many of the formerly imprisoned people were re-arrested, others found jobs, and still others had no money for the bus fare. While she was concerned with the well-being of these group members, she generally accepted disappearances as an inevitable part of the NGO's work and quickly moved on. But for Elias, their final encounter was a painful revelation. It wasn't just that Magnólia's care had fallen short, although he clearly thought that even if she had no contact at the hospital, there was still something she could have done. But that night spent in a van outside the hospital, with his pregnant wife in pain, seemed to reveal that the relationship Elias understood to exist between them was hollow. In that moment, the figure of the caring, maternal resocialization worker seemed to dissolve in an instant, revealing to Elias that he and his new family were alone.

Prison Is a Mother

Diogo and I sent letters to each other over two years. Sometimes we handed these to each other during my visits to René Dotti; on a few occasions, Pastor Bruno would deliver them between us. We resorted to the post only if those options were unavailable. Diogo had learned to read and write a few years prior, after entering the prison system, but he quickly became prolific in both. He tried to write each day—to me, to the Ministry of Justice, to various NGOs, or to himself. Paper and pens were hard to come by. I would fold blank sheets into my letters, or else slide them into the books that I brought for him, but they were far from enough. The canteen only stocked food and basic hygiene products, so he relied on the informal prison economy, where a single sheet of paper sold for one real (about thirty U.S. cents at the time), and a pen for five.

Diogo had no visitors to support him financially, and he refused to participate in any of the money-making endeavors within René Dotti that he saw as illicit. So to keep writing, he would wash the sheets and clothes of his cellmates at a tap that stuck out of the wall just outside his cell, the same single tap that supplied the entire wing with drinking water. I tried to speak to him in person about this once; he grew uncomfortable and quickly changed the subject. In his next letter, he wrote to explain:

> You spoke about something that you've never spoken about before, and I felt kind of unable to speak because there were people around but also because that's not the focus of our friendship, it [the question] was about my time here and the day-to-day: like I've said, I wash clothes to "survive" [...] I don't like to talk about this because I don't want to seem like I'm destitute or a beggar.

The next month, he wrote another letter with more detail, describing the pain that ran down his back from the hours he spent hunched over this tap each day. Like every other men's prison in Rio de Janeiro, René Dotti had no dedicated space to wash or dry clothes, towels, and sheets. After washing them at the tap, incarcerated people would hang them up next to the small windows or grates in their cells to facilitate drying. This reduced air circulation and increased humidity, both of which amplified the risk of contracting tuberculosis and other airborne diseases.

But there were laundries in the women's prisons. Talavera Bruce—Rio's first dedicated women's prison, and still its largest—was built in the 1940s. Before this point, those who the state identified as women were held in segregated wings or cells. As the historian Elça Mendonça Lima highlights, Talavera Bruce was not built to improve their welfare; instead, the project aimed to "preserve the internal peace and security of men's prison" against women's supposedly destabilizing presence.[35] For the first few years, the people confined in Talavera Bruce were responsible for washing not just their own clothes but those of the nearby men's prisons as well. The prison was mostly staffed by Catholic nuns, but its first warden was a man named Vitório Caneppa, who noted that "in every aspect one can see a feminine touch: the position of a towel, the availability of utensils, the alignment of the tables and chairs, flowers on top of tables—nothing resembles what one might imagine in the first instance as a prison."[36]

Do prisons have a gender? Beyond the designation of specific penitentiaries for men or women, some have suggested that these institutions constitute a *masculine* or even "ultramasculine" form of security.[37] This can be seen, for example, in Angela Davis's argument that prisons are built around the image of a particular gendered subject, that the project of incarceration has always anticipated and imagined men as its primary targets.[38] But it also extends to the claim that prisons embody and monumentalize what Wendy Brown calls the *masculinism of the state*: "those features of the state that signify, enact, sustain, and represent masculine power as a form of dominance."[39] Loïc Wacquant, for example, argues for a model of a state concentrated around two poles, identified as the left and right hands of the Leviathan.[40] Here the "feminine" left hand acts through welfare, education, health, and housing, while the "masculine" right hand represents the punitive force of prisons, policing, and market deregulation. Specifically, Wacquant points to a qualitative historical shift in the governance of urban marginality from the left to the right hand since the late twentieth century, as the "muscular" forces of punitivism became increasingly central to governance. This gendering finds an echo in the words of Talavera Bruce's warden; regardless of the veracity of Caneppa's description, it suggests that the more feminine his prison appeared, the more it ceased to resemble a prison at all.

Both Wacquant and Davis use masculinity as a point of entry to understand prisons and parse their effects. This method pulls different objects into focus, from sentencing reforms and systematic beatings to the shape of a cell, the lack of a laundry, or the pain that shot up Diogo's spine as he bent over the tap, twisting his body around a space that was never built for feminized labor. But it also preemptively distances punishment from the "feminine" domains of care, compassion, and treatment, a gesture that Rio de Janeiro's resocialization workers also employed to separate and shield their own work from the violence of imprisonment. Lívia, Mariana, and many others were able to style themselves as defenders of imprisoned people because they understood their labor as materially and symbolically distinct from the custodial imperative. Motherhood was the figure that gave form to this split.

Motherhood also offers a view onto a much broader constellation of relationships and questions regarding gender, punishment, development, and the regulation of desire. It develops alongside and in counterpoint to sons, brothers, and fathers, the discursive center of a field where gender and statecraft shape one another.[41] This point of contact is where surrogate mothers proliferate, where Black cisgender manhood is deferred, and where the capacity of Black women to socialize their children is continually placed under question. Invocations of motherhood name and enact a tension at the center of the project of incarceration; that tension and the provisional solutions to relieve it shape the governance and the experience of imprisonment itself. Emerging from this problem space, Edilaine's image of the hand of a mother, outstretched to hit her child, represents the promise of imprisonment: an act of violence that is already looking toward who and what will emerge from the blow.

FIVE

Evasion

Hillary once asked me if I knew that prisons were first built to hold slaves. We were sitting on a roof ledge, together with a man named Wagner whom she had introduced as a friend of her husband, Lucas. All three were imprisoned in a nearby penitentiary called Crispim Ventino, which held those who had been approved for day release as part of an open security regime and was designated for men—although it also held travestis like Hillary. Underneath our feet was the third-floor apartment that she had rented with a few others from the prison as a place to rest, pass the time, and shelter from the heat. It was late afternoon; we faced away from the street to avoid staring directly into the sun that now hovered over the skyline of Rio de Janeiro's North Zone, just past a field dotted with rusting industrial equipment.

I was surprised by the question. Hillary spoke of herself as *preta*, a term that referenced her unambiguous Blackness and darker skin tone within Brazil's chromatic order. *Preta* also signaled her engagement with a new generation of Brazil's Black movement, one that had shifted toward the term (and away from *negra*) as a marker of pride, solidarity, and resistance. Hillary's embodiments of travesti femininity and Blackness were entwined, both informed by a transatlantic imaginary that took inspiration from West African textiles, North American music and television, and Afro-Brazilian religion. Although imprisonment had placed limits on these forms of embodiment, she was planning to open a beauty salon after her release, and she wanted it to be *bem afro* (very Afro). Still, a few weeks earlier, when I asked if she had experienced racism in prison, she responded with an emphatic no.

"Did you know that prisons were first built to hold slaves?" Looking back, the

147

question seems like a return to that earlier conversation, but on different terms. Hillary reframed her prison sentence as a repetition, part of a longer, ongoing project of Black confinement. At the same time, she had flipped our roles, pushing me to do the accounting that I had fished for earlier. I told her what I knew then from my research—that at least one prison in Rio was built on the same site as a jail that had held recaptured fugitives, and that the city's police force was first organized in response to elite anxieties surrounding a growing emancipated Black population.[1] Hillary responded, "It's like my friend said, prisons are made to control Black people." We raised ourselves off the ledge and turned around to watch the sky turn red, my notepad closed for the moment in the grip of my hand.

It was around six thirty p.m., so there were a few hours left before the deadline for Hillary, Wagner, and all those held in Crispim Ventino to return to the prison. When they arrived at the front gates, Wagner would be led back to his shared cell. But Hillary would be escorted to a segregated cell known as the *castigo* (which literally means *punishment*), where she would be held for up to ten days with her right to day release suspended. She had spent the last two weeks as an *evadida*, "evaded," a fugitive living outside the grasp of her prison sentence. Having decided to turn herself in, she would not enjoy another sunset for a while. But she knew all of this already. She had evaded before and she would do it again, repeatedly, sometimes alone and sometimes together with others from the prison. This cycle was so routine that I often did not know if Hillary was completing her sentence or if she was instead living as an *evadida*, most often in this apartment, only a short walk from the prison itself.

Unlike closed penitentiaries like René Dotti or the semi-open regime of Tobias Barreto, Crispim Ventino is the only prison in Rio de Janeiro designated as fully "open." For those held there, it was the final stage of confinement before parole. It therefore stood at the pinnacle of resocialization's forward momentum, marking the threshold between punishment and release. Because of this, it also held out the possibility of another kind of exit. This unit, which held less than five hundred people in its custody at any one time, registered more than two thousand escapes annually during my fieldwork. Evasions were ordinary, expected, and largely temporary. Some fled immediately after their transfer to Crispim Ventino, never to return. Most left for a moment, coming back after a few days or weeks. But even if Hillary seemed to end up back where she started, these evasions stretched and cut at the binds of her sentence, carving out room to move.

Day release and escape mirrored one another, composing two different rhythms of release and recapture—one sanctioned by the law, the other against it. By moving back and forth between the two, Hillary and others played them against each other, disturbing the terms of their confinement in the process. This chapter follows their movements, which took advantage of an opening afforded by resocialization but redirected it toward other ends. Along the way, this is also my attempt to come up with a better answer to Hillary's question. By drawing a line between slavery and her own confinement, she reframed the latter as evidence of an enduring project, a persistent condition of Black unfreedom and a symptom of the unfulfilled promise of emancipation itself. Crispim Ventino—a prison that held her under the pretext of preparing her for eventual release—recapitulated that promise while shunting it further down the line.

But there is more to it than this. Because if Hillary's imprisonment was a repetition, her evasions were another, part of a fugitive tradition that responds to the racial calculus of slavery, surveillance, and captivity. The constant cycle of escapes and returns disturbed any linear history of emancipation in the Americas; it also undermined the prison system's own telos, its premise of progression through a sentence that might carry the incarcerated person toward freedom. This temporal breakdown was, in turn, an opportunity to pivot between the state's qualifications on emancipation and the liberties that could be seized in spite of them. But those who fled also confronted the impossibility of a life lived fully outside incarceration, a project that extended far beyond the prison walls.

I first met Hillary, along with her friend, another incarcerated Black travesti named Diana, through my work with a prison reform activist. We spent several days outside the gates of Crispim Ventino collecting *denúncias* (denunciations, or formal complaints) to present to the penal court. Neither of us entered the prison. Since it operated under an open security regime, the unit was paradoxically closed off to those whom I normally accompanied in my fieldwork—technicians, missionaries, and public defenders—under the premise that those in prison could access these and other services outside. Although the activist left after a week, I continued visiting many of those I had met in the neighborhood surrounding the prison, connecting them with legal, health, and social services where I could. It took me a few months to perceive and recognize the cycle of prison escapes and returns that whirled around this place. Still, it is important to stress that there is no secret to evasion. What I outline here was well-known by the prison administration, courts, and imprisoned people alike. I am also not describing a felony. To escape prison custody does not constitute a crime in Brazil unless it is accompanied by the use or threat of violence, although it carries other consequences, like the *castigo* waiting on the other side.

To chart this landscape also reveals some of the experiences of travestis within Brazil's project of incarceration. Although evasion is not the exclusive domain of any gender, there is, as Dora Santana argues, a resonance between the "movement" of trans embodiment and "those routes of escape that also define blackness."[2] This movement echoes the insistence of José Muñóz that queerness is always *in* (not on, or beyond) the horizon, while "the here and now is a prison house."[3] Somewhere between confinement and fugitivity, between the prison and the apartment on the third floor, lay the possibility of a different mode of life, something like what Marquis Bey calls the trans *anarchitect*: one for whom "unstitching the enclosure of the house's structural architecture is in fact far more livable for some ways of becoming and unbecoming than the presumed house."[4] An attention to this anarchitectural work orients us to what is unmade and what endures along these edges of incarceration.

Travestilidade as Gender and Politics

This book is an ethnography of men's prisons and so far has largely centered the experiences of and the institutional concern with cisgender men. But Hillary's position within this system, and the forms of critique that she articulated as a travesti, shift the grounds on which we might approach the relationship between gender and incarceration. When they do not misgender them outright, many scholars often subsume travestis under the category of trans women, while others insist on a mutual exclusivity or even antagonism between the two modes of identification. The supposed "problem" of the relationship between the two terms stems from a demand for commensurability, which is itself inflected by anxieties about race, class, medicalization, and respectability. Rigid definitions of travesti have also been weaponized against those who identify with the category, rendering their lives and desires as "untranslatable" within law and medicine.[5] In any case, they largely fall short of capturing the experiences of people who inhabit and improvise gender in strikingly fluid ways, including while incarcerated.[6]

Still, to understand the position of incarcerated travestis, it is important to begin by noting that they are legally designated as male at birth, an ascription that follows them into the criminal justice system. Depending on the resources available to them, travestis cultivate feminine bodies and subjectivities. Many speak of themselves as women; others don't. But this is not the distinction upon which travesti identity or community turns. Dora Santana observes that "there is a political distinction but also an overlap and at times interchangeable naming among *travesti, transexual* and *mulher trans* in the country. The term *travesti* has been attached to a history of exclusion that has become classed and racialized in Brazil."[7] The most detailed and often the only accounts of this history lie in police and court files, archives built out of an ongoing proximity with the punitive edge of the law.[8]

The criminalization of travestis and trans people is rendered invisible in statistical terms, since virtually all imprisoned people are classified in accordance with the sex they were legally assigned at birth. Despite this, classification and segregation processes shape the passage of queer, trans, and gender nonconforming people generally, and travestis specifically, through their sentences: state prison administrators develop norms for their custody; these groups also organize to demand recognition and rights while imprisoned; and Brazil's factions maintain codes of conduct that in some cases exclude those who fall outside a particular model of masculinity and in others explicitly embrace gender and sexual diversity. The combined result of these forces varies among states and even among specific prisons. In São Paulo, for instance, a small number of units hold the majority of travestis together with other openly queer and trans incarcerated people in separate cells or wings from the rest of the imprisoned population.[9]

The situation in Rio de Janeiro is distinct. Beyond the classification of closed, semi-open, and open prisons, units designated for men are also assigned to one of the handful of factions, militias, and other collectives of incarcerated people that operate in the state. One of the largest, the People of Israel, explicitly prohibits homophobia and transphobia within its statute. This group is largely composed of those who, until the mid-2000s, were collectively referred to as neutral, meaning that they belonged to neither militia groups nor factions. They included those convicted of rape, violence against women, and homicides, as well as gay cisgender men, travestis, and trans women. Through the People of Israel, they built a network of survival and a system of internal governance similar to those already existing in other factions, including a statute that governs conduct within their prisons and offers some protection against transphobic attacks and violence from other incarcerated people. Like other factions, the group also nominated official representatives that advocated for incarcerated people, offering some limited support in resisting or responding to violence from correctional officers. Most travestis were held in units dominated by the People of Israel, and most People of Israel prisons had a nominated travesti representative among their leadership. The notable exception to this was Crispim Ventino; as the only "open" prison in the state, it was also the only unit designated for men in which different factions were confined together. Regardless of the prison, however, travestis and trans women in Rio were generally imprisoned in the same cells as cisgender men.

The statute of the People of Israel arguably offers the most concrete set of protections for incarcerated travestis and trans people. But in 2015, Rio's prison administration also adopted a resolution that established specific rights for incarcerated LGBT people. It obliges prison workers to recognize the self-determined gender and sexual orientation of imprisoned people and to treat them accordingly, including by referring to them with what in Brazil is known as their *social name (nome social)*. It also guarantees the right of travestis and trans women to wear feminine clothing and prohibits guards from shaving their heads. Finally, it guarantees the right of trans women—but not travestis or trans men[10]—to choose whether to be held in a men's or women's unit. The resolution's impact was minimal beyond formalizing what was already established in many prisons as an informal arrangement, often as a result of the People of Israel. Most prison staff were unaware that it existed, and many of its directives were not applied during my fieldwork. For example, travestis continued to be registered as male in all documents produced by the prison administration and penal court. However, the resolution did create a platform by which activists inside and out of prison have attempted to hold the administration accountable for its treatment of queer, trans, and travesti people.

In the closed unit of René Dotti, it was Renata, the prison psychologist, who worked to make both staff and incarcerated people aware of the resolution. She was the founder and coordinator of a program that she had named the LGBT Group. On paper, the group was housed under the umbrella of Project Life, the psychologist-run education program discussed in Chapter 2. But it was structured differently. Any of the ninety or so people that Renata had registered on her "LGBT list" were invited to each event, with no selection process and no graduation. Through the group, she regularly invited speakers to discuss the 2015 resolution and to outline participants' rights. Other topics included sexual and reproductive health and the process of gaining legal recognition for one's social name.

A few months before my conversation with Hillary on the roof, Renata invited me to run a workshop with the LGBT Group inside René Dotti. After guards checked my paperwork, I was back in the yellow education hall. It was empty when I arrived aside from Renata and Leo, who was helping her set up the room. As I ran through my plan for the workshop, Leo pulled chairs from the stacks sitting against the wall and arranged them in rows facing the front. Renata asked him to find the microphone, but he responded that a church group had borrowed it for a special event. Clearly irritated, Renata responded that they could have left at least one for us. People slowly started to arrive; after about fifteen minutes there were thirty participants sitting in front of me, around half of whom I read as feminine presenting.

The basic outline of the workshop was like others that I had run for Project Life. It moved through a conversation on various ideas related to punishment, resocialization, freedom, and citizenship. Once again, the fans made it difficult for me to introduce myself, but by this point most recognized me from my work in the prison. After a brief discussion, I suggested that we split into groups to work through the futures that participants imagined for themselves and the barriers that they faced. One of the participants stood out to me: Jéssica was a Black travesti whom I had met almost one year prior, before her imprisonment, when she briefly dated my friend. When I reminded her of our first encounter, her face lit up and we talked about our mutual acquaintance before she asked, "So, what is it you want from us here? Is this about what we want to do, or is this about reality?" I said both, but that I was mostly thinking about the former. "Okay," she responded, "so you want a utopia." I searched for a way to reframe her response in a way that would push forward my planned conversation rather than derailing it, but I couldn't find one, so I just nodded.

As we approached the end of the two hours we had been given to use the hall, we came back together to share our thoughts. Jéssica was the first to speak. She explained that her group had divided their ideas between utopia and reality. She started with the former: "Get a job. Go back to my family. Find somewhere to live. See an endocrinologist, because we use way too many hormones in prison and we could end up with thrombosis." Then she switched to reality: "Nobody's going to hire us. Our families don't accept us, and we can't find anywhere to live. The endocrinologists we need don't exist, and even if they do, they won't see us. Schools won't accept us. Honestly, when I leave prison, I'm going to steal."

Her response split the room along gendered lines. While most joined in a huge round of applause, many of the masculine-presenting participants made a point of keeping their arms folded. One of them stood up after the clapping and told the crowd that anything was possible if they stayed strong (*se manter firme*). This was the affirmation that I was used to hearing in workshops. Jéssica let him have the last word, but after the workshop finished I spoke to her again. While she wrote down her address for me to pass on to an acquaintance who might be able to send her money, I asked what she thought of the event. She replied that it was good to open the conversation and vent a little, "but people here are so naïve. The doors are closed to us unless we break them down."

Jéssica refused the utopia, the call to situate herself within the unfulfilled promise of resocialization. She also undid my planned discussion, since I was expecting the kinds of personal affirmation I had grown used to hearing in these spaces. In doing so, she brought a tension into the room that we moved through for the rest of the workshop without ever resolving it. In fact, we could not resolve it because the discussion, the program, and this yellow educational hall were all constituent parts of the impasse being named. This chafed against the aspirations of others who were committed to weathering the storm, who were assured by the promise of something better, or who were at least hoping to find in the workshop a place to affirm their worth and their potential. But Jéssica's point was that conviction and resilience were irrelevant, since even the most optimistic futures had no space for her and for most of the people in that room. This is *travestilidade* (travesti-ness) as politics, a critique borne out of the friction between Jéssica's existence and the horizons of this institution. That same friction rendered her and other travestis as trouble cases, a designation that profoundly influenced the shape of their confinement.

Bad Behavior

I hadn't seen Hillary for a while. I tried calling the phone—the one she shared with Diana, the one they left in the apartment when they were inside Crispim Ventino—but nobody picked up for two days. So I figured that one or both might have returned to the prison following an *evasão* and were spending their time in the *castigo*. But then I ran into Diana on the street and she corrected me: Nobody had evaded. A few days ago, Hillary had returned to the prison a few minutes before the deadline. When she reached the front of the line to enter, a guard insulted her and physically assaulted her by aggressively patting her down. When Hillary pulled herself from him and began to defend herself verbally, two other guards intervened to hold her while the first completed his search. She received one infraction for "formulating a complaint or accusation with impudence revealing a reprovable motive."[11] But because of the conflict, she signed in late, so she received a second for "disobedience of regulatory schedules."[12] The two infractions would be written up in her Disciplinary Record Transcript, and Diana reasoned that Hillary would be in the *castigo* for at least another week.

Diana was generally more reserved than Hillary, although her quiet voice often carried an acerbic wit that spared nobody but her mother, whom she adored, and who had visited and supported her throughout her imprisonment. She also self-consciously took a different approach to correctional officers than her friend. As she explained to me once during an interview, "I always respected the guards, you know, when I arrived, I would always say 'yes, sir,' 'thank you, sir,' so I never had much of a problem." Hillary, by contrast, had a repertoire of tactics to confront her abusers that she called her "basic scandals" (*escândalos básicos*). These included shouting her demands to speak to the warden from inside the *castigo* and threatening *denúncias* against individual staff and the prison itself. *Denúncias* rarely offer a viable path for travestis to address harm, and often open new avenues of violence and retribution.[13] Still, the constant repetition of the threat also denied the guards any peace inside the unit. When I finally met up with Hillary after her time in the *castigo*, she retold this event to me, her voice still hoarse, offering as an explanation the phrase *"estou sempre em evidência."* The phrase roughly means "I always attract attention" and reflects her hypervisibility in a unit designated for men. But another, more literal translation might be "I am always in evidence," which speaks to her gender as already invested with accusations of culpability or poor behavior that she could not shake off. Where Diana aimed to pass by undetected, Hillary saw this project as impossible from the start, since her body would always be read as incriminating evidence.

In the previous chapter, I describe how cisgender men were first infantilized and then redeemed by a reformative project that placed them on a trajectory from childhood to fatherhood. This project was a deliberate counterpoint to the image of the innate and incurable criminal, the *bandido*. It did not extend to women's prisons, where social workers, missionaries, and public defenders would declare that their clients were in fact victims of their husbands, brothers, or sons. The claim denied any capacity for criminal agency to those that the state recognized as female, instead pointing to the men who either framed them for their own crimes or forced them into committing felonies against their will. Such a predicament was exemplified in the figure of the wife or girlfriend conscripted into acting as a drug mule, one that served as an icon of both cisgender feminine criminality and victimhood.

Incarcerated travestis fell outside both explanatory frameworks. They did not evoke the fear or the compassion afforded to cisgender men, nor did they elicit the pity extended to cisgender women. Occasionally, they were seen as comic figures; the public defender Lívia once told me at the end of a day's work in Tobias Barreto, "I like working with travestis because they're always so funny." For evangelicals, by contrast, travestis represented the most visible face of a broader problem inside the prison system that they identified as *homossexualismo* (homosexualism), a "vice" comparable to addiction in which gender and sexual confusion had emerged from of a lack of emotional or spiritual support. Broadly speaking, though, travesti criminality was both taken for granted and diminished, at least in relationship to cisgender men. Given travestis' invisibility within prison statistics, it is difficult to establish a trend in sentencing patterns. But my fieldwork and that of other researchers suggest that in comparison to cis men, the surveillance, policing, and imprisonment of travestis largely occurs outside or on the peripheries of the network of security policies and narratives that constitute Brazil's War on Drugs, including the occupation of Rio's favelas.[14] None of the travestis that I worked with were convicted on drug charges. Instead, they were most often sentenced for theft or assault, and while most were residents of Rio's favelas, they were arrested while in the policed middle- or upper-class neighborhoods that were linked to the tourist economy.

Those differences had consequences for their passage through the prison system. Travestis' convictions generally did not fall under the group of crimes designated as heinous (*hediondo*), a category that defers progression to later stages of a sentence. This meant that prison sentences for travestis were, on paper, often shorter than for others within the men's prison system. It also meant that they followed a standard (rather than delayed) calculation in determining the dates that they become eligible for regime progression and parole. As Chapter 1 highlights, this progression is not automatic; instead, it is based on an evaluation of subjective criteria, including evidence of the incarcerated person's resocialization. It is worth returning here to the Disciplinary Record Transcript, which lists the infractions incurred during a person's imprisonment and uses them to assign a behavioral classification along an ascending ladder of terms. Correctional officers often wrote up infractions for imprisoned people based on seemingly innocuous incidents or even administrative errors. These infractions were important because they represented the only means for correctional officers to exert a direct influence on the sentences of those under their custody. But travestis were far more likely than others to incur these infractions. Through the Disciplinary Record Transcript, these became a legal record of insubordination and resulted in their continual designation as "badly behaved," a mark that often served as justification to deny them parole.

In a prison system in which the two main subjective criteria for parole were behavior and the intended plans of the incarcerated person upon release, travestis seemed to fall short on both fronts. This apparent failure was written up in documents that then came to represent them in the state's penal courts. Incidents like the assault that Hillary suffered upon returning to prison became evidence that they had failed to reorient themselves away from delinquency and toward forms of social life deemed as lawful or respectable. Thus, travestis often became caught within the progressive gears of a system that only seemed capable of registering them as incorrigible, antisocial, and badly behaved.

The dissonance between the demands of reform and the actual possibilities open to those in prison also provides some explanation for why Hillary and Diana found themselves in Crispim Ventino in the first place. For cisgender men who became eligible for an "open" prison regime, the far more common path was house arrest. But an incarcerated person's eligibility for such measures depended on their capacity to produce a credible claim to having a home in the first place. And here home depended, above all, on the support of people whom the law recognized as family—most often mothers and wives, but with the occasional grandmother or father. These kin needed to sign a declaration in which they agreed to take responsibility for the incarcerated person during their confinement and to provide some proof of residence.

Public defenders like Lívia and Ângela would distill these requirements down to a single question during their appointments with clients: *Do you have family who can take you in?* For Hillary, Diana, Jéssica, and many other travestis, the short answer was no. This is not to say that all travestis had cut ties with their families. But their relationships were often strained by conflicts that made this kind of support impossible. Diana, for instance, was close to her mother, who would visit and send money when she had the chance. But her mother lived with her father—Diana's maternal grandfather—who refused to allow Diana to enter the house unless she returned to presenting as a man. The options remaining for her were to "progress" to Crispim Ventino or to remain in a semi-open unit and forgo day release until parole or the end of her sentence. This combination of being "always in evidence" and yet illegible within the parameters of the law is what funneled Diana, Hillary, and others into Crispim Ventino. It is also what pulled them into the *castigo*. The two travestis seemed to cycle through the segregated cell regardless of their own actions. As I describe in the following chapter, Hillary was also placed there by the warden under the pretext of keeping her safe after being beaten by cellmates and facing the threat of further violence.[15] To be always in evidence meant to be followed by bad behavior, to be familiar with the *castigo*, to anticipate one's return to it.

These modes of violence offer some explanation for why the two evaded, why they would step out of the often unbearable conditions of their confinement. But they also place the act of escape itself under a different light. To put it directly, there just wasn't much at stake in the decision to evade, since the consequences of flight did not differ from Hillary's and Diana's routine experiences of imprisonment. Regardless of what they did, the two were always in evidence. So if the repercussions of evasion were the same as those faced for simply existing, if the *castigo* was waiting for them anyway, then what was the harm in leaving for a day or two?

The Big Exit

On the morning of January 19, 2023, three imprisoned men left their cells and fled the closed men's prison of Lemos Britto after sawing through iron bars and descending the external wall with a rope made of sheets, in what one news outlet described as a "cinematic escape."[16] Such dramatic circumstances helped to capture and frame the attention of the media, who reported on the story over the following days and weeks. But the event also drew scrutiny because the fugitives were identified by the prison administration as "highly dangerous" leading figures within organized crime. The prison administration's recapture division was deployed in an ultimately unsuccessful search for the three. A judge from Rio's VEP demanded that the prison's warden produce a report on the circumstances of the escape, since the fugitives were held in separate cells, the flight had occurred during a power outage, and the backup generator had not been switched on. Although these details suggested that they may have acted with the collaboration of guards, the final report instead pointed to severe understaffing of the prison itself, a shortage that left several guard posts along the external wall unoccupied. The unfolding story became a diagnostic event for both the prison administration and the courts, one that revealed several failures in security infrastructure and that the correctional officers' union exploited for its ongoing campaign for greater staff funding.

But less than one month before this, 393 people escaped Rio's prisons. This time, there was no sense of scandal or emergency. On the contrary, it was something of a yearly ritual, one that had been going on for more than a decade. Christmas was one of five moments throughout the year where thousands left prison under Periodic Family Visitation, the temporary furlough that in Rio was commonly referred to as the *saidão*, meaning *big exit* or *big excursion*.[17] These thousands constituted a small portion of the entire prison population; most were ineligible to apply, and fewer still received authorization. Those who left were obligated to return by the end of the week. But the new year, like all years, was marked by reports documenting the official number of those who had not returned—a number that, from 2014 to 2024, floated around four hundred.[18]

This was both the largest and the most predictable fugitive event in Rio de Janeiro, one whose escape route ran through the front gates of prisons. And yet unlike ropes fashioned out of bedsheets, elaborate tunnel constructions, or attempts to flee in disguise,[19] the big exit captured little attention, was not broadcast on television, provoked no demands for a formal explanation, and sparked neither an accusation nor an admission of systemic failure. During my fieldwork, regular mass escapes simply did not rise to the level of an event for the prison administration, the courts, or the broader public.[20] There was no apparent conspiracy, no collusion. Nor was there any clear breach to identify and fix within the physical or administrative structures of confinement. People left prison in accordance with the law. Escape arguably took place at some later point, in a moment of inaction, or in the decision to stay, or to go somewhere else, or to just wait a while.

Lying behind the term *evasion* is an incredible diversity of motives, conditions, and strategies, most of which bear little resemblance to any popular image of escape. *Evadidos* might never return, but they might also simply be running late. Sometimes they just have no money for the bus fare back. In other cases, incarcerated people plan and organize evasions to mitigate crowding. A psychologist stationed at one men's prison explained to me that most who did not return to the unit after a *saidão* had drawn the short straw in a lottery run by the unit's dominant faction. By forcing some to flee, the faction opened space for others among its ranks to transfer into a penitentiary that was considered relatively calm. An evasion might also represent an administrative error. In my work with public defenders, I learned of a case in yet another prison where a client's transfer between units was never registered. He was assumed to be an *evadido* for months before the mistake was found. The ambivalence of an absence can also present an opportunity. In Porto Alegre, a city in Brazil's south, Helena Lancellotti documents the case of a woman issued an ankle monitor during her house arrest who regularly evaded surveillance by covering it with aluminum foil while working or visiting family.[21] She reasoned with Lancellotti that since the GPS signal in her neighborhood was so patchy anyway, nobody would notice if it dropped out for an extra hour or two.

Collectively, these examples point to an ecology of evasive practices that surround Brazil's prison system. At the same time, each case emerged out of the processes of confinement that were established and justified through a mandate to resocialize. Transfers, house arrest, and the big exit represent some of the benefits (*benefícios*) that become available to those who have completed set portions of their sentences. They reflect the nominally progressive shape of incarceration and enact the law's conception of punishment as a gradual process of opening. Evasions hijack this momentum and veer away from the linear path of a sentence.

While the dynamic between resocialization and flight stretched across the prison system, it found a very particular and public expression in Crispim Ventino. As the only open prison in the state, it represented the culmination of progress, the final stage of imprisonment, and a form of confinement with less restrictions on movement. The benefits of day release were real and tangible, and they provided at least some respite from the institution itself. For some, it meant finally being able to see family again, or to access healthcare, or to spend time at the beach. But public defenders often warned clients against transferring here, even if they were unable to apply for house arrest. This is because the prison was also among the least resourced and most inhospitable units in the system. People held there were forced out every weekday morning with no support and no food. Those without money for transport were confined to the surrounding neighborhood. Many sought shade in a nearby plaza, where they waited for a pastor who sometimes stopped by with a few free meals; or else they managed their hunger pains until eight p.m., the earliest time they were permitted to return to their cells and receive dinner.

Under these conditions, the question of why someone would escape is perhaps less of a puzzle than why they would ever return. But the cycle of evasions made confinement a less totalizing mode of life. While it did not resolve the predicament of captivity, it made it possible to renegotiate its conditions and to produce other rhythms of existence. Crispim Ventino was a monument to these braided logics of progression and flight, a back-and-forth that spread out from the prison itself and into the surrounding neighborhood, including the apartment on the third floor. But Hillary's question—*Did you know that prisons were first built to hold slaves?*—also suggested that there was nothing necessarily new about this dynamic. Arguably, it had been established long ago, as part of Brazil's own emancipation.

To Speak of Emancipation

That afternoon on the roof, as we faced the glare of the sun, Hillary and I looked out from the ledge and onto a relatively quiet landscape. But if we could turn back the clock on that view by about 180 years we might have seen, just past the field of abandoned equipment, a site that Flávio Gomes has identified as one of Rio's largest urban *quilombos*, fugitive communities that emerged at the edges of the nineteenth-century capital of Brazil's slaveholding empire.[22] Many *quilombos* that are better-known today were located far from its colonial cities, in part because that distance allowed them to endure. But Rio's peripheries, like those of many other cities, were also marked by fugitive settlements and a continual movement of people across them. Their presence in the city's margins marked the limits of slaveholder domination, while also providing a visible reminder of the possibility of escape.[23] They were also vulnerable to violent interventions that aimed to either destroy them or recapture their inhabitants. Alongside this constant threat, *quilombos* were also dependent on trade and commerce with settler society. Even as they defied the grasp of colonial power, *quilombolas* (inhabitants of *quilombos*) across the margins of Rio de Janeiro confronted the impossibility of fully extricating themselves from it.

While fugitives were seizing this precarious autonomy, the state was building its own thresholds of emancipation. As the free Black population grew in Brazil across the nineteenth century, the juridical category of *liberto* (freedperson) tethered this freedom to new modes of tutelage and control, including a legal obligation to work.[24] Manumissions were frequently obtained only under the condition of continued labor, while those born in Africa were deemed ineligible for Brazilian citizenship. After the prohibition of the Atlantic slave trade, those held on ships intercepted by the Brazilian or British navies were given their own legal status as *africanos livres* (free Africans), but this freedom was still tied to wardship and fourteen years of indentured servitude.[25] One of the most important public works constructed by the labor of *africanos livres* was Rio's, Brazil's, and Latin America's first penitentiary, the House of Correction.[26] The Brazilian Empire tailored these new qualifications to both manage and defer emancipation, a task that was later taken up by its newly established police force.

Rio's *quilombolas* and *libertos*, its fugitives and freedpeople, were thus not only suspended in positions that "blurred the distinction between slavery and freedom";[27] they also found themselves caught between emancipations ascribed the by the state and those seized in spite of it. The forms of partial autonomy that lay along this second axis anticipated and arguably propelled the formal abolition of slavery in Brazil in 1888. Yet neither offered a definitive or immediate exit from the predicament posed by the slave state's violence. At the same time, neither of these positions entirely precluded the other. Despite the formal distinction between fugitive and conditionally free, separated by their relation to the law, in practice the two constantly overlapped and bled into one another. *Libertos* escaped servitude and found refuge in *quilombos* alongside those who had fled enslavement.[28] The latter also used flight as a negotiating tactic to secure better terms for their manumission.[29] Thus, it was movement across this field that allowed many Black Brazilians to exploit both the opportunities and the hypocrisies of the law's promises of liberation.

There is much more to say about contestations of power among Brazil's *quilombolas* and *libertos*. But even this brief history highlights an enduring tension between the circumscribed liberties held out by the state and the fugitive strategies that pushed beyond them. This is not the same *quilombo* as the one reclaimed and remade by contemporary Black activists—that is, a blueprint for projects of political autonomy and freedom from anti-Black genocide.[30] Rather, both *quilombos* and prison escapes mark encounters with the limits of freedom, with an enduring condition of life that Rinaldo Walcott identifies as "long emancipation"—the ongoing era in which "each push by the formerly enslaved is an eruption of a potential Black freedom, but each push is also contained by the juridical and legislative elasticity of the logic of emancipation as partial, as incremental, as apprenticed."[31]

My claim here is that the relationship between flight from slavery and an ersatz emancipation is substantially the same as that between evasion and the progressive promise of imprisonment. The promises of resocialization, and of day release specifically, echo the slaveholding state's vision of emancipation as tutelary, incremental, and constantly deferred. Escapes called the bluff of this linear narrative, even as they remained in close proximity to the forms of governance that it engendered. Neither side of the equation held out any clear or unambiguous figure of freedom. But between the two lay a field of movement where the possibilities of life might be challenged and reconfigured, even if only for a moment.

Looking out over that ledge, pondering if it had always been like this for Black people, Hillary was spending her final hours as an *evadida* along the outer edges of Brazil's emancipatory project. Beside her was Wagner, who kept her company in her escapes even as he remained inside the routine of day release himself. Beneath the three of us was the apartment, one of several spaces in this favela that had been rented out to those imprisoned nearby. Farther below, some were walking down the neighborhood's unpaved streets with their ankle monitors showing, a condition and visible marker of their house arrest. Others, knowingly or not, were targeted by one of the 360,000 arrest warrants that are, at any one moment, open and active in Brazil.[32] And everyone in this community was surveilled by a constant armed police occupation—just as these police were also watched from windows and rooftops so that others could avoid them, making their way down the back streets.

It was, in other words, a landscape saturated by a constant navigation between the qualified liberties held out by the state and the practices of autonomy cultivated despite it. That navigation underscored the "impossible project" of Black citizenship within the polis.[33] But if oscillation makes for a general mode of life for Black Brazilians,[34] there is also something specific in evasion that challenges the operative binary of captivity/freedom that gives incarceration its coherence. Not all escapes do this. In fact, prisons constantly anticipate flight; this anxiety shapes their concrete form and organizational structure. As Gilles Chantraine and Tomas Max Martin put it, "escapes not only *break* the prison, they also *make* the prison as a central issue through which the institution is imagined, built, organized, justified, reproduced, resisted and transformed."[35] But while Hillary's evasions could be metabolized by this logic, her returns could not. If imprisonment hinges on the limits of a sentence and the borders of a wall, she and others would repeatedly and without huge consequence pass through them *in both directions.* The figure traced by this movement, this anarchitectural work, is itself a reevaluation of what is possible within the time and the territory of incarceration.

The Apartment on the Third Floor

And then there was that time over Christmas when we were drinking in the favela, and time was passing, time was passing, and suddenly it was almost midnight, so we went to the [prison] gate, but the guard said, "Look, you're already late, you'll be going to the *castigo* either way." So I looked at Hillary and we decided to go back for another drink.

Diana, recorded interview

Evasions rarely came as a surprise. This was true in many prisons, but perhaps most of all in Crispim Ventino, where they took place almost every day. As the preceding quote from Diana suggests, flight was something of a non-event both for the guard and for herself. Standing at the front gate with Hillary, the correctional officer not only suggested that she evade but also offered a justification: Whatever they had to lose was already lost; the *castigo* would be waiting for them regardless. In that moment, the three of them were playing with the terms imposed on them by a criminal conviction. What did it mean to stand outside the prison in the dark, facing the supposedly inexorable fact of one's own sentence, and decide: *Not tonight?*

A prison sentence sequesters time from the convicted person. This act is formalized by the ceremony of the court and the authority of the judge. In Brazil, as much as elsewhere, a sentence is often understood through the metaphor of debt. At the same time, it carries an assurance of its eventual end. Chapter 1 offers a historical overview of how Brazilian penal and criminal law tinkered with the interval brought forth by a sentence. Progression introduces stages and gradients, all justified through the promise of resocialization. But this structure also routinely produces delays and deferrals. Diana, for example, had reached eligibility for parole around the time that I first met her; it took five months for her to finally receive the judge's approval.

Facing both the promise and the constant postponement of release, incarcerated people evaded to take time into their own hands. To escape from prison, even by walking away for another drink, fractured the state's claims to the imprisoned person's time. A sentence was no longer an uninterrupted interval; instead, it became a task one might leave and come back to. For many, including Hillary, this transformed the obligation of confinement into something more flexible. The trade-off was a further delay in her ultimate release date; since the days spent outside prison custody did not count toward completing a sentence, evasions pushed back eligibility for release or parole. But in Diana's case, this point was completely irrelevant since the latter date had already passed. Rather than redefining the terms of her "debt," evasion took back what the law owed her.

Crispim Ventino had its own rhythm, one that was built around a particular image of the working day. Federal legislation justifies open prison regimes in part to incentivize imprisoned people to work. The prison's schedule—release by seven a.m., return by ten p.m., and confinement during weekends and public holidays—reflected this premise.[36] But the few work opportunities that existed for those held in the unit did not fit easily into this time frame because they involved early starts and long commutes across the city's peripheries. Evasion offered a partial fix because it untethered people from this timetable and widened their field of movement. Incarcerated cisgender men would often evade to spend several weeks working on civil construction projects, where opportunities were scattered around the city, work started early and ran over the weekends, and projects were far from the prison. Hillary faced a different dilemma. She was a *faxineira*, a cleaner for the houses of friends and neighbors who lived near her childhood home, almost two hours away by bus. She could sometimes manage this while imprisoned, but it was difficult to arrive at work on time, and she had already lost a few clients after showing up late. The money was important because it helped cover her share of the rent and allowed her to buy food and medicine to make her time in prison at least a little more bearable. This is why, one afternoon, she explained to me that she would probably evade tomorrow.

We were sitting under the awning of a bar just down the road from Crispim Ventino itself. I had been waiting there for Diana to arrive, but she was over an hour late at that point and not answering the phone, so Hillary suggested that we make our way to the apartment. Almost immediately past the entrance to the favela, we ran into four police officers standing idly by with their guns drawn. These were members of the Pacifying Police Unit, which I had grown used to seeing in the neighborhood by now. I generally stood out here because I was white and not familiar to the community—when I was alone, residents often asked if I was looking to buy drugs. But now, as always, I barely warranted a glance from the officers as we walked past. When we turned the corner off to a side street, a group of adolescents who clearly recognized Hillary asked if the police were behind us. She nodded as we kept walking.

Before the UPP arrived in this community, police would periodically invade during special operations. But for the last five years, pacification had made their occupation permanent, justified in the name of reclaiming the territory from organized crime.[37] The UPPs broadened both the intensity and scope of residents' exposure to the criminal justice system. One direct consequence, as I have described in the Introduction, was an acceleration in the already rapid rise of Rio's prison population. Pacification ratcheted up arrest and conviction numbers in the state, bringing unprecedented strain to an already hypercrowded system.

But the UPPs also produced an entire landscape marked by the constant anticipation of and negotiation with their intimate presence. For instance, while our exchange with the teenagers lasted only a few seconds, it conscripted Hillary into the back-and-forth of surveillance and countersurveillance between the UPPs and the faction that claimed the neighborhood as its own territory, and on whose behalf the children were asking the question.

The short walk between the prison and the apartment took us through overlapping territorial claims that were unavoidable and that demanded of Hillary a constant calibration of proximity to and distance from either side. That demand is unremarkable in Rio's peripheries, particularly for feminine subjects whose movement is predicated on navigating between the "masculine" forces of factions, police, and militias. Anthropologist Hollis Moore identifies these pressures as part of a gendered imperative of "ongoing relations between antagonists."[38] But if Hillary did evade tomorrow, she would also contend with an added threat: the risk of being apprehended by the police. In such cases, the punishment was far more severe than for those who returned of their own accord. Generally, it meant "regression" back to a semi-open or closed prison and the suspension of eligibility for parole or house arrest for twelve months.

And yet while some in the favela needed to actively avoid the police, Hillary did not seem openly concerned with them, regardless of whether she was currently evading or not. This stance initially confused me, given the possibility of being detained. But eventually I became more attuned to her constant labor to remain out of focus by cultivating good relationships with neighbors and by avoiding open conflict. I once joked that she seemed to know everyone in the community, even though she had arrived only a few months ago. But this was because she, like other feminine subjects in the neighborhood, went out of her way to befriend people, to learn how to navigate the community, and to present herself as a member of it rather than a threat. That work became clearer to me when Diana, who sometimes engaged in sex work, ended up in a fight with a client inside the apartment and was expelled by the others for almost two weeks as a result. The problem was not the damage done to the furniture but that in drawing attention to the apartment, she had risked the intervention of either the UPP or the neighborhood's faction within a space that was meant to provide some refuge for both.

When we arrived at the apartment building, Hillary unlocked the front door

and we climbed the concrete stairs to the third floor. The apartment was unoccupied when we arrived. It was small. There were two rooms—a bedroom with a
double bed, a desk, and a single window overlooking the street; and a combined
kitchen and living room furnished with a small fridge, a sink and countertop, a
chocolate brown couch, and a fold-out chair. There was also a bookcase with a
stack of English-language workbooks piled up on the bottom shelf, which the
residents would occasionally work through with me. The walls and the floor
were bare concrete, but a rug covered most of the ground in the living room.
Some of this furniture had come as a gift from Diana's mother. The bathroom
was just outside the apartment's front door and was shared with the other unit
on this floor. The window had a few iron bars but no glass pane and no curtain.
When the heat of the afternoon sun began to stream through, they would cover
it up with a sheet of cardboard. But the street outside was quiet most of the time,
and so were the neighbors, which lent the apartment a feeling of calm. Hillary,
Diana, and a few other friends from Crispim Ventino had found this place a few
months before I met them. While it was always a struggle to pull together the
money for each month's rent, they had nevertheless managed to keep a hold of
it for now.

The apartment on the third floor was a site for cultivating the kinds of do-
mesticity and kinship that Brazilian law found impossible to ascribe to travestis.
Today, it was also part of the binds of Hillary's prison sentence, a satellite of her
confinement. Tomorrow, when she evaded, it would become something different: a fugitive place, one that gave her room to maneuver outside the confines of
her imprisonment. What was striking about the apartment was the superimposition between these two modes of existence, the ordinariness of their coexistence
within a space so close to the prison itself, and a neighborhood enveloped by
a constant police occupation. It smoothed the pivot between the subject positions of imprisoned and *evadida*, affording some stability through this shift. It
was this oscillation that allowed Hillary, Diana, and others to bridge the limited
forms of autonomy offered by either side, and to play one off the other.

What might a theory of incarceration look like from the apartment on the
third floor? The space was not free from the operations of policing and punishment; in fact, it attests to the impossibility of a constitutive outside or a definitive exit. There was little room here for what Rinaldo Walcott calls the "romance
story" of fugitivity, no heroic dash toward freedom and little chance that what

was built would last.[39] But as a counterweight to Crispim Ventino, it also redirected the momentum of progressive imprisonment against itself. Punishment and progress were both felt here, but so was the movement of flight. The apartment held these forces together awkwardly, never resolving or transcending them, but making it possible to find a path through. This is what Katherine McKittrick has described as a "usable paradoxical space"—a claim she develops through the garret that both concealed and confined Harriet Jacobs during her flight from slavery in the United States.[40] To occupy these spaces is to situate oneself across, rather than directly against, a set of tensions shaped by slavery and incarceration.[41] Up on the roof of the apartment, we looked over a landscape that bore the marks of this ongoing struggle. The space offered no clear blueprint for abolition, but it still laid bare the unstable edges of Brazil's penal landscape and the potential that might be seized from within them.

Inhabiting the Predicament

In 1840, an *africano livre*—enslaved in Africa, emancipated upon arrival to Brazil, then immediately placed under indentured servitude—fled from the construction site of Rio's House of Correction. This was the third registered escape of a man given the name of João, someone whose ostensible "freedom" also provided the legal pretext for wardship.[42] In João's case, that meant working alongside other freed, enslaved, and convict laborers to shape the bricks for Latin America's first penitentiary. João was reported missing for five months. In the end, he was discovered in Niterói, a city just across the bay from Rio. But João was not in hiding; instead, he was working in a quarry operated by the state, still maintaining his status as an *africano livre*.

Black fugitivity and marronage in the Americas historically emerged in and through a precarious, generally asymmetrical form of dependence on slaveholding centers of power, the "outcome of an encirclement of unfreedom."[43] Under these conditions, flight could neither lead to nor easily create a "beyond" to slavery. Instead, as Gary Wilder argues, it faced this very impossibility head-on: to escape was "to confront and inhabit the predicament."[44] João fled one site of unfreedom for another, in search of a different way to inhabit a landscape of captivity. But his case also illuminates a particular moment when the landscape itself was shifting. João's path out of slavery, part of Brazil's unfinished project of abolition, is also the story of how the bricks were made for a new project of confinement.

Almost two centuries stand between João and Hillary, a distance that I cannot bridge in this book. But João's experience offers another place from which to answer the question posed by Hillary that afternoon on the apartment roof. The two moments speak to one another, bringing to light an ongoing negotiation between the concessions offered by the state and the opportunities forcibly seized from it. Evasion builds an insurgent mode of safety through movement. It remains distinct from the forces of both state security and criminal collectives, even as it is caught between them. This kind of safety flits in and out of sync with Brazil's project of incarceration, finding moments of temporary reprieve, then moving again.

From the perspective of the prison administration and the courts, evasion signifies something different: an absence, a subject that has become legally unaccounted for. Absence opened a set of possibilities for those imprisoned in Rio, and particularly in Crispim Ventino, to shift the terms of their confinement. It was not, however, the unmaking of their imprisonment. Crispim Ventino outlived the apartment on the third floor. The cycle of flight and return that I have followed in this chapter did not extricate Hillary or Diana or anyone else from the law's violence. Neither did release. Instead, what it offered was an opportunity for the two to rework the edges of their imprisonment, to make day release the foothold for something else to break through.

That afternoon, when Hillary led me from the bar into the apartment on the third floor, we didn't stay for long. Almost immediately after we arrived, she suggested that we head out again. She had recently been introduced to another bar nearby that apparently sold the cheapest beer in the favela. But she couldn't remember the name, so after circling the block we just settled for the closest one. Standing around a table on the street, we shared a bottle between us. When we brought our glasses together, I offered her a *saúde* (cheers). She replied with an *axé*, a call for good energy or high spirits that had made its way into Brazilian Portuguese from Yoruba.[45] Both of us were surprised to see Diana walk past; when we called her over, she corrected our choice of bar and led us across the street, where we now stood resting our backs against the wall. Hillary and I prodded Diana for a few details on a new romance, but she instead turned to her frustrated attempts to find work. As we talked, Hillary was pulled into another conversation with women from the neighborhood who were passing by. But when she asked me the time, and found out with a shock that it was verging on eight p.m., she excused herself quickly and left. With two hours left before she needed to get back, I don't know where she was headed.

Resocialize to Conquer the Future

The end of imprisonment begins with a legal order called the *alvará de soltura*, the *release license*. Judges from Rio's penal court produce this document when someone's application for house arrest or parole is approved, as well as for those who complete the entire length of their sentence. After the prison administration receives it, there is still a delay of a few days for release. This is because the final obligation of those held in prison is to attend a "freedom ceremony"—a ritual that, despite its magisterial name, is largely a bureaucratic formality. The ceremonies are officiated by members of Rio de Janeiro's Penitentiary Council (Conselho Penitenciário) who travel around the state, visiting prisons with an ink pad and a set of green booklets that will soon serve as a record of attendance at the state parole office. Those about to leave are called out of their cells with the phrase *cantou a liberdade*: freedom sang.

Semi-open and open prisons, where releases are common, hold one or two freedom ceremonies per week, most often in an unoccupied room within the administration building. The council member first distributes booklets to those present, instructing them to press their thumb into the ink pad and mark the final page with their fingerprint. Some of them congratulate newly released people and offer words of advice or encouragement. Most are instructed to appear at the state's Patronato—the institute responsible for overseeing house arrest and parole—within the next ten days. The entire process generally takes less than fifteen minutes. Next, those assembled are taken to the prison's classification office to verify their identities and sign out. Finally, they are brought to the front gates and led outside, one by one. Some have family members waiting for them on the other side. Others step out alone.[1] When I began research in 2014, those leaving prison were given a prepaid transportation card holding twenty reals (about US$6 at the time) to help them make their way home. Two years later, this provision had been cut. The experience was quick, often unexpected, and largely unceremonious.

This is the back end of imprisonment, an outflow that administrators and prison staff refer to as the *porta de saída,* or "exit door." Over the course of my research, tens of thousands of people went through the freedom ceremony and were led out of prison, averaging about a hundred per day.[2] It was a point that so much of a criminal sentence looked toward; the moment foretold in the prison administration's motto, *Resocialize to Conquer the Future*; the horizon against which futures were made and broken, evaluated and analyzed, promised and deferred. It was the time that Colonel Gilson and Diogo spoke of at the start of this book to make their claims for what prisons were and what they could be. When my imprisoned interlocutors talked about the future, they were always talking about a time and a place after release. Whatever months or years they still had to spend in confinement were part of the institution's long, drawn-out present.

And yet release from prison also marked the point at which these modes of anticipation began to unravel, where the promise of resocialization loosened its grip. Those leaving prison might still face the demand to prove that they had changed to family members, neighbors, churches, potential employers, or even themselves. If they were under house arrest or parole, they still lived within the structure of gradual social reintegration set out by the law, which included restrictions on movement.[3] But progress through the remainder of their sentence was no longer tied to any evaluation of their reform. At the same time, release forced an encounter between resocialization's plot and other ways of making and marking time. In particular, what became known during my fieldwork as *the crisis (a crise)* was rippling through Rio de Janeiro and Brazil, swallowing individual and collective futures in its wake.

In the middle of a profound economic downturn, rising unemployment, and the breakdown of old motors of social mobility, the optimism that had defined Brazil's development for the previous decade rapidly evaporated. By 2016, the nation was embroiled in a massive recession, a corruption probe that had uncovered the largest bribery scheme in history, and the coup-by-impeachment of president Dilma Rousseff. Rio's state and municipal governments negotiated with federal agencies for emergency loans to complete some of the construction projects required for the 2016 Olympic Games so they might maintain some semblance of order for international visitors. But those plans and that dependence on the construction industry left the city hit hard by the recession. In June of that year, a few weeks before I arrived to continue my fieldwork, the state government declared a "state of calamity" that remained over the entire course of my research. Unemployment and homelessness ballooned, and rising public fears about crime led the city's newly elected mayor to request federal military intervention on the streets. Christ the Redeemer, that iconic symbol of Rio, still loomed large over the city, but it now looked out on crumbling infrastructure, an upsurge of violence, and half-built construction projects pointing toward a future that had never arrived.

If contemporary experiences of time are marked by an "evacuation of the temporal frame of the 'near future,'" as anthropologist Jane Guyer has claimed, the crisis only amplified and deepened this vacuum.[4] It offered a language through which Brazilians connected their own struggle with a broader national, collective predicament. None of this was limited to the prison system itself; it was a much broader malaise, a general condition of life that Brazilians found themselves in. But crisis also directly collided with the temporalities of resocialization. It undercut the sense of individual authorship over one's future. As the past surged unexpectedly back into view, it also threatened the notion of linear progress and the promise of development itself. Finally, crisis directly brought into question the nature and worth of the "social" itself as a space of belonging. The walls of the penitentiary and the mandates of prison law had provided something of a buffer between the times of resocialization and crisis, but release brought them face to face.

In this epilogue, I follow Elias and Hillary, two figures introduced in previous chapters, as they tried to leave imprisonment behind and pursue new futures for themselves—and, in doing so, navigated the impasse between resocialization and crisis. After leaving prison, both were forced to grapple with the vanishing future, the confinement of the present, and the resurgence of a past that had ostensibly been overcome. Both also turned to divine time, to prophecy and rebirth, to reclaim time for themselves. The paths that each took through this moment draw attention to resocialization's long shadow as well as its limits in Rio's urban peripheries.

The Tip of the Revolver

In the two years following Elias's release from prison, he and his family were forced to move neighborhoods several times over. First, there was the evangelical shelter that took him in when he had nowhere else to go; then longer-term accommodation in a more distant neighborhood in the city's North Zone, where he was living when he married Rosa. Soon after, they moved into a favela neighboring Madureira, which was their home when I first met them. But when a conflict with neighbors threatened to turn violent, the couple were forced even further into the urban periphery. By mid-2017, the family was living along the outer edge of Nova Iguaçu, one of Rio's satellite cities. It took me a little over three hours to reach their home from my central apartment by public transport.

On my first visit, Rosa greeted me at the door and led me into their home. Elias wasn't physically able to stand; instead, he waved from the kitchen table, covered in bruises and sporting a neck brace. About a week beforehand, a car had collided with him on one of his first days at a new construction project. While the man who hit him was initially helpful, providing money and assisting in Elias's application for an insurance payout, he eventually stopped answering his calls; the man's wife told Elias not to contact them again, backing up this warning by reminding him that she was a lawyer. As a result, he now lacked the money to travel to the hospital for a checkup. A friend had called him recently, asking if he could start working next week on housing renovations. Elias insisted that he would be fit enough to work by then. That seemed overly optimistic to me, but his main concern was that he needed a car to transport himself, and he had recently lost his van in a police blitz[5] that confiscated the unregistered vehicle.

As we continued talking, Rosa and their son, Elias Junior, moved into the bedroom to watch television, while Elias began to recount a scene on the street from two days earlier:

> I'm walking along like this and I see an old lady with a cane leaving a bank, counting almost two thousand reais [approximately US$600] in her hand. That's what I calculated, I saw her walking with her cane, she stopped, she counted a few bills, kept walking, stopped again, counted a few more bills, and I was just staring at her on the street and I thought, shit, why not throw some of that my way? [Laughing] And, you know, problem solved! You know? And why? Be-

cause I had this need, trying to find a solution for this need. So what did I do? So I wouldn't—so it wouldn't invade my mind, so it wouldn't enter my heart and grow roots, what did I do? She was going this way; I went that way. I went in the opposite direction to her, even though I was supposed to be going her way, but if I go her way, it could enter my heart, grow roots, and once it's grown roots then it's done, it's over [*já era*], there's no going back.

He never named the solution, the thing that might enter his heart. I don't know if he stopped himself because it was too dangerous or just too obvious to state that he could have robbed this woman. Still, he made it clear that there was another path he could have followed, one that might have led him out of the situation he now found himself in, even as he reminded himself that this path would inevitably lead to ruin.

As we kept talking, he brought up a more recent conversation:

This morning I went over to talk to Pablo [Elias' prospective employer] and I ran into an old friend, we started talking, I said I needed a car, all that, and he said "Fuck, man, there's an easy solution to all this, go find two cars, sell them, buy one for yourself!" You know? He said it's easy, find two cars, buy one for yourself. People say it's easy, but what if I go find two cars, I could end up spending years in prison again, lose another chance to see one of my children grow up. But to take care of him, for the rest of the month, we have fifty reals [about US$15]. So, what am I going to do? Explain this to me.

It wasn't the first time that Elias produced these counterhistories. I first noticed it in a conversation we'd had about a month earlier. In moments of frustration or disappointment, Elias would openly ponder what he—or, at least, a former version of himself—might have done. On another occasion, he was fired on his first day working at a farmer's market when a conflict with his new boss, whom he described first as a lesbian, then later more pejoratively as a "dyke" (*sapatão*), escalated; in an attempt to publicly shame her for her sexuality, Elias fell to his knees and began loudly praying for her soul. Afterward, he told me that this former employer should have known how easy it would have been for him to rent a weapon to kill her. By dwelling on moments that never took place, Elias identified a concrete and consequential choice. These accounts always ended with the choice to expel such thoughts, to refuse to allow them to enter his heart. He didn't rob the woman leaving the bank; he wouldn't steal the cars; he never retaliated against the boss who had fired him. These decisions reframed what might otherwise have been felt as humiliation as a mark of strength in overcoming the temptation of revenge or easy money. They transformed inaction into agency, a demonstration of his worth as a new man, a provider for his family, and a moral subject. But the result was that he remained stuck in the problems of the present; as he explained later that afternoon, "On the side of the *good*, I can't see an exit. I can only see an exit on the side of evil. My mind is very creative, it works twenty-four hours, since I can't create anything, you know?"

Elias insisted that this moment was ephemeral, that it would soon give way to a future that had yet to reveal itself to him. He described this feeling as sitting "at the tip of the revolver," searching for the trigger that would propel him forward. The image of waiting in the barrel of a gun, like a bullet, carried a strange resonance with the growing armed violence in his neighborhood between paramilitary militia groups and the local faction. But it also articulated a Christian sense of waiting as a discipline, of holding out for a future moment that was both assured and unknowable until it arrived in the realization of God's plan, and in God's time. Hirokazu Miyazaki points to a similar metaphor of waiting in a Christian community in Suvavou, Fiji, as they battled for land rights: to "prick the taro leaf."[6] There, if the leaf was finally punctured in the right place, water would immediately flow out in abundance, and their struggles would be over. Here, Elias was waiting for the right trigger. He continued to wake up at four every morning to pray, asking both for this future to arrive and for the strength to hold out until it did. The "side of the good" was not creative—it was set by God, waiting to be revealed through adherence to a community and a specific set of values. Evil, on the other hand, was working through Elias's own mind to creatively imagine diversions from this path.

At the same time, Elias split himself from his own mind. In the preceding conversation, the "I" that emerged was a subject of volition, not of thought, and Elias strived to maintain that distinction. The mind was endowed with an agency separate from his own. It could not be entirely controlled but could still be subordinated to his will. There was, therefore, no categorical distinction to be made between the suggestion of a friend and one that arose within his own thoughts—both were *external* moral hazards that threatened his integrity. That split was a response to the immense strain that Elias felt as he saw a world of possibilities around him, knowing that they would all lead to ruin. To reject his own mind was to rebuke the near futures that gestured toward him in favor of a time of prophecy, but it also meant another day of living in the gap between the two.

Elias's recognition of his own potential, however frustrated its realization, stands against a broader context of antipathy and violence against those labeled as criminal. Teresa Caldeira has drawn attention to a constant discourse in Brazil on insecurity that she identifies as "talk of crime."[7] In the context of another decade and the shadow of another crisis, Caldeira contends that talk of crime offered Brazilians a way of making sense of urban violence, one that resonated with broader experiences of precarity. When people recounted their experiences as victims of theft, assault, kidnapping, or robbery, they built rigid boundaries of an innocent "before" and a wiser but more fearful "after." Crime offered a readily available symbol of evil and disorder, and the criminal was marked as an essentially incorrigible figure. Through this talk, Brazilians sutured their personal experiences with broader urban and national shifts of the 1980s and 1990s including the transition to democracy, the economic recession and hyperinflation, and a growing sense of insecurity. Talk of crime consolidated a set of standard narratives of victimhood, innocence, and evil; in doing so, it provided a way of making sense out of disorder. It also fed into a broader spatial transformation of urban life, as communities sought to wall themselves off in search of security.

Talk of crime left no space for Elias and his claims of resocialization. On the contrary, it framed the criminal as invasive and inherently malignant, something that must be cut out of the social body. Elias reconfigured this moral universe through his faith, distancing himself from crime not through space but by a rupture in time. As discussed in Chapter 3, the Elias of the present was not the same as the one who was responsible for the crime for which he was sentenced. The counterhistories indicated moments when the break was threatened but ultimately maintained. The past seemed to percolate into the present through these possibilities that Elias saw, as if the evil he thought he had left behind was still alongside him, looking out onto the world with the same set of eyes and reminding him of the obvious, yet existentially dangerous fact that despite its risks, crime was in fact a rational and relatively secure form of existence, at least compared to his current life. At the same time, he acutely felt the lack of respect that he had once commanded as "Elias the Rottweiler," including the wealth that his involvement in drug commerce had brought him. Still, these stories all ended up back at the same point: a disavowal of crime and a commitment to a different kind of life for himself and his new family.

Eventually, Elias told me not to worry, that God knew he was just "letting off steam" and would forgive him. In fact, he assured me that things were working out for him—particularly since he had begun to visit local evangelical radio stations where he gave his testimony and advertised his music. There, testimonies of self-identified former criminals (*ex-bandidos*) were not only recognized but actively valued, celebrated, and even commodified, alongside other stories of transformation such as the ex-addict, the ex-paraplegic, or the ex-travesti—a collection of former lives that Mariana Cortês describes as the "ex-everything."[8] Given the support that the church provided during this time, even under the strain produced by the crisis, Elias saw the clearest possibility for his social, economic, and spiritual flourishing within this community. Maybe the trigger was somewhere in there. Maybe it would be a new career within the evangelical music industry, a space where some seemed to go viral overnight, like a revolver going off. But until then, the weight of the present remained:

> I'm going to tell you something from the heart. I'm hoping something's going to happen, because I feel, how can I explain this to you . . . I feel like I'm at the bottom of a pit, there has to be a way out of this pit, there has to be a light at the end of the tunnel. But a natural light, because artificial light I already know how to make, you know? So I'm waiting in the hope of that natural light, man. That's the truth, I'm waiting for natural light, I can create artificial light, but . . . every minute, every second, every split second, I'm killing the lion, you know? The thing is, this whole thing is humiliating, right? It's humiliating.

The night after my visit, the electricity to his house was cut.

Making Saints

Hillary never went through the freedom ceremony. Instead, her exit from prison was swift, unorthodox, and violent. After a fight broke out with a member of one of Rio de Janeiro's factions, ostensibly over her refusal to change the channel on the cell's shared television, both she and her husband were severely beaten before a correctional officer pulled them out. For two days, the pair were kept in the *castigo*, the segregated cell described in the previous chapter, while they waited to see a doctor. Hillary insisted that remaining in prison would constitute a threat to her life, and her lawyer requested an emergency transfer to house arrest. While waiting for a decision from the penal court, they were moved into the prison's evangelical cell. Those held there refused to let Hillary sleep along-side them, so the couple spent their last night lying on the concrete floor next to the cell door. As she recounted this moment to me a few weeks later, she re-membered looking at the few possessions she had managed to retrieve from her former cell:

> And my old fan was plugged in, whirring around and making a clicking noise, and I was looking at my stuff, wondering who would take it after I was gone. And I remember thinking, "I hope nobody takes it. They don't deserve it." And it must have been magic because just like that, I'm looking at the fan, and it starts to catch fire.

The judge accepted the request for an emergency transfer. Hillary was placed under a stringent form of house arrest in her old childhood home, a place she once told me she never wanted to return to. Her husband moved back in with his mother, who did not approve of his relationship and agreed to take him in only if he cut off all contact with Hillary.

It was a two-hour bus ride from my home near the city center to Hillary's house—a large, autoconstructed building perched on top of a small hill.[9] Like Elias, Hillary was adopted, one of seven Black children who spent their first years of life in an orphanage before being visited by a single white man who became their father and took them all to live in this house on the hill. As they grew older, he built a second floor on top of the first, the space that Hillary had now made her home. Two of her brothers lived downstairs, while their father, who continued to own the property and who had signed the forms allowing Hil-lary to stay there during house arrest, now lived with his boyfriend in another area of the city. The other siblings were dispersed around the metropolitan area. One of them, Hillary stated, was a *bandido* (criminal), and she once suggested offhand that I might want to get in contact with him to learn more about crime. I started visiting the house every week or two to catch up and help her set up the front room, where she planned to open her beauty salon, the one she had been thinking about since she was imprisoned. About two months into these visits, I stopped short when she opened the front door to let me in. Her hair had been shaved short and she had what looked like at least a week's worth of stubble on her face. Instead of the colored prints she normally wore, today she was in a white pants and shirt—"like a little man" (*bem homenzinho*), as she put it.

Rio's prison administration used the crisis as justification to withhold payments to the private company that manufactured and serviced ankle monitors for those under house arrest. Eventually, the company stopped providing them at all. So when Hillary began house arrest, she was told that "the monitoring has to be in your own mind." It wasn't exactly that Hillary ignored the legal mandate to stay at home, but she had other demands to attend to. She still cleaned the house of a neighbor one day a week. And she was beginning to visit a *terreiro*, a communal sacred space for the Afro-Brazilian religious tradition of Candomblé. She assured me that she was still a Spiritist, the religion she was raised within, but she started going to the *terreiro* on the advice of her friend, who was also the boyfriend of the temple's leader, the *pai-de-santo* (father-of-the-saint). Now she was in the middle of her initiation, a ritual known as the *feitura de santo* (saint-making) that would present her to the *orixás*, the divine spirits within many West African and diasporic religious traditions. Normally, this meant three weeks of isolation at the *terreiro*, but to balance the ritual's requirements with her house arrest she wound up moving back and forth between the two spaces.

Like Elias, Hillary often found herself confined to one of these two sites because of the gun violence that had taken over the neighborhood. The main street that my bus passed through served as a line demarcating the old border between two rival factions. The relationship between the two had been peaceful in recent years. But when members of one faction defected to the other, these territorial claims were suddenly up for contestation. From her house, we could sometimes hear gunshots in the distance. For those living in Rio's peripheries, it was this soundscape, more than delayed salaries or deteriorating public services, that most clearly represented the crisis. Rio's homicide rate—including those committed by on-duty police officers—was rapidly climbing after years of steady decline. At the same time, the gap between homicide rates for Black and white Brazilians was widening.[10] Territorial skirmishes and stray bullets produced a pervading atmosphere of danger and confined people to their houses. For most residents, these conflicts were not new, but their increased frequency and ferocity had shifted the rhythm of communal life and presented a new force to be navigated through or around.[11]

The upsurge in violence within Hillary's and Elias's neighborhoods repeated itself across the city's peripheries. Schools were shutting down more often to avoid student casualties, while many people remained in their homes for hours or days as they waited for the quiet that might signal that they could return to the streets and their jobs. At Rio de Janeiro's parole office, staff knew that many of their clients were failing to show because they could not safely arrive at their scheduled appointments, but this did not stop them from passing on their names to the Court of Penal Execution. Arriving one or two days late might save the parolee from further problems, but then again, it might not—many were considered as no longer fulfilling the terms of their sentence and determined to be fugitives. Likewise, the evangelical missionary Magnólia began to open each meeting of her church group with a collective prayer for an end to violence in the city. She praised those who continued to arrive each month, while lamenting the growing number of empty seats left by those she described as not "committed" to the project. These absences were noted by volunteers; after three of them, a participant's right to the monthly food baskets provided by the church was revoked.

Hillary was worried about her own scheduled visit to the parole office, where she was required to visit each month until her sentence was complete. But the gunfire was also bad for business. The recently opened salon was failing to attract any customers outside of her immediate neighbors, since people were far less willing to travel—especially up the hill and into the favela. Even if they could, nobody seemed to have money to pay her. She had first reached out to the *pai-de-santo* for an herbal infusion that she sprayed around the salon to attract prosperity. But as she returned to the *terreiro* and became more interested in Candomblé, she decided to undergo the *feitura*. It wasn't just the salon. Everything had felt stagnant since she left prison. Aside from the end of her marriage, she was also struggling to quit Rivotril, a benzodiazepine she had begun using while in prison. It used to help her pass the time of her sentence, but now she found that it just clouded her mind and left her anxious. She needed something that would allow her to get out of this situation, to regain some momentum in her own life. Hillary hoped that the *feitura* would give her back some movement.

As part of this process, the *pai-de-santo* told her that she needed to dress and present herself as masculine.[12] We spent a while in the kitchen, preparing lunch together. During the initiation period, she was advised to not break anything, so she passed me the eggs to crack into the skillet. As they sizzled in hot oil next to some black beans—which were for me, since she was prohibited from eating black foods—she continued explaining some of the ritual's details, like the bracelets she was wearing on both arms. She told me that her *orixá* was Iansã, the deity of the wind. As she spoke, the long grass on the hill outside the window was rustling in the breeze. I saw that her nails had grown long and thought that this might have been a way for her to preserve some femininity in her body. She noticed me looking and told me that she was not allowed to cut them during the initiation. It was the same for her toenails, which now sometimes touched the ground when she walked barefoot.

Hillary was looking forward to the end of her *feitura*: "I look at myself in the mirror and can still recognize myself, but I don't like to see me like this." She felt different, too—aside from the clothes, the *pai-de-santo* told her to stop taking hormones until after she had completed the ritual. She felt uncomfortable, estranged from herself as she noticed her body changing in response to the lack of estrogen. But even with this discomfort, she conceded that she had begun to see things more clearly, that she was feeling lighter, more free. She had finally stopped taking the benzodiazepines, and she felt like she had a new outlook on life. She only had a few days left for the ritual; in a few months, her house arrest would be over as well. From here on, she told me, she could finally move forward.

Youth Reaction

I met up with Elias, Rosa, and the now six-month-old Elias Junior at a train station close to the end of the line. Elias was doing a little better this time—he had managed to borrow enough money from neighbors to buy an old car and was working intermittently on the renovation sites, which at least meant that he could pay the electricity bills. He was out of the neck brace and he seemed to be in less pain. He had invited me to join them for a street event called Youth Reaction (Reage Juventude) that had been organized by a pastor friend. It was scheduled to begin in the early evening, but the family wanted to arrive early to prepare. Elias was slated to perform in front of the crowd. He was excited for the opportunity to speak about his life and to use his music to reach young people, whom he considered most in need of his message. My job was to film the performance on an old digital camera Elias had borrowed from a friend at church. The camera was designed for still photos rather than video, but it would have to do.

Elias wanted the footage to make a DVD that he could sell at future events and send to other churches as a kind of demo reel.

They picked me up from the station and we drove off in their recently purchased car, which was struggling to hold itself together. The smell of gasoline wafted through the interior, while the engine made a harsh growling noise as we drove. Worse still, the streets were lined with speed bumps at regular intervals. If Elias did not take them at a snail's pace, the tailpipe would inevitably come loose and start dragging on the road. We would then stop for a minute, and he would take off his shirt to keep it clean before disappearing underneath the car to fasten it back on. The second time this happened, Rosa and I sat anxiously in the car as we watched a mugging at gunpoint unfold on the street fifty meters ahead. Rosa called for Elias to get back in and just leave the tailpipe hanging, but it was fastened back on soon enough. As we drove on, Elias warned me that we were entering a dangerous territory, one that was currently contested between the neighborhood's faction and incoming militias—a conflict that made today's event and its message all the more vital.

Once we arrived, we were greeted by the pastor, who led us to a small reception building in the local church. There, we spent a few hours getting ready. Elias was eager to speak to the band who would be backing up his music, and anxious about the time slot that would be allocated to him. The pastor said that the event would start at around six in the evening. He had arranged for Elias to speak and perform at nine p.m., which was when most people would have arrived and settled themselves in the audience. The church had hired a *trio elétrico*, a semi-trailer equipped with a stage and sound system that would cut off traffic to the street and project the sounds of the event through the surrounding streets. The sound itself was another territorial claim, marking out the neighborhood as belonging neither to factions nor militias but to God.[13] Talking to me privately, Elias asked me not to record the first part of his talk, since he would say things about his past that might put his life in danger if they were broadcast. Meanwhile, the pastor was busy recording a promotional audio clip for the event to boom out from the sound system, letting passersby know that there would be a special performance from "Elias, formerly known as Elias the Rottweiler."

By six, the *trio elétrico* had arrived, and we had set up around eighty plastic chairs in front of it for the audience. As we waited, Elias gave me more directorial suggestions for the video. He asked me to take some footage of the audience arriving, to make sure I had a good angle to record, and to occasionally pan between himself and the crowd to capture their reactions. As time began to drag on, I filmed a few sweeps of an audience which, despite the event's name, was largely composed of elderly women. It began a little after seven, with the pastor giving a speech on the importance of youth and the mission to take over the streets. Afterward were a series of shorter performances—one by a group of five in their early teens, another by a choir of older adolescents. Once they had finished, another pastor came to give a sermon; meanwhile, Elias watched with clear irritation as the previous performers, who collectively had constituted almost all the youth present, began to split from the main crowd and walk off down the street.

He was finally called up to the stage about an hour late. Since the streetlights were shining directly into the camera from my vantage point, I moved to the other side of the road, a few meters in front of him and off to the side. While Elias spoke of his former life, I waited for him to give me a nod, the signal to start recording. "... But that's not what I'm here to talk about," he continued through the speaker system after the nod. "I'm here to talk to you about what God has done in my life since I accepted him." From here, he began with the same testimony I had heard many times before—the night of his attempted suicide, the moment God rescued him, and the gift of music that he received from his prison cell. As he spoke, Rosa handed out sheets of paper with the lyrics to many of his songs written on both sides. Elias alternated between testimony and music. At one point he pulled out the prepaid funeral receipt his mother had bought for him, handed it to a woman sitting in the front row, and asked her to read it out. I kept the camera trained on him most of the time but panned to the audience as they sang along or applauded at certain points in his narrative. I had fifty minutes of recorded footage by the time Elias finished his performance. By then, it had reached eleven at night. The crowd had thinned out a little more; about half the seats were empty. When the pastor took back the microphone, he asked everyone to stand and spread out into a single line down the street, holding hands. Elias and Rosa joined the line while I walked up and down with the camera, recording as they sang.

Before the event's close, the pastor took a collection of donations for Elias and Rosa, "who have shared their lives with us tonight." As soon as we were done, the *trio elétrico* drove off, and we had to stack the chairs and move them off the road quickly to make room for the cars that were waiting to pass through the street. When we came back to the church it was after midnight. Elias Junior was asleep in his mother's arms, while his father expressed his frustration that the event could have been planned better; that he should have been given an earlier time slot; that they should have done the collection earlier, before the audience had begun to disperse. We waited for the pastor to arrive before immediately saying our goodbyes and leaving in the car. This time, I sat in the front to give Rosa more room with a sleeping Junior in the back. By now, there was no public transport to take me home, so the family offered for me to stay the night. Elias drove a little slower this time, although the tailpipe still fell off twice. But we also had to take the side streets back to their house, because there was bound to be another blitz on the main road, just like the one that saw him lose his van a few months ago. We arrived at one in the morning; Rosa handed me a spare blanket from the cupboard and I fell asleep on the living room couch almost immediately.

Youth Reaction was a staged intervention within the neighborhood, an effort to reclaim the streets from armed conflict, to forge a connection between the church and young people, and to thereby draw them away from the influence of both factions and the militia. Elias performed as an agent of security, laying out his testimony as both a warning and a beacon of hope that could reshape the neighborhood. But he came to the event with an added objective: the video recording, one that could potentially reach a far greater audience. He offered a far more triumphant, less ambivalent portrait of himself than the one he had given me a few weeks earlier at his home, injured and struggling to find a car for work. In both moments, he presented an image of his former self, only to denounce it. But this evening, at least, the distance between the two seemed firmer; the blue slip of paper was for another man's funeral, someone safely sequestered in the past. Elias had earned an invitation to this event through his performance on a local Christian radio station; he hoped that, in turn, Youth Reaction would lead to more opportunities.

But the event's proceedings seemed to fall short of fully achieving either of these goals. The most important problem was the absence of youth. While the evening spoke *to* young people from the neighborhood, the only youths who took part were performers who were already members of the church, and they had left before Elias even had a chance to speak. In part, his distress at their exit was motivated by a concern about the optics of the film we were making—my pans to the audience now largely consisted of women in their fifties and sixties, rather than the young people he was reaching for. Those who remained seemed unable or unwilling to fully play their roles within his carefully choreographed plan.

That included me. Apparently, at least ten minutes of the footage I recorded was unusable because I had muffled the sound by covering the microphone with my index finger. The compact camera that I used was also not of the quality that he was expecting. It could only record twenty minutes at a time, so there were several cuts that he needed to work around in the final edit. He had hoped to speak from the stage on top of the *trio elétrico*, but the band equipment and sound system left no room for him, so he ended up on the road. As a result, I filmed him from eye level rather than a low angle, which might have made for a more impressive shot. Aside from their age, the audience was smaller and less enthusiastic than he had hoped. Although they had been given the lyrics to his music, many of the songs were so fast that they could not keep up, so most gave up the attempt to sing along after a few lines.

Redemption, as ethnographer Nikki Jones contends, is a dialogic process performed with and alongside others.[14] The work of "making good," in the language of Jones's interlocutors, requires the validation of others for reform to be maintained and recognized.[15] Elias did this work largely within the evangelical community. Here, his transformation was not only affirmed but celebrated—which was far from insignificant, given the weight of suspicion and antipathy that he was exposed to among others because of his criminal record. But his attempts to translate this support into material resources were constantly frustrated. Youth Reaction was supposed to demonstrate and record the power of Elias's music and testimony, a power that he might be able to market and use to at least supplement his income. The fact that it did not live up to his expectations was not merely a disappointment; it was a loss of the entire family's substantial investment of time and money into the event.[16]

Perhaps more than anyone else I worked with, Elias most closely represented a success story within the parameters of resocialization. After his imprisonment and conversion, he had built a new family, found employment, and remained steady in his commitment to building a life outside of crime. Moreover, he was immensely proud of this achievement and understood it as the reward of years of hard labor. But the conditions that enabled this success were neither stable nor entirely legal. Elias was able to work at his job and attend Youth Reaction because he drove an unregistered car. This wasn't a criminal offense, but it still left him exposed to the police, just like his previous van. In a fugitive zigzag that echoed Hillary's and Diana's cycle of evasions and returns, Elias tacked between the main roads and the side streets, skirting the figure of the law in the middle of the night.[17] His success never felt secure. Instead, it left him bearing the weight of combined financial, spiritual, and family strains, all while being stalked by the figure of a former self he thought he had left behind.

The next time I visited the family, Elias was at home looking after his son while Rosa visited her aunt. As soon as I arrived, he showed me the stack of DVDs that he had made from the event. The cover of the disc included a still image from the footage—in the first batch, these had come out a little blurry, but the second was much clearer. He had sold a few copies to neighbors for ten reals (worth about US$3 in 2017) and planned to give others to the pastors that often visited his local church. But he also mailed off four DVDs, each one accompanied by a hand-written letter detailing his life history, to prominent Christian singers from Rio de Janeiro, including the Latin Grammy Award–winning artist Fernanda Brum. As he explained, even if only one of the four responded to him, the relationship would undoubtedly open doors. "When you sing *in the media*," he explained, leaning on those words, "everything starts to take off." To make sure that the parcels would be opened by their recipients, he spent a little more on the postage so that a signature would be required upon delivery, a price he considered a small investment in his future. But there was another event coming up in two weeks where he planned to record a second video. This one would be longer and have better image quality—and, I assumed, a more skilled operator behind the camera.

We sat down together on the same couch I had slept on to watch the DVD. The total run time was thirty minutes, meaning that he had used more than half the footage I provided. There were a few rough cuts between moments and the audio wasn't great, but overall it seemed far better than I had feared. After watching for about five minutes, we turned our attention away from the television and started talking, although Elias's recorded voice continued to sing in the background. The recording had reminded him of a video he recently received on WhatsApp, so he took out his phone to show me. The message combined stock footage of natural landscapes with a voice-over that explained that humanity was the dream of God, that our dreams were also his dreams, and so to pursue them was to fulfill his will. It was October. Elias assured me that by the end of the year, things would be looking up.

All Our Tomorrows

The motto for Rio's prison system wasn't always *Resocialize to Conquer the Future*. It used to be *Fronde Virere Nova*, Latin for "to be green with new leaf," a quote from Virgil's *Aeneid* that was accompanied by the image of a sun smiling over a barren tree, patiently waiting for it to grow again. I found it in the state archives, stamped on documents dated over sixty years ago—a moment when Rio had just lost its status as the capital of Brazil, but before the coup that inaugurated Brazil's most recent dictatorship. Considered against this former motto, the militarism of the newer one, its image of the future as unclaimed territory waiting to be conquered, stands out. But together, the two phrases point to an enduring insistence that a better future is waiting to be found, that imprisonment itself is an act of optimism, of promise.

This impulse to search for something better just over the horizon is one that anthropology often shares. Rehabilitation narratives and ethnographic writing both often hold out the promise of an "otherwise" by finding some small window of change, some potential for transformation, within the suffering of the present.[18] That is one way to conclude an ethnography. But this book is already saturated with redemptive turns. Rather than recapitulate them, I have tried to reckon with the weight of the future, to follow people across a prison system that illuminated and bound them within the promises of reform. Resocialization pinned incarcerated people under a vision of their own reform that they struggled to inhabit. It also offered a channel for some to resignify their confinement, to build new strategies of self-making and self-narration, to hold the image of their eventual release in view, and to hijack this reformative impulse toward fugitive ends. Some of these responses to resocialization's predicament are what anthropologist Zöe Wool would call "in-durable sociality," forms of living that push against the conditions of the present while offering little chance of any concrete or lasting transformation.[19] Others sweep the present into grand narratives of triumph or salvation.

The stories continue outward, beyond the moments I have described here.

I could follow them to offer another kind of conclusion. I could show you the day when a social worker announced her retirement, elated to be done with a career that she had compared, repeatedly, to a prison sentence. I could write of the moment when someone I had met in prison was finally released, simultaneously elated and terrified. I could also describe the afternoon when I was grading papers in a windowless office in California, and received an unexpected call to let me know that someone I knew and cared for had died while still in prison. But those tomorrows neither resolve nor dissolve the "present" that I have laid out in this book. Incarceration finds its justification in a vision of progressive movement toward a future. This ethnography has been an attempt to freeze that movement, or at least to view it in slow motion, to grapple with how resocialization unfolds from one day to the next, as a document, a gesture, an interview, a game, or an offhand phrase. Things shift in these moments, while other temporalities become folded into the operations of punishment, from evangelical horizons of rebirth to the stalled project of Black emancipation. But my point is, if resocialization is already here—that is, if we refuse to wait for its future arrival, the final realization of its promise—then we can reckon with what it has already wrought. Without this deferral, perhaps the carceral present becomes less workable.

Acknowledgments

This book has been crafted out of the generosity of people caught at different points across Rio's prison system who decided to share something of themselves with me. I have tried to do justice to their lives and to thread my gratitude across these pages. But I need to offer a special thanks to those currently and formerly imprisoned people, as well as their families, who have worked with me over the years. Their confidence in this project kept me going. For the ones who have been asking me for years now, *"e o livro?"*—"and the book?"—I hope that this is a worthy answer.

Long before it was a book, it was a partially formed question, a lingering feeling that something needed a better explanation. At the University of California, Berkeley, I met friends and colleagues who took that feeling seriously and encouraged me to see where it could lead. James Holston has always been a bedrock of support, while insisting on a level of clarity and purpose that I continue to aspire toward. I thank Teresa Caldeira for the gift of her insight, and for welcoming me into an intellectual community. Nancy Scheper-Hughes was a companion and friend whose passion for the work of anthropology continues to push me forward. Laura Nader and Lawrence Cohen offered companionship and advice as we charted the terrain of anthropological inquiry. Brittany Birberick, Candace Lukasik, Anthony Wright, Jonathan Wald, Nicole Rosner, Lana Salman, Ricardo Rivera, Caylee Hong, Jesús Gutiérrez, and many others were a source of companionship and a reminder that scholarship is something we do together.

Thank you to my Brazilian colleagues, who welcomed me and invited me into a new set of conversations. Flávia Medeiros opened the doors of this incredible community for me and has accompanied the project as a friend, roommate, critic, and supporter. I can see my conversations with her—and with Everton Rangel and Luisa Bertrami d'Angelo—across the pages of this book. I am grateful for the opportunity to work at Rio de Janeiro's Public Defense Office, and the hospitality that was offered me there. Staff at the National Archive and the Public Archive of the State of Rio de Janeiro were both extremely supportive of this amateur historian. The Institute for Comparative Studies on the Administration of Conflicts (InEAC) at the Universidade Federal Fluminense also took me in and supported me both during and after my fieldwork.

When I was an undergraduate student at the University of Sydney, Vek Lewis, Danielle Celermajer, and Erin Taylor encouraged me to ask my own questions and showed me how. In Germany, the Max Planck Institute for Social Anthropology welcomed me into their community. The School for International Studies at Simon Fraser University in Vancouver provided an intellectual home during my postdoctoral fellowship, when most of this book was written. There, I was fortunate enough to find the guidance of Tamir Moustafa, Megan MacKenzie, Ellen Siew Meng Yap, Kathleen Millar, Chris Gibson, Liz Cooper, Sally Sharif, Irene Pang, and Darren Byler. This research has also been supported by two grants from the Social Science Research Council; a John L. Simpson Memorial Fellowship from UC Berkeley's Institute for International Studies; the Simons Foundation, Canada, Postdoctoral Fellowship; and a Hunt Postdoctoral Fellowship from the Wenner-Gren Foundation.

I want to express my profound gratitude to the scholars who engaged with my work and encouraged me to continue, including Emily Avera, Nell Haynes, Hollis Moore, Daniel Silva, Ana Chiritoiu, Samuel Maull, and Laurie Denyer Willis. Chapter 5 of this book has been reworked from an article previously published in *Cultural Anthropology*—thank you to AbdouMaliq Simone and the anonymous reviewers, whose feedback made that work and this one stronger. At Stanford University Press, Dylan Kyung-Lim White was the driving force behind getting this book out into the world. I owe so much to the reviewers who engaged deeply with the manuscript, who affirmed its potential and pushed me to see what it could become.

There are many others who found a thousand different ways to support me. My students at UC Berkeley, Simon Fraser University, and San Quentin Penitentiary have all been a joy to work with, challenging me to understand the place of my work in the world. Friends like Thalles, Eliot, James, Lis, Bernardo, Pinah,

Nicholas, André, Dandara, Nico, Gene, Moe, and Fabrício kept me going through good times and bad. Writing would have been a much lonelier experience without Vicente, my beautiful cat, asleep on my lap. My partner, Robson, has been an accomplice in it all, giving me strength and keeping me tethered to the world. My family in Australia is an anchor, a constant reminder that I will always have a home. My little sister, Gemma, has always been a source of joy and a model of how to pursue justice in the world. Her sudden death, soon after I began writing the book, is a scar that runs through me. But I am so proud to be her brother.

Finally, this book is dedicated to my parents, Chris and Jocelyn, whose love travels with me everywhere I go. I owe them everything. To them, and to all of you—this book is yours.

Notes

Introduction

1. Most people referred to Gilson with the title "Colonel," even though he had never worked in the military. But the term was used as an honorific within the prison administration because many of those appointed at higher levels were, in fact, also current or former members of Brazil's armed forces.

2. Sánchez et al., "Mortalidade e causas de óbitos nas prisões do Rio de Janeiro, Brasil."

3. Secretaria Nacional de Políticas Penais, "Relatório de informações penais."

4. The state and its capital city are both named Rio de Janeiro. Almost all prisons in Brazil, including those I discuss in this book, are administered at the level of the state.

5. The term *reabilitação* is not used as a synonym for resocialization in Brazil. In the context of criminal and prison law, it has a far more narrow, technical meaning: the sealing of criminal records two years after the completion of a criminal sentence.

6. Their use of the term *sistema* offers a counterpoint to the arguments of Luiz Claudio Lourenço and Hollis Moore, both of whom suggest that Brazil's prisons "cannot be understood as a system," given the autonomy of individual penitentiaries and the lack of standardization or oversight. Although *sistema* was used most often by incarcerated people and their families, prison staff, volunteers, and administrators also referred to Rio's prisons as a system at times. In doing so, they drew attention the *systematicities* that shaped incarceration, from shared bureaucratic processes to widespread illegalities to the systematic targeting of Black Brazilians and residents of Rio's favelas. I also suggest that, in contrast to Bahia where Moore and Lourenço both conducted research, Rio's prisons were subject to a greater (though still limited) degree of centralized oversight. See Moore, "The Gender of Inmate Governance in Northeast Brazil," 343; Lourenço, "O jogo dos sete erros nas prisões do Brasil."

7. Infopen, "Levantamento nacional de informações penitenciárias."

8. Caldeira and Holston, "Democracy and Violence in Brazil."

9. Khan, "Judges as Agents of Coloniality."

10. These groups are often glossed as "gangs" in English, which tends to understate

their scope and to flatten the multiple valences of the original term. Factions are simultaneously (1) collectives of survival and forms of political self-organization for those incarcerated in Brazil, particularly within men's prisons; (2) consolidated networks of organized crime that are generally centered in the commerce and exportation of narcotics but have also spread to arms dealing, extorsion and deforestation; (3) providers of infrastructure and social and cultural programs within Brazil's urban peripheries, where they claim and compete for territory; (4) organized, armed opposition to police forces and to state violence; and (5) parallel systems of justice, security and punishment that operate within and outside prisons.

11. Franco, "UPP—A redução da favela a três letras"; Machado, "The Church Helps the UPP, the UPP Helps the Church."

12. Militias (*milícias*) refer to paramilitary groups, founded and largely formed by security agents (including military and civil police, correctional officers, and firefighters). Like the factions, militias claim and dispute territories within Rio de Janeiro and its satellite cities. Initially justified as a mode of resistance against factions, militias have diversified from racketeering and extrajudicial killings to service and infrastructure provision (including forced monopolies on utilities), drug trafficking, and real estate. They increasingly hold influence in state and federal politics, particularly in Rio de Janeiro. See Lessing, "Milicianization."

13. Members of the People of Israel (Povo de Israel) offered multiple origin stories for the collective's name. Most suggested that it was a reference to the biblical Israel as a nation surrounded by enemies. An older name given to the group, which had mostly fallen out of usage by the time of my fieldwork, was Enemies of Enemies (Inimigos dos Inimigos), which was itself an inversion of the name of one of Rio de Janeiro's factions, Friends of Friends (Amigos dos Amigos).

14. Here I use the official terms within the Brazilian census and other statistical instruments that refer to categories of color (*cor*), which are considered as a proxy for race (*raça*) but not identical to it. Today, many social scientists consider as Black (*negro*) those who identify or are identified as *preto* or *pardo*. However, Indigenous scholars and activists have argued that the practice erases Indigenous (including Afro-Indigenous) identity and ancestrality within the category of *pardo*. In addition, those caught by the criminal justice system are virtually all racially profiled by police, rather than through self-identification; one result is the registration of many Indigenous people as *pardos* at the moment of their arrest. As in the case of gender, statistics thus tend to obscure specific patterns of criminalization and racism. Nevertheless, most imprisoned people I met during my fieldwork identified themselves as Black, and the visual impression of Rio's prisons as sites of Black confinement was clear to me and most of my interlocutors. See Silva, "O Índio, o pardo e o invisível."

15. Alves, *The Anti-Black City*; Smith, *Afro-Paradise*.

16. Infopen, "Levantamento nacional de informações penitenciárias."

17. Moore, "Extralegal Agency and the Search for Safety in Northeast Brazil"; Biondi, *Sharing This Walk.*

18. Vargas, "Gendered Antiblackness and the Impossible Brazilian Project."

19. The main administrative division within Rio's prison system was between the subsecretaries of treatment (*tratamento*) and custody (*custódia*), although the latter was far larger and better resourced than the former.

20. McLennan, "America's Human Rights Crisis in Historical Perspective"; Wacquant, *Punishing the Poor.*

21. Lourenço Filho, *Ressocializado na cidade do caos.*

22. Lourenço Filho, *Ressocializado na cidade do caos*, 31.

23. Lourenço Filho, *Ressocializado na cidade do caos*, 79.

24. The Brazilian phrase *world of crime* (*mundo do crime*) is not synonymous with illegality. Instead, it refers to a social landscape that largely orbits around the lower rungs of Brazil's drug trade, as well as the forms of self-fashioning that this "world" makes possible. In Rio, it is also closely tied to the physical space of favelas. People can be *in crime* (*no crime*), or even *of crime* (*do crime*). Rather than signifying a specific act, *crime* points to a place and a set of social relations, somewhere you can enter, inhabit, leave and return.

25. BRAZIL. Legislation no. 7.210, July 11, 1984 (Lei de Execução Penal). Article 1.

26. BRAZIL. Legislation no. 7.210, July 11, 1984 (Lei de Execução Penal). Article 10.

27. Crewe and Ievins, "The Prison as a Reinventive Institution."

28. Wacquant, *Punishing the Poor*; Sufrin, *Jailcare.*

29. Comfort, *Doing Time Together.*

30. Carr, *Scripting Addiction*; Fassin, *Prison Worlds.*

31. Ricoeur, *Freud and Philosophy*; Sedgwick, "Paranoid Reading and Reparative Reading."

32. Foucault, *Wrong-Doing, Truth-Telling.*

33. Gilmore, *Golden Gulag.*

34. Burton, *Tip of the Spear.*

35. Meiners, *For the Children?*

36. Throughout this book, I alternate between the terms *guard* and *correctional officer* to refer to those who were known during my research as either Inspetores de Segurança e Administração Penitenciária (Inspectors of Security and Prison Administration, or ISAPs) or, more informally, *agentes penitenciários* (prison agents). After the conclusion of my fieldwork, a 2019 constitutional amendment reclassified these guards as a police force, the Polícia Penal (Penal Police).

37. Life sentences and the death penalty were outlawed under the 1890 Penal Code, and these prohibitions were reaffirmed in Brazil's most recent constitution, alongside others for forced labor, banishment, and "cruel" punishment. The maximum legal penalty for a single conviction is thirty years, the upper limit codified in the Penal Code

for a small set of crimes including homicide, kidnapping resulting in death, and rape. Multiple convictions can stack, producing sentences that can, hypothetically, reach into the centuries. But when those penalties are "unified," the time exceeding a legal ceiling is effectively disregarded. During the time of my fieldwork, that ceiling was thirty years; in 2020, under the presidency of Jair Bolsonaro, it was raised to forty. The Brazilian constitution also outlines a single exception for the death penalty prohibition: for military crimes committed during times of war, and only with the authorization of the Brazilian president. The measure has never been used.

38. Forum Brasileiro de Segurança Pública, *Anuário brasileiro de segurança pública, ano 10.*

39. Caldeira, *City of Walls.*

40. Povinelli, *Economies of Abandonment.*

41. Thomas, *Political Life in the Wake of the Plantation*, 129.

42. Walcott, *The Long Emancipation*, 72–73; Shange, *Progressive Dystopia.*

43. Walcott, *The Long Emancipation.*

44. Lombroso, "Illustrative Studies in Criminal Anthropology III."

45. Freyre, *The Masters and the Slaves.*

46. Fabian, *Time and the Other*, 31.

47. Throughout this book, I use the terms *cisgender* and *cis* in line with the use of *cisgênero/cis* by Brazilian trans and travesti scholars and activists. But I also recognize a tension between this use and the critique within Anglophone scholarship that such terms represent a "categorical ruse disingenuously hailing those who nevertheless do not and cannot sit comfortably within it," particularly since they are propped up by white standards of gender that Black people, among others, do not inhabit. Bey, *Cistem Failure*, xiv.

48. One defining characteristic of prison architecture in Brazil is that administrative offices are always located in their own building, close to but physically separated from the wings or galleries holding incarcerated people. See Cordeiro, *Até quando faremos relicários?*

49. Godoi, *Fluxos em cadeia.*

50. McKittrick, "On Plantations, Prisons, and a Black Sense of Place"; Silva, "To Be Announced."

51. For example, Lourenço Filho, *Ressocializado na cidade do caos*; Nascimento, *Pensamentos livres*; Silva, *Eu sinto julho.*

Chapter 1

1. The site was originally named the Bangu Prison Complex after the region surrounding it. In 2004, a municipal decree split the area off from Bangu, forming the new neighborhood of Gericinó, and the name of the complex followed suit. By this point, however, *Bangu* had become synonymous with the prison complex itself, and the old name stuck.

2. Han, *Letters of the Law*, 97.

3. Shammas, "The Perils of Parole Hearings."

4. Samples of sentencing certificates and TFDs are publicly available through the Rio de Janeiro's Justice Tribunal (TJRJ). I have chosen not to cite them here, since they are not properly anonymized. I was also given access to (unfilled) templates of sentencing certificates and TFDs through Lívia, Ângela, and the coordinator of NUSPEN. Prison psychologists, social workers, and psychiatrists shared templates of their criminological exam reports with me—these are prepared and organized by resocialization workers themselves, rather than following a model established by the prison administration or penal courts. The composite report, included later in this chapter, draws on the five criminological exams where I received authorization from both the prison psychologist and the incarcerated interviewees to access and use these records.

5. Petersilia, *When Prisoners Come Home*.

6. Ignatieff, *A Just Measure of Pain*.

7. Melossi and Pavarini, *The Prison and the Factory*.

8. Jean, " 'A Storehouse of Prisoners.' "

9. The term was a specific reference to those enslaved in Africa after the British prohibition of the slave trade; if discovered by the British navy or Brazilian armed forces upon their arrival to Brazil, they would be formally emancipated, although subject to indentured labor by the state. Chapter 5 includes further detail on this category of partial freedom.

10. Araújo, "Cárceres imperiais: A Casa de Correção do Rio de Janeiro. Seus detentos e o sistema prisional no Império, 1830–1861" (PhD diss., Universidade Estadual de Campinas, 2009), 19.

11. BRAZIL. Decree no. 847, October 11, 1890 (Código Penal dos Estados Unidos do Brazil). Article 157.

12. BRAZIL. Decree no. 847, October 11, 1890 (Código Penal dos Estados Unidos do Brazil). Article 50.

13. BRAZIL. Decree no. 16.665, May 6, 1924. Article 1.

14. BRAZIL. Decree no. 16.665, May 6, 1924. Article 4.

15. Santos, "Os porões da república."

16. Carrilho, "Psicogênese e determinação pericial da periculosidade"; Dias, "Páginas de ciência, crime e loucura."

17. BRAZIL. Legislation no. 7.210, July 11, 1984 (Lei de Execução Penal). Article 1.

18. Fields for missing information or that were inapplicable to the particular case were either left blank or populated with zeros. The exception was the field for "Father's Name," which, like other documents, would be listed as *não declarado* (not declared), or *ND* for short.

19. Registro Geral (General Register), one of two main identification numbers for all Brazilians in use during my fieldwork.

20. Article 5 of the 1988 Brazilian constitution states that "the law will consider as

ineligible for bail, amnesty or pardon, the crimes of torture, the illicit traffic of narcotics and other drugs, terrorism and those defined as heinous crimes." The open-ended nature of this definition of *heinous* left space for successive legislations to include an increasing number of crimes within the category. The acts listed alongside heinous crimes, such as trafficking, are considered "equivalent" (*equiparado*) to them and are subject to identical restrictions. See Constitution of the Federal Republic of Brazil of 1988, Article 5.

21. "Harmonization" (*harmonização*) was a yes/no field that identified whether the imprisoned person was currently under a specific juridical provision—assigned to one regime of punishment but occupying a more open regime because of lack of space. This might involve, for example, home arrest for someone who would otherwise be held in a semi-open prison. In the state of Rio de Janeiro, I never encountered this measure being used; administrators and penal judges were extremely tolerant of overcrowding.

22. In the case of those convicted of nonheinous crimes, these fields were populated with zeros.

23. Based on my fieldwork, that assertion seemed to underestimate the collective legal literacy of incarcerated people.

24. SEI, or Sistema Estadual de Identificação (State System of Identification), is a centralized database for identification used by state agencies and in juridical or administrative processes.

25. GRP, or Guia de Recolhimento à Prisão (Guide for Delivery to Internment), refers to information released to the prison system by the criminal court. The mug shot is included to the right of this section—the digital version is in color, but the printed documents brought in by public defenders are in black and white.

26. This field lists whether the incarcerated person is actively serving their sentence ("active") or has fled prison custody ("evaded").

27. This is a six-letter code; the first four are always SEAP, referring to the state prison administration, while the last two identify the specific prison unit (for example, SEAPTB for Tobias Barreto).

28. The count (*confere*) refers to the daily ritual of confirming the number of people present in each cell of a prison.

29. Costa, "Exame criminológico," 26.

30. Costa, "Exame criminológico," 233.

31. BRAZIL. Legislation no. 10.792, December 1, 2004.

32. BRAZIL. Summary (Súmula) no. 439, April 28, 2010.

33. In 2024, after I concluded my fieldwork, the ruling was overturned by a new bill that reinstated the criminological exam as a mandatory element for any regime progression or parole across Brazil. See BRAZIL. Legislation no. 14.843, April 11, 2024.

34. Current and formerly incarcerated people—including Diana and Elias, introduced in subsequent chapters—spoke of the extremely long waiting times to schedule an exam, resulting in months of delays for their applications. Their main impression of the

interview process itself was its velocity: an extremely short exchange where specific questions or exchanges rarely stuck in their memories.

35. Rauter, *Criminologia e subjetividade no Brasil.*

36. Rauter, *Criminologia e subjetividade no Brasil*, 102.

37. Vargas, *Never Meant to Survive.*

38. Roth-Gordon, *Race and the Brazilian Body.*

39. Cunha, "Stigmas of Dishonor."

40. Corrêa, "Repensando a família patriarcal brasileira."

41. Bakhtin, "Reported Speech as an Index of Social Change."

42. Hull, *Government of Paper.*

43. Cunha, "Stigmas of Dishonor."

44. Conselho Federal de Psicologia. Resolution no. 009, June 9, 2010.

45. Secretaria de Administração Penitenciária, Subsecretário de Tratamento Penitenciário. Circular no. 004, August 2010.

46. "Everyone, in the judicial and administrative sphere, is guaranteed reasonable duration of process and measures that guarantee the celerity of processing" (*a todos, no âmbito judicial e administrativo, são assegurados a razoável duração do processo e os meios que garantam a celeridade de sua tramitação*). BRAZIL. Constitutional Amendment no. 45, December 30, 2004. Article 5, Section LXXVIII.

47. Stevenson, *Life Beside Itself.*

Chapter 2

1. "These three lines of approach lead to the final goal, of which an Ethnographer should never lose sight. This goal is, briefly, to grasp the native's point of view, his relation to life, to realise *his* vision of *his* world." Malinowski, *Argonauts of the Western Pacific*, 63.

2. By the time of my fieldwork, that unit held approximately three thousand incarcerated people and had only one part-time psychologist.

3. Spiritism (also known as Kardecism) is a religious movement founded in the nineteenth century by French writer Allen Kardec, with an estimated four million followers in Brazil. Spiritism centers on communication with the spirit world and cycles of reincarnation.

4. O'Neill, *Secure the Soul*; Fogarty-Valenzuela, "Pedagogies of Prohibition."

5. Fogarty-Valenzuela, "Pedagogies of Prohibition."

6. Oliveira, "Pacificação e tutela militar na gestão de populações e territórios."

7. Holston, *Insurgent Citizenship.*

8. Oliveira, "Pacificação e tutela militar na gestão de populações e territórios," 138.

9. Geertz, *Interpretation of Cultures*; Wacquant, *Body and Soul*; Archetti, *Masculinities.*

10. Silva, "No-Bodies."

11. Kropotkin, *Mutual Aid.*

12. This question was designed to ask about the experience of arrest, pretrial

detention, and transfer to the unit, not the crimes for which participants had been convicted.

13. Foucault, "Truth and Juridical Forms."

14. Deleuze, "Postscript on the Societies of Control."

15. Foucault, *Discipline and Punish*.

16. Riles, *The Network Inside Out*.

17. Luan repeatedly impressed on me this this sense of both overcoming and undercutting factional authority in a story he told me multiple times over the course of my fieldwork. A few years earlier, he had organized games inside a prison dominated by the Terceiro Comando Puro ("Pure Third Command," or TCP), what was then Rio's second-largest faction. The players apparently picked up on the guidelines quickly, but after a few games Luan had to stop his visits. When he came back a few months later, he found that a teacher from the prison's school had kept up the game. But he was surprised to see that to distinguish between the teams, one side had begun wearing red vests. Red, the color of the TCP's rival faction, the Comando Vermelho (Red Command), was prohibited by both the TCP and correctional officers. For Luan, this small gesture demonstrated that peaceball had melted away factional politics in favor of the game.

18. Burton, *Tip of the Spear*.

19. Meiners, *Right to Be Hostile*; Ngai, *Ugly Feelings*.

20. The differences between this biography of Shakespeare and the standard historical account of the playwright's life push Leo's story into a narrative of human flourishing common among Brazilian evangelicals like him in which one patiently endures the present while remaining attentive to the possibility of an opportunity for future success that will eventually present itself. Chapters 3 and 6 examine other manifestations of this narrative.

21. Boal, *Theatre of the Oppressed*, 98.

22. Smith, *Afro-Paradise*, 203.

23. The term *deadname* was not commonly used in Brazil during my fieldwork. Instead, trans people and travestis distinguished between the name recorded at birth, otherwise known as a *civil name* (*nome civil*) or *registered name* (*nome de registro*), and the *social name* (*nome social*). It is extremely difficult to modify a registered name (although the process was somewhat simplified in 2022), but Brazilian law recognizes the right to a social name.

24. Patterson, *Slavery and Social Death*.

Chapter 3

1. Thompson, "Evangelical Christianity as Infrastructure in Brazil's Penal System."

2. Biondi, "The Effects of Some Religious Affects."

3. Gillespie, "Moralizing Security."

4. Meranze, *Laboratories of Virtue*; Green, "Penal Optimism and Second Chances."

5. Foucault, *Discipline and Punish*; Bounds, "What Must I Do to Be Saved?"

6. Graber, *Furnace of Affliction.*

7. Green, "Penal Optimism and Second Chances."

8. Teixeira and Reis, "Mulheres evangélicas para além do voto"; Denyer Willis, *Go with God.*

9. At the same time, new pragmatic alliances arose between evangelicals and conservative Catholics, as exemplified in the authoritarian president Jair Bolsonaro—a nominal Catholic, married to an evangelical, baptized twice (by a priest and an evangelical pastor), who rose to the presidency with the vocal support of evangelical politicians and public figures.

10. Lima, *Origens da prisão feminina no Rio de Janeiro.*

11. BRAZIL. Legislation no. 7.210, July 11, 1984 (Lei de Execução Penal). Article 3.

12. Johnson, *If I Give My Soul.*

13. As used by evangelicals, the term excludes Catholics.

14. The main distinction between Pentecostals and other evangelicals is the former's emphasis on believers' direct access to the gifts of the Holy Spirit as demonstrated in the New Testament, such as speaking in tongues, healing, and casting out demons.

15. Godoi et al., "Epistemopolíticas do dispositivo carcerário paulista."

16. The letters APAC stand both for Association for the Protection and Assistance of the Convicted (Associação para a Proteção e Assistência aos Condenados) and Loving Your Neighbor, You Will Love Christ" (Amando o Próximo, Amarás a Cristo). The two names refer to the same organization.

17. Thompson, "Evangelical Christianity as Infrastructure in Brazil's Penal System."

18. The word is used as a catch-all term for Afro-Brazilian (and sometimes Indigenous) spiritual practices. Its valence depends on the speaker and context; when used by Christians, as in this case, it carries derogatory connotations and is considered synonymous with witchcraft and devil worship.

19. Giordano, "Lying the Truth"; Stephen, "Bearing Witness."

20. Most imprisoned people in Rio, and Brazil, were convicted and sentenced solely on the basis of police testimony—a practice that had legal grounding in a 2003 ruling from Rio's Justice Tribunal (Tribunal de Justiça). This was particularly true of drug-related convictions—a 2016 study by the state's Public Defense Office found that 71 percent of convictions for trafficking were based entirely on the word of police officers, with no other evidence presented to the courts. In December 2024, after I concluded fieldwork, the Justice Tribunal revised its earlier ruling, stating that other evidence was needed to corroborate police reports. The accused themselves are rarely given an opportunity to testify—most remain detained during their trials, and many only learn of the outcome weeks or months later through their public defender. See Defensoria Pública do Estado do Rio de Janeiro, "Relatório final."

21. My extensive quotation of this testimony is, in part, an attempt to fulfill that role.

22. Teixeira, "O testemunho e a produçao de valor moral."

23. Another iteration of this testimony appears in Chapter 6. I also accompanied Elias

to churches and Christian radio stations, where he was invited to testify, and where he often received donations afterward.

24. Stephen, "Bearing Witness"; Garcia, "Serenity."

25. Lambek, "The Continuous and Discontinuous Person."

26. Teixeira, "De 'corações de pedra' a 'corações de carne.' "

27. Dias, *A igreja como refúgio e a Bíblia como esconderijo*, 270.

28. Varella, *Estação Carandiru*.

29. Mafra, "Saintliness and Sincerity in the Formation of the Christian Person."

30. This is what Clara Cristina Jost Mafra identifies as an ethic of "saintliness," one that continues a Catholic understanding of the immanence of good and evil but marks a clear, geographic border between the two.

31. *Bocas de fumo*, or "mouths of smoke," are sites of small-scale drug commerce that are often located just past the entrance to favelas.

32. Teixeira, "O testemunho e a produção do valor moral."

33. For example, see Mariz, *Coping with Poverty*; Chesnut, *Born Again in Brazil*.

34. Zaluar, "O crime e a não-cidadania," 130.

35. Zaluar, "O crime e a não-cidadania," 130.

36. Harding, "Representing Fundamentalism."

37. Both the figure of the *bandido* and the person who has left that identity behind are almost exclusively masculine figures.

38. Damasceno, *Segredos da boa aparência*.

39. Vargas, *Never Meant to Survive*.

40. Taking Magnólia's time frame at its word, it seems likely that the man had been a pretrial detainee and that the charges against him were subsequently dropped.

41. Júnior, Franco, and César, *Como anunciar o Evangelho entre os presos*, 99.

42. Júnior, Franco, and César, *Como anunciar o Evangelho entre os presos*, 94.

43. Júnior, Franco, and César, *Como anunciar o Evangelho entre os presos*, 100.

44. Denyer Willis, *Go with God*.

Chapter 4

1. During my fieldwork, the name of this furlough flipped to Periodic Home Visitation (Visita Periódica ao Lar), then back again.

2. Alves, *The Anti-Black City*; Denyer Willis, "Eating Pizza in Prison."

3. The moment I describe in that chapter—of Reinaldo criticizing his young student's behavior in prison while running his hands down her imagined body—also suggests that male prison staff and volunteers projected their own desires for these women onto incarcerated people.

4. Júnior, Franco, and César, *Como anunciar o Evangelho entre os presos*, 79.

5. This is not to deny the existence of desire itself. Diogo once described the experience of his own frustrated sexuality in a letter to me: "In these years inside the system, I can confirm that the annihilation of any heterosexual relationship is the biggest cause of my

suffering, of agony, of mixed feelings and sensations that blossom when there is a 'hot' scene on TV or beautiful women in newspapers and magazines, but it's not just about sex, pleasure in itself, it's this convergence of not being able to construct a family, of not having a companion to talk, caress, sleep alongside." Anthropologist Donna Goldstein also offers an account of resisting an incarcerated man's sexual advances during her visit to Rio's now-decommissioned Ilha Grande penitentiary. In that case, Goldstein invoked sisterhood rather than motherhood as a rebuff, although in doing so she alluded to the authority of their shared "mother." Goldstein, "Perils of Witnessing and Ambivalence of Writing."

6. Kunzel, *Criminal Intimacy*.

7. Conduct within men's prisons is governed by statutes, created and enforced by the faction or collective that dominate the particular unit. All of them demand that imprisoned people never remain shirtless in the presence of a woman. Factions also prohibited excessive public displays of affection between men and their visiting spouses or girlfriends, and forbade anyone from speaking to female visitors unless given explicit permission by their incarcerated family member or partner. As mentioned in Chapter 3, within evangelical cells, the elected "pastor" was responsible for screening incoming reading materials such as newspapers or magazines and blacking out any images that they considered overtly sexualized. Karina Biondi outlines even more stringent forms of conduct in São Paulo's prisons; while she was visiting her imprisoned husband, other incarcerated men were forbidden from looking at Biondi and would approach with their backs turned "to avoid turning [their] genital region toward the *senhora*." The extent to which these forms of "respect" extended toward incarcerated trans women and travestis varied depending on the prison and the faction governing it, as I outline in Chapter 5. See Biondi, *Sharing This Walk*.

8. In her case, Mariana saw the category of *parda* as distinct from Black, white, or Indigenous.

9. Infopen, "Levantamento nacional de informações penitenciárias."

10. Rhodes, *Total Confinement*; Gillespie, "Moralizing Security."

11. Rhodes, *Total Confinement*, 124.

12. To put it directly, there were no surrogate fathers among resocialization workers. In part, this reflects the dominance of women in these fields. But the men who worked in the same areas, like Reinaldo, Luan, or Pastor Bruno, made no gestures toward fatherhood or parenthood as metaphors, paradigms, sources of inspiration, or experience in their encounters with incarcerated people.

13. Maya Mayblin elaborates on the divine status of motherhood in Brazil, whereby children learn what it is to be loved and to love others only through exposure to the love of a mother. This understanding also emerges in the Brazilian phrase *amor só de mãe*, roughly meaning *the only real love is a mother's love*, which I frequently encountered tattooed on the forearms of imprisoned men. Mayblin, "The Madness of Mothers."

14. Feltran, *Irmãos*.

15. Silva, "No-Bodies," 228.

16. In 2007, the news site G1 published an interview with then governor of Rio de Janeiro, Sérgio Cabral, in which he expressed alarm at the fertility rate within the city's favelas, calling them "factories for producing marginals." Ten years later, during a meeting I attended with family members of the imprisoned, a Black favela resident and mother stated that she would never forget how Cabral had called her a "criminal factory" (*fábrica de bandido*). See Aluízio Freire, "Cabral defende aborto contra violência no Rio de Janeiro." *G1*, October 24, 2007, https://g1.globo.com/Noticias/Politica/0,,MUL155710 -5601,00.html.

17. Silva, "No-Bodies."

18. Lombroso, "Illustrative Studies in Criminal Anthropology III"; Lombroso, *Criminal Man*.

19. Nina Rodrigues, *As raças humanas e a responsabilidade penal*. Nina Rodrigues was considered by Lombroso to be the "Apostle of Criminal Anthropology in the New World," according to Augusto and Ortega, "Nina Rodrigues e a patologização do crime no Brasil," 226–227.

20. Corrêa, "Repensando a familia patriarcal brasileira."

21. Corrêa, "Repensando a familia patriarcal brasileira," 6.

22. Corrêa, "A babá de Freud e outras babás."

23. Goldstein, *Laughter out of Place*, 75; Hordge-Freeman, *Second-Class Daughters*.

24. During the presidency of Jair Bolsonaro, the program was rebranded as Auxílio Brasil (Brazil Assistance) but reverted to its original name after Lula returned to power in 2023.

25. Sorj and Gomes, "O gênero da 'nova cidadania' "; Silva, "No-Bodies."

26. Azimute Comunicação, "Cartilha 'Mulheres da Paz.' "

27. One requirement was meeting a certain threshold for children's school attendance. In many cases, this stipulation severely limited contact between children and their incarcerated parents. Since visiting days for many prisons fell on school days, bringing children to visits meant jeopardizing the family's continued enrollment within the Bolsa Família program.

28. Alves, *The Anti-Black City*.

29. While I noticed some trends within specific professions or areas of work, resocialization workers fell across the traditionally defined political spectrum and included avowed Marxists as well as members of Brazil's rising authoritarian movement.

30. Father's Day in Brazil falls on the second Sunday in August.

31. Shange, "Play Aunties and Dyke Bitches."

32. Jones, *The Chosen Ones*.

33. Millar, "The Precarious Present."

34. Most Brazilians use marital terms without distinction between civil and common-law partnerships, a practice that I follow in this book. For Elias, Rosa, and many other evangelicals, however, marriage "on paper" (*no papel*) was integral to the recognition of

their relationship by their church and community. Medeiros, *Marriage, Divorce and Distress in Northeast Brazil.*

35. Lima, *Origens da prisão feminina no Rio de Janeiro.*

36. Lima, *Origens da prisão feminina no Rio de Janeiro,* 60.

37. Sabo, Kupers, and London, "Introduction: Gender and the Politics of Punishment," 3–18.

38. Davis, "Race, Gender and Prison History."

39. Brown, *States of Injury,* 167.

40. Wacquant, *Punishing the Poor.*

41. Vianna and Lowenkron, "O duplo fazer do gênero e do estado"; Brown, *States of Injury.*

Chapter 5

1. Holloway, *Policing Rio de Janeiro.*

2. Santana, *"Mais Viva!,"* 218.

3. Muñóz, *Cruising Utopia,* 1.

4. Bey, *Cistem Failure,* 4.

5. Jarrin, "Untranslatable Subjects."

6. Zamboni, "O barraco das monas na cadeia dos coisas."

7. Santana, *"Mais Viva!,"* 213.

8. York, Oliveira, and Benevides, "Manifestações textuais (insubmissas) travesti."

9. Zamboni, "O barraco das monas na cadeia dos coisas."

10. For information on the experiences of trans people in women's prisons, see D'Angelo et al., "Performatividades de gênero em unidades prisionais femininas do Rio de Janeiro."

11. *"formular queixa ou reclamação, com improcedência reveladora de motivo reprovável."* RIO DE JANEIRO, Decree no. 8897, March 31, 1986. Article 59.

12. *"desobedecer os horários regulamentares."* RIO DE JANEIRO, Decree no. 8897, March 31, 1986. Article 59.

13. York, Oliveira, and Benevides, "Manifestações textuais (insubmissas) travesti."

14. Zamboni, "Travestis e transexuais privadas de liberdade."

15. This experience of "protection" as punishment is shared by incarcerated queer and trans people in North America. For example, Hébert, "Trans Rights as Risks"; Stanley, *Atmospheres of Violence.*

16. *R7 Notícias,* "Usando corda feita de lençóis, três presos fogem do presidio de Bangu." January 29, 2023, https://noticias.r7.com/rio-de-janeiro/usando-corda-feita-de -lencois-tres-presos-fogem-do-presidio-de-bangu-29012023.

17. In other Brazilian states, it is called the *saidinha* (little exit).

18. Carolina Heringer, "Beneficiados com 'saidão' de Natal no Rio, 422 não retornam à cadeia." *O Globo,* December 31, 2019, https://oglobo.globo.com/rio/beneficiados-com -saidao-de-natal-no-rio-422-presos-nao-voltam-cadeia-24166292.

19. *O Dia*, "Túnel de dez metros é descoberto no complexo de Gericinó." January 7, 2019, https://odia.ig.com.br/rio-de-janeiro/2019/07/5658924-tunel-de-dez-metros-e -descoberto-no-complexo-de-gericino.html; *Extra Online*, "Traficante preso é pego tentando fugir da cadeia vestido de mulher em Bangu." August 3, 2019, https://extra. globo.com/casos-de-policia/traficnte-preso-pego-tentando-fugir-da-cadeia-vestido-de -mulher-em-bangu-23853277.html.

20. This situation shifted in 2024, when a proposed legislation banning Periodic Family Visitation was debated, passed, and then partially vetoed; the result was the continuation of such visits, with some increased restrictions on eligibility. See BRAZIL. Legislation no. 14.843, April 11, 2024.

21. Lancellotti, "Tecnologias de governo, vigilância e transgressão."

22. Gomes, "Africans and Petit Marronage in Rio de Janeiro, ca. 1800–1840."

23. Réis and Silva, *Negociação e conflito*.

24. Chalhoub, "The Precariousness of Freedom in a Slave Society."

25. Collins, *Revolt of the Saints*.

26. Jean, "A Storehouse of Prisoners."

27. Chalhoub, "The Precariousness of Freedom in a Slave Society," 406.

28. Gato, *O massacre dos libertos*.

29. Réis and Gomes, "Introdução: A história da liberdade."

30. A. Nascimento, *Quilombismo*; B. Nascimento, "O conceito de quilombo e a resistência cultural negra"; Pinho, *Cativeiro*.

31. Walcott, *The Long Emancipation*, 4.

32. Conselho Nacional de Justiça (CNJ), "Banco nacional de monitoramento de presos."

33. Vargas, "Gendered Antiblackness and the Impossible Brazilian Project," 5.

34. Díaz-Benítez and Rangel, "Evocações da escravidão."

35. Chantraine and Martin, "Introduction: Toward a Sociology of Prison Escape," 2.

36. The gendered nature of this expectation is evident in the difference between this schedule and the more restricted one for those held in the "open" wing of a prison designated for women, who were released at eight a.m. and expected to return before six p.m.

37. Vargas, "Taking Back the Land"; Penglase, *Living with Insecurity in a Brazilian Favela*.

38. Moore, "Extralegal Agency and the Search for Safety in Northeast Brazil."

39. Walcott, *The Long Emancipation*, 107.

40. McKittrick, *Demonic Grounds*, 42.

41. Echoing Hortense J. Spillers, McKittrick articulates this occupation as "garreting," transforming noun into verb, place into action. See Spillers, "Mama's Baby, Papa's Maybe."

42. Araújo, "Arquitetando a liberdade."

43. Walcott, *The Long Emancipation*, 107.

44. Wilder, "The Promise of Freedom and the Predicament of Marronage," 5.

45. The concept of *axé* is central to Afro-Brazilian religions such as Candomblé; it is also shared in Black religious traditions across the Americas. In Anglophone contexts, it is often rendered as *ashe* or *ase*.

Epilogue

1. While some have the opportunity to inform their families or friends, many are informed of their impending release only a few hours beforehand.

2. The prison administration's own records indicate that 42,400 people were released between January 2017 and April 2018. The figure does not include evasions or deaths in custody.

3. Those under parole required a judge's authorization to leave the state of Rio. The requirements of house arrest varied, but generally people were also prohibited from leaving their homes for reasons other than work or medical care.

4. Guyer, "Prophecy and the Near Future," 409.

5. *Blitz* refers to an action by off-duty police, who use their vehicles and uniforms to set up checkpoints, stop traffic, and solicit bribes from drivers with faulty or unregistered vehicles.

6. Miyazaki, *The Method of Hope*, 32.

7. Caldeira, *City of Walls*.

8. Cortês, "O mercado pentecostal de pregações e testemunhos," 200.

9. The term *autoconstruction* is used by poor and working-class Brazilians to refer to the process by which they build and expand their own houses, often over long periods of time, in the urban hinterland. See Holston, "Autoconstruction in Working-Class Brazil."

10. Instituto de Pesquisa Econômica Aplicada (IPEA), "Atlas da violência."

11. Penglase, *Living with Insecurity in a Brazilian Favela*.

12. Afro-Brazilian religious communities and traditions generally affirm and celebrate queerness and have historically provided sanctuary and support for queer cisgender people. But the status of trans or travesti identities and of transition itself are points of contemporary debate within Candomblé and Umbanda. See Allen, " 'Brides' Without Husbands"; Nascimento and Odara, "Gênero na encruzilhada."

13. Oosterbaan, "Sonic Supremacy."

14. Jones, *The Chosen Ones*.

15. Jones, *The Chosen Ones*, 60.

16. Rosa calculated that the amount they received from donations was less than what they had spent on gasoline for the round trip.

17. The blitzes were also illicit police operations, although that distinction was not particularly useful or relevant to those who were pulled over.

18. Wool, "In-Durable Sociality."

19. Wool, "In-Durable Sociality," 81.

Bibliography

Allen, Andrea Stevenson. "'Brides' Without Husbands: Lesbians in the Afro-Brazilian Religion Candomblé," *Transforming Anthropology* 20, no. 1 (2012): 17–31. https://doi .org/10.1111/j.1548-7466.2011.01141.x

Alves, Jaime. *The Anti-Black City: Police Terror and Black Urban Life in Brazil.* University of Minnesota Press, 2018.

Araújo, Carlos Eduardo Moreira. "Cárceres imperiais: A Casa de Correção do Rio de Janeiro. Seus detentos e o sistema prisional no Império, 1830–1861" [Imperial prisons: Rio de Janeiro's House of Correction. Its detainees and the prison system of the Empire, 1830–1861]. PhD diss., Universidade Estadual de Campinas, 2019. https://doi .org/10.47749/T/UNICAMP.2009.438954

———. "Arquitetando a liberdade: Os africanos livres e as obras públicas no Rio de Janeiro imperial" [Constructing liberty: Freed Africans and public works in imperial Rio de Janeiro], *História Unisinos* 14, no. 3 (2010): 329–333. https://doi.org/10.4013/htu .2010.143.08

Archetti, Eduardo. *Masculinities: Football, Polo and the Tango in Argentina.* Routledge, 1999.

Augusto, Cristiane Brandão, and Francisco Ortega. "Nina Rodrigues e a patologização do crime no Brasil" [Nina Rodrigues and the pathologization of crime in Brazil], *Revista Direito GV* 7, no. 1 (2011): 221–236. https://doi.org/10.1590/S1808-24322011000100011

Azimute Comunicação. "Cartilha 'Mulheres da Paz: Levando a cultura da paz para sua comunidade'" [Pamphlet 'Women of Peace: Bringing the culture of peace to your community']. April 12, 2011. https://issuu.com/azimutecom/docs/cartilha_mpaz_ familias_visitadas

Bakhtin, Mikhail. "Reported Speech as Index of Social Change." In *The Bakhtin Reader: Selected Writings of Bakhtin, Medvedev, Voloshinov,* edited by Pam Morris. Arnold, 1994.

Bey, Marquis. *Cistem Failure: Essays on Blackness and Cisgender.* Duke University Press, 2022.

Biondi, Karina. "The Effects of Some Religious Affects: Revolutions in Crime." In *Precarious Democracy: Ethnographies of Hope, Despair, and Resistance in Brazil*, edited by Benjamin Junge, Sean T. Mitchell, Carmen Alvaro Jarrin, and Lucia Cantero. Rutgers University Press, 2021.

——. *Sharing This Walk: An Ethnography of Prison Life and the PCC in Brazil*. Translated by John F. Collins. University of North Carolina Press, 2016.

Boal, Augusto. *Theatre of the Oppressed*. New ed. Pluto Press, 2008.

Bounds, Elizabeth M. "What Must I Do to Be Saved? Punishment and Redemption Under Incarceration," *Political Theology* 23, no. 4 (2022): 298–316. https://doi.org/10.1080/1462317X.2022.2039345

Brown, Wendy. *States of Injury: Power and Freedom in Late Modernity*. Princeton University Press, 1995.

Burton, Orisanmi. *Tip of the Spear: Black Radicalism, Prison Repression, and the Long Attica Revolt*. University of California Press, 2023.

Caldeira, Teresa Pires do Rio. *City of Walls: Crime, Segregation, and Citizenship in São Paulo*. University of California Press, 2000.

Caldeira, Teresa, and James Holston. "Democracy and Violence in Brazil," *Comparative Studies in Society and History* 41, no. 4 (1999): 691–729.

Carr, E. Summerson. *Scripting Addiction: The Politics of Therapeutic Talk and American Sobriety*. Princeton University Press, 2011.

Carrilho, Heitor. "Psicogênese e determinação pericial da periculosidade" [Psychogenesis and expert determination of danger], *Arquivos de Neuro-Psiquiatria* 6, no. 1 (1948): 24–45.

Chalhoub, Sidney. "The Precariousness of Freedom in a Slave Society (Brazil in the Nineteenth Century)," *International Review of Social History* 56, no. 3 (2011): 405–439. https://doi.org/10.1017/S002085901100040X

Chantraine, Gilles, and Tomas Max Martin. "Introduction: Toward a Sociology of Prison Escape." In *Prison Breaks: Towards a Sociology of Escape*, edited by Tomas Max Martin and Gilles Chantraine. Springer International, 2018.

Chesnut, R. Andrew. *Born Again in Brazil: The Pentecostal Boom and the Pathogens of Poverty*. Rutgers University Press, 1997.

Collins, John F. *Revolt of the Saints: Memory and Redemption in the Twilight of Brazilian Racial Democracy*. Duke University Press, 2015.

Comfort, Megan. *Doing Time Together: Love and Family in the Shadow of the Prison*. University of Chicago Press, 2008.

Conselho Nacional de Justiça (CNJ). "Banco nacional de monitoramento de presos" [National database for prisoner monitoring], accessed August 15, 2024. https://portalbnmp.cnj.jus.br

Cordeiro, Suzann. *Até quando faremos relicários? A função social do espaço penitenciário* [For how long will we build relics? The social function of penal space]. EdUFAL, 2006.

Corrêa, Mariza. "A babá de Freud e outras babás" [Freud's nanny and other nannies],

Cadernos Pagu, no. 29 (2007): 61–90. https://doi.org/10.1590/S0104-8333200700020 0004

———. "Repensando a família patriarcal brasileira" [Rethinking the patriarchal Brazilian family], *Cadernos de Pesquisa*, no. 37 (1981): 5–16.

Cortês, Mariana. "O mercado pentecostal de pregações e testemunhos: Formas de gestão de sofrimento" [The Pentecostal market in preaching and testimonies: Forms of administrating suffering], *Religião e Sociedade* 34, no. 2 (2014): 184–209. https://doi.org/10.1590/S1984-04382014000200010

Costa, Álvaro Mayrink da. *Exame criminológico* [Criminological exam]. Editora Jurídica e Universitária Ltda, 1972.

Crewe, Ben, and Alice Ievins. "The Prison as a Reinventive Institution," *Theoretical Criminology* 24, no. 4 (2019): 568–589. https://doi.org/10.1177/1362480619841900

Cunha, Olívia Maria Gomes da. "The Stigmas of Dishonor: Criminal Records, Civil Rights, and Forensic Identification in Rio de Janeiro, 1903–1940." In *Honor, Status, and Law in Modern Latin America*, edited by Sueann Caulfield, Lara Putnam, and Sarah C. Chambers. Duke University Press, 2005.

Damasceno, Caetana. *Segredos da boa aparência: Da "cor" a "boa aparência" no mundo do trabalho carioca (1930–1950)* [Secrets of good appearance: From "color" to "good appearance" in Rio de Janeiro's labor world (1930–1950)]. Editora UFRRJ, 2011.

D'Angelo, Luisa Bertrami, Vanessa Pereira de Lima, Vanessa de Andrade da Costa, et al. "Performatividades de gênero em unidades prisionais femininas do Rio de Janeiro" [Gender performativities in Rio de Janeiro's feminine prison units], *Psicologia: Ciência e Profissão*, no. 38 (2018): 44–59. https://doi.org/10.1590/1982-3703000212199

Davis, Angela. "Race, Gender, and Prison History: From the Convict Lease System to the Supermax Prison." In *Prison Masculinities*, edited by Don Sabo, Terry A. Kupers and Willie London. Temple University Press, 2001.

Defensoria Pública do Estado do Rio de Janeiro. "Relatório final: Pesquisas sobre as sentenças judiciais por tráfico de drogas na cidade e região metropolitana do Rio de Janeiro" [Final report: Studies on judicial sentences for drug trafficking in the city and metropolitan region of Rio de Janeiro], 2016.

Deleuze, Gilles. "Postscript on the Societies of Control," *October* 59 (1992): 3–7.

Denyer Willis, Graham. "Eating Pizza in Prison: Failing Family Men, Civil Punishment, and the Policing of Whiteness in São Paulo," *American Ethnologist* 49, no. 2 (2022): 221–233. https://doi.org/10.1111/amet.13071

Denyer Willis, Laurie. *Go with God: Political Exhaustion and Evangelical Possibility in Suburban Brazil*. University of California Press, 2023.

Dias, Allister Andrew Teixeira. "Páginas de ciência, crime e loucura: A trajetória e o projeto médico-intelectual de Heitor Carrilho" [Pages of science, crime and madness: The trajectory and the medico-intelectual project of Heitor Carrilho], *Temporalidades* 3, no. 2 (2011): 78–97.

Dias, Camila Nunes. *A igreja como refúgio e a Bíblia como esconderijo: Religião e violência na prisão* [The church as a refuge and the Bible as a hiding place: Religion and violence in prison]. Humanitas, 2008.

Díaz-Benítez, María Elvira, and Everton Rangel. "Evocações da escravidão: Sobre sujeição e fuga em experiências negras" [Evocations of slavery: On subjection and flight in black experiences], *Horizontes Antropológicos* 28, no. 63 (2002): 39–69. https://doi.org/10.1590/S0104-71832022000200002

Fabian, Johannes. *Time and the Other: How Anthropology Makes Its Object*. Columbia University Press, 1983.

Fassin, Didier. *Prison Worlds: An Ethnography of the Carceral Condition*. Polity Press, 2017.

Feltran, Gabriel. *Irmãos: Uma história do PCC* [Brothers: A history of the PCC]. Companhia das Letras, 2018.

Fogarty-Valenzuela, Benjamin. "Pedagogies of Prohibition: Time, Education, and the War on Drugs in Rio de Janeiro's Zona Norte," *Cultural Anthropology* 37, no. 2 (2022): 286–316. https://doi.org/10.14506/ca37.2.09

Forum Brasileiro de Segurança Pública (FBSP). *Anuário brasileiro de segurança pública, ano 10* [Brazilian annual report on public security, year 10], 2016.

Foucault, Michel. *Discipline and Punish: The Birth of the Prison*. Translated by Alan Sheridan. 2nd ed. Random House, 1995.

———. "Truth and Juridical Forms." Translated by Lawrence Williams and Catherine Merlen. *Social Identities* 2, no. 3 (1996): 327–342. https://doi.org/10.1080/13504639652213

———. *Wrong-Doing, Truth-Telling: The Function of Avowal in Justice*. Translated by Stephen W. Sawyer. University of Chicago Press, 2014.

Franco, Marielle. "UPP—A redução da favela a três letras: Uma análise da política de segurança pública do estado do Rio de Janeiro" [UPP—The reduction of the favela to three letters: An analysis of public security politics in the state of Rio de Janeiro]. Master's diss., Universidade Federal Fluminense, 2014.

Freyre, Gilberto. *The Masters and the Slaves: A Study in the Development of Brazilian Civilization*. Translated by Samuel Putnam. 2nd ed. University of California Press, 1986.

Garcia, Angela. "Serenity: Violence, Inequality and Recovery on the Edge of Mexico City," *Medical Anthropology Quarterly* 29, no. 2 (2015): 455–472.

Gato, Matheus. *O massacre dos libertos: Sobre raça e república no Brasil (1888–1889)* [The massacre of the freedpeople: On race and republic in Brazil (1888–1889)]. Editora Perspectiva, 2020.

Geertz, Clifford. *The Interpretation of Cultures*. Basic Books, 1973.

Gillespie, Kelly. "Moralizing Security: 'Corrections' and the Post-Apartheid Prison," *Race/ Ethnicity: Multidisciplinary Global Contexts* 2, no. 1 (2008): 69–87.

Gilmore, Ruth Wilson. *Golden Gulag: Prisons, Surplus, Crisis and Opposition in Globalizing California*. University of California Press, 2007.

Giordano, Cristiana. "Lying the Truth," *Current Anthropology* 56, no. S12 (2015): S211–S221. https://doi.org/10.1086/683272

Godoi, Rafael. *Fluxos em cadeia: As prisões em São Paulo na virada dos tempos* [Penal flows: Prisons in São Paulo in the turning times]. Boitempo, 2017.

Godoi, Rafael, Marcelo da Silveira Campos, Fabio Mallart, and Ricardo Campello. "Epístemopolíticas do dispositivo carcerário paulista: Refletindo sobre experiências de pesquisa-intervenção junto à Pastoral Carcerária" [Epistemopolitics of the Sao Paulo prison apparatus: Reflecting on research-intervention experiences with the Pastoral Carcerária], *Brazilian Journal of Empirical Legal Studies* 7 (2020): 143–158.

Goldstein, Donna. *Laughter out of Place: Race, Class, Violence and Sexuality in a Rio de Janeiro Shanty-town*. University of California Press, 2003.

———. "Perils of Witnessing and Ambivalence of Writing: Whiteness, Sexuality and Violence in Rio de Janeiro Shantytowns." In *Women Fielding Danger: Negotiating Ethnographic Identities in Field Research*, edited by Martha K. Huggins and Marie-Louise Glebbeek. Rowman & Littlefield, 2009.

Gomes, Flávio. "Africans and Petit Marronage in Rio de Janeiro, ca. 1800–1840," *Luso-Brazilian Review* 47, no. 2 (2010): 74–99. https://doi.org/10.1353/lbr.2010.0020

Graber, Jennifer. *The Furnace of Affliction: Prisons and Religion in Antebellum America*. University of North Carolina Press, 2011.

Green, David A. "Penal Optimism and Second Chances: The Legacies of American Protestantism and the Prospects for Penal Reform," *Punishment and Society* 15, no. 2 (2013): 123–146. https://doi.org/10.1177/1462474513477789

Guyer, Jane I. "Prophecy and the Near Future: Thoughts on Macroeconomic, Evangelical, and Punctuated Time," *American Ethnologist* 34, no. 3 (2007): 409–421. https://doi.org /10.1525/ae.2007.34.3.409

Han, Sora. *Letters of the Law: Race and the Fantasy of Colorblindness in American Law*. Stanford University Press, 2015.

Harding, Susan. "Representing Fundamentalism: The Problem of the Repugnant Cultural Other," *Social Research* 58, no. 2 (1991): 373–393.

Hébert, William. "Trans Rights as Risks: On the Ambivalent Implementation of Canada's Groundbreaking Trans Prison Reform," *Canadian Journal of Law and Society/La Revue Canadienne Droit et Société* 35, no. 2 (2020): 221–244. https://doi.org/10.1017/cls .2020.11

Holloway, Thomas H. *Policing Rio de Janeiro: Repression and Resistance in a Nineteenth-Century City*. Stanford University Press, 1993.

Holston, James. "Autoconstruction in Working-Class Brazil," *Cultural Anthropology* 6, no. 4 (1991): 447–465.

———. *Insurgent Citizenship: Disjunctions of Democracy and Modernity in Brazil*. Princeton University Press, 2008.

Hordge-Freeman, Elizabeth. *Second-Class Daughters: Black Brazilian Women and Informal Adoption as Modern Slavery*. Cambridge University Press, 2022.

Hull, Matthew. *Government of Paper: The Materiality of Bureaucracy in Urban Pakistan*. University of California Press, 2012.

Ignatieff, Michael. *A Just Measure of Pain: The Penitentiary in the Industrial Revolution.* Macmillan, 1978.

Infopen. "Levantamento nacional de informações penitenciárias" [National survey of penitentiary data]. Ministério da Justiça, 2017.

Instituto de Pesquisa Econômica Aplicada (IPEA). "Atlas da violência" [Atlas of violence]. 2018.

————. "Reincidência criminal no Brasil: Relatório de atividades da pesquisa sobre reincidência criminal, conforme acordo de cooperação técnica entre o Conselho Nacional de Justiça e o IPEA" [Criminal recidivism in Brazil: Report on research activities on criminal recidivism, within the technical cooperation agreement between the National Justice Council and the IPEA], 2015.

Jarrin, Carmen Alvaro. "Untranslatable Subjects: Travesti Access to Public Health Care in Brazil," *Transgender Studies Quarterly* 3, no. 3–4 (2016): 357–375. https://doi.org/10 .1215/23289252-3545095

Jean, Martine. " 'A Storehouse of Prisoners': Rio de Janeiro's Correction House (Casa de Correção) and the Birth of the Penitentiary in Brazil, 1830–1906," in *Atlantic Studies* 14, no. 2 (2017): 216–242. https://doi.org/10.1080/14788810.2016.1240915

Johnson, Andrew. *If I Give My Soul: Faith Behind Bars in Rio de Janeiro.* Oxford University Press, 2017.

Jones, Nikki. *The Chosen Ones: Black Men and the Politics of Redemption.* University of California Press, 2018.

Junior, Antônio Carlos, Cristiano Rezende Franco, and Elben M. Lenz César. *Como anunciar o Evangelho entre os presos* [How to announce the Gospel among prisoners]. Editora Ultimato, 2016.

Khan, Omar Phoenix. "Judges as Agents of Coloniality: Understanding the Coloniality of Justice at the Pre-Trial Stage in Brazil," *British Journal of Criminology* 64, no. 5 (2024): 1045–1062. https://doi.org/10.1093/bjc/azae009

Kropotkin, Petr Alekseevich. *Mutual Aid: A Factor of Evolution.* Penguin Press, 1972.

Kunzel, Regina G. *Criminal Intimacy: Prison and the Uneven History of Modern American Sexuality.* University of Chicago Press, 2010.

Lambek, Michael. "The Continuous and Discontinuous Person: Two Dimensions of Ethical Life," *Journal of the Royal Anthropological Institute* 19, no. 4 (2013): 837–858.

Lancellotti, Helena Patini. "Tecnologias de governo, vigilância e transgressão: Um estudo etnográfico sobre as tornozeleiras eletrônicas" [Technologies of government, surveillance and transgression: An ethnographic study of electronic ankle bracelets], *Mediações: Revista de Ciências Sociais* 23, no. 1 (2018): 141–169. http://dx.doi.org/10 .5433/2176-6665.2018v23n1p141

Lessing, Benjamin. "Militarization: Dark Innovation at the State-Crime Frontier." In *Rio as Method: Collective Resistance for a New Generation*, edited by Paul Amar. Duke University Press, 2024.

Lima, Elça Mendonça. *Origens da prisão feminina no Rio de Janeiro: O período das freiras*

(1942–1955) [Origins of the women's prison in Rio de Janeiro: The period of the nuns (1942–1955)]. OAB/RJ, 1983.

Lombroso, Cesare. *Criminal Man.* Duke University Press, 2006.

———. "Illustrative Studies in Criminal Anthropology III: The Physiognomy of the Anarchists," *The Monist* 1, no. 3 (1891): 336–343.

Lourenço, Luiz Claudio. "O jogo dos sete erros nas prisões do Brasil: Discutindo os pilares de um sistema que não existe" [The game of seven errors in Brazil's prisons: Debating the pillars of a system that does not exist], *O Público e o Privado*, no. 30 (2017): 285–301.

Lourenço, Samuel, Filho. *Ressocializado na cidade do caos* [Resocialized in the city of chaos]. Editora Multifoco, 2022.

Machado, Carly. "The Church Helps the UPP, the UPP Helps the Church: Pacification Apparatus, Religion, and Boundary Formation in Rio de Janeiro's Urban Peripheries," *Vibrant: Virtual Brazilian Anthropology* 14, no. 3 (2017): 1–16. https://doi.org/10.1590/1809-43412017v14n3p075

Mafra, Clara Cristina Jost. "Saintliness and Sincerity in the Formation of the Christian Person," *Ethnos: Journal of Anthropology* 76, no. 4 (2011): 448–468. https://doi.org/10.1080/00141844.2011.610513

Malinowski, Bronislaw. *Argonauts of the Western Pacific: An Account of Native Enterprise and Adventures in the Archipelagos of Melanesian New Guinea.* Dutton, 1961.

Mariz, Cecília Loreto. *Coping with Poverty: Pentecostals and Christian Base Communities in Brazil.* Temple University Press, 1994.

Mayblin, Maya. "The Madness of Mothers: Agape Love and the Maternal Myth in Northeast Brazil," *American Anthropologist* 114, no. 2 (2012): 240–252. https://doi.org/10.1111/j.1548-1433.2012.01422.x

McKittrick, Katherine. *Demonic Grounds: Black Women and the Cartographies of Struggle.* University of Minnesota Press, 2006.

———. "On Plantations, Prisons, and a Black Sense of Place," *Social & Cultural Geography* 12, no. 8 (2011): 947–963.

McLennan, Rebecca. "America's Human Rights Crisis in Historical Perspective," *Social Justice* 42, no. 2 (2015): 177–184.

Medeiros, Melanie. *Marriage, Divorce and Distress in Northeast Brazil: Black Women's Perspectives on Love, Respect and Kinship.* Rutgers University Press, 2018.

Meiners, Erica R. *For the Children? Protecting Innocence in a Carceral State.* University of Minnesota Press, 2016.

———. *Right to Be Hostile: Schools, Prisons, and the Making of Public Enemies.* Routledge, 2010.

Melossi, Dario, and Massimo Pavarini. *The Prison and the Factory: Origins of the Penitentiary System.* Translated by Glynis Cousin. Palgrave Macmillan, 1981.

Meranze, Michael. *Laboratories of Virtue: Punishment, Revolution, and Authority in Philadelphia, 1760–1835.* Omohundro Institute of Early American History & Culture, 1996.

Millar, Kathleen. "The Precarious Present: Wageless Labor and Disrupted Life in Rio de Janeiro, Brazil," *Cultural Anthropology* 29, no. 1 (2014): 32–53. https://doi.org/10.14506/ca29.1.04

Miyazaki, Hirokazu. *The Method of Hope: Anthropology, Philosophy, and Fijian Knowledge.* Stanford University Press, 2004.

Moore, Hollis. "Extralegal Agency and the Search for Safety in Northeast Brazil: Moving Beyond Carceral Logics," *Cambridge Journal of Anthropology* 38, no. 1 (2020): 33–51. https://doi.org/10.3167/cja.2020.380104

———. "The Gender of Inmate Governance in Northeast Brazil." In *Geographies of Gendered Punishment*, edited by Anastasia Chamberlen and Mahuya Bandyopadhyay. Palgrave Macmillan, 2024.

Muñóz, José. *Cruising Utopia: The Then and There of Queer Futurity.* 10th anniversary ed. New York University Press, 2019.

Nascimento, Abdias do. *O quilombismo: Documentos de uma militância pan-africanista* [Quilombism: Documents of a Pan-Africanist militancy]. 3rd ed. Editora Perspectiva, 2019.

Nascimento, Beatriz. "O conceito de quilombo e a resistência cultural negra" [The concept of *quilombo* and Black cultural resistance], *Revista Afrodiáspora* 3, no. 67 (1985): 41–49.

Nascimento, Thiago H. G. *Pensamentos livres* [Free thoughts]. Editora Multifoco, 2017.

Nascimento, Wanderson Flor do, and Thiffany Odara. "Gênero na encruzilhada: Um olhar em torno do debate sobre vivências trans no Candomblé" [Gender at the crossroads: A look around the debate on trans experiences in Candomblé], *Revista Periódicus* 1, no. 14 (2020): 50–72. https://doi.org/10.9771/peri.v1i14.38132

Ngai, Sianne. *Ugly Feelings.* Harvard University Press, 2007.

Nina Rodrigues, Raymundo. *As raças humanas e a responsabilidade penal* [The human races and penal responsibility]. Companhia Editoria Nacional, 1894.

Oliveira, João Pacheco de. "Pacificação e tutela militar na gestão de populações e territórios" [Pacification and military tutelage in the administration of populations and territories], *Mana* 20, no. 1 (2014): 125–161. https://doi.org/10.1590/S0104-93132014000100005

O'Neill, Kevin. *Secure the Soul: Christian Piety and Gang Prevention in Guatemala.* University of California Press, 2015.

Oosterbaan, Martijn. "Sonic Supremacy: Sound, Space and Charisma in a Favela in Rio de Janeiro," *Critique of Anthropology* 29, no. 1 (2009): 81–104.

Patterson, Orlando. *Slavery and Social Death: A Comparative Study.* Harvard University Press, 1982.

Penglase, Ben. *Living with Insecurity in a Brazilian Favela: Urban Violence and Daily Life.* Rutgers University Press, 2014.

Petersilia, Joan. *When Prisoners Come Home: Parole and Prisoner Reentry.* Oxford University Press, 2003.

Pinho, Osmundo. *Cativeiro: Antinegritude e ancestralidade* [Captivity: Antiblackness and ancestrality]. Segundo Selo, 2022.

Povinelli, Elizabeth. *Economies of Abandonment: Social Belonging and Endurance in Late Liberalism.* Duke University Press, 2011.

Rauter, Cristina. *Criminologia e subjetividade no Brasil* [Criminology and subjectivity in Brazil]. Revan, 2003.

Réis, João José, and Flávio Gomes. "Introdução: A história da liberdade" [Introduction: The history of freedom]. In *Liberdade por um fio: História dos quilombos no Brasil* [Freedom by a thread: The history of *quilombos* in Brazil], edited by João José Réis and Flávio Gomes. Companhia das Letras, 1996.

Réis, João José, and Eduardo Silva. *Negociação e conflito: A resistência negra no Brasil escravista* [Negotiation and conflict: Black resistance in slaveholding Brazil]. Companhia das Letras, 1989.

Rhodes, Lorna. *Total Confinement: Madness and Reason in the Supermaximum Security Prison.* University of California Press, 2004.

Ricoeur, Paul. *Freud and Philosophy: An Essay on Interpretation.* Translated by Denis Savage. Yale University Press, 1970.

Riles, Annelise. *The Network Inside Out.* University of Michigan Press, 2000.

Roth-Gordon, Jennifer. *Race and the Brazilian Body: Blackness, Whiteness, and Everyday Language in Rio de Janeiro.* University of California Press, 2017.

Sabo, Don, Terry Kupers, and Willie London. "Introduction: Gender and the Politics of Punishment." In *Prison Masculinities*, edited by Don Sabo, Terry Kupers, and Willie London. Temple University Press, 2001.

Sánchez, Alexandra, Celina Roma Sánchez de Toledo, Luiz Antônio Bastos Camacho, and Bernard Larouze. "Mortalidade e causas de óbitos nas prisões do Rio de Janeiro, Brasil" [Mortality and causes of death in the prisons of Rio de Janeiro, Brazil], *Cadernos de Saúde Pública* 37, no. 9 (2021), 1–13. https://doi.org/10.1590/0102-311X002 24920

Santana, Dora Silva. "*Mais Viva!* Reassembling Transness, Blackness, and Feminism," *Transgender Studies Quarterly* 6, no. 2 (2019): 210–222. https://doi.org/10.1215/ 23289252-7348496

Santos, Myrian Sepúlveda dos. "Os porões da república: A colônia correcional de Dois Rios entre 1908 e 1930" [The cellars of the Republic: The correctional colony of Dois Rios between 1908 and 1930], *Topoi* 7, no. 13 (2006): 445–476. https://doi.org/10.1590/ 2237-101X006013006

Secretaria Nacional de Políticas Penais. "Relatório de informações penais: 16o ciclo SISDEPEN, 1o semestre de 2024" [Penal information report: 16th SISDEPEN cycle, 1st semester of 2024], 2024.

Sedgwick, Eve. "Paranoid Reading and Reparative Reading; Or, You're So Paranoid, You Probably Think This Introduction Is About You." In *Novel Gazing*, edited by Eve Sedgwick. Duke University Press, 1997.

Shammas, Victor L. "The Perils of Parole Hearings: California Lifers, Performative Disadvantage, and the Ideology of Insight," *PoLAR: Political and Legal Anthropology Review* 42, no. 1 (2019): 142–160. https://doi.org/10.1111/plar.12275

Shange, Savannah. "Play Aunties and Dyke Bitches: Gender, Generation, and the Ethics of Black Queer Kinship," *Black Scholar* 49, no. 1 (2019): 40–54. https://doi.org/10.1080/00064246.2019.1548058

———. *Progressive Dystopia: Abolition, Antiblackness and Schooling in San Francisco.* Duke University Press, 2019.

Silva, Cristhian Teófilo da. "O Índio, o pardo e o invisível: Primeiras impressões sobre a criminalização e o aprisionamento de indígenas no Brasil" [The Indian, the mixed-race and the invisible: First impressions on the criminalization and imprisonment of Indigenous people in Brazil], *Antropolítica* 34 (2013): 137–158. https://doi.org/10.22409/antropolitica2013.0i34.a41521

Silva, Dandara Dias da. *Eu sinto julho* [I feel July]. Editora Multifoco, 2024.

Silva, Denise Ferreira da. "No-Bodies: Law, Raciality and Violence," *Griffith Law Review* 18, no. 2 (2009): 212–236. https://doi.org/10.1080/10383441.2009.10854638

———. "To Be Announced: Radical Praxis or Knowing (at) the Limits of Justice," *Social Text* 31, no. 1 (2013): 43–62. https://doi.org/10.1215/01642472-1958890

Smith, Christen. *Afro-Paradise: Blackness, Violence and Performance in Brazil.* University of Illinois Press, 2016.

Sorj, Bila, and Carla Gomes. "O gênero da 'nova cidadania': O programa Mulheres da Paz" [The gender of 'new citizenship': The Women of Peace program], *Sociologia & Antropologia* 1, no. 2 (2011): 147–164. https://doi.org/10.1590/2238-38752011v127

Spillers, Hortense J. "Mama's Baby, Papa's Maybe: An American Grammar Book." In *The Transgender Studies Reader Remix.* Edited by Susan Stryker and Dylan McCarthy Blackston. Routledge, 2022.

Stanley, Eric A. *Atmospheres of Violence: Structuring Antagonism and the Trans/Queer Ungovernable.* Duke University Press, 2021.

Stephen, Lynn. "Bearing Witness: Testimony in Latin American Anthropology and Related Fields," *Journal of Latin American and Caribbean Anthropology* 22, no. 1 (2017): 85–109. https://doi.org/10.1111/jlca.12262

Stevenson, Lisa. *Life Beside Itself: Imagining Care in the Canadian Arctic.* University of California Press, 2014.

Sufrin, Carolyn. *Jailcare: Finding the Safety Net for Women Behind Bars.* University of California Press, 2017.

Teixeira, César Pinheiro. "De 'corações de pedra' a 'corações de carne': Algumas considerações sobre a conversão de 'bandidos' nas igrejas evangélicas pentecostais" [From 'hearts of stone' to 'hearts of flesh': Some considerations on the conversion of 'criminals' in Pentecostal evangelical churches], *Dados* 54, no. 3 (2011): 449–478. https://doi.org/10.1590/S0011-52582011000300007

———. "O testemunho e a produção do valor moral: Observações sobre um centro de recuperação evangélica" [Testimony and the production of moral value: Observations on an evangelical recovery center], *Religião e Sociedade* 36, no. 2 (2016): 107–134. https://doi.org/10.1590/0100-85872016v36n2capo6

Teixeira, Jaqueline Moraes, and Lívia Reis. "Mulheres evangélicas para além do voto: Notas sobre processos de engajamento, política e cotidiano," *Debates do NER* 22, no. 2 (2022): 11–64. https://doi.org/10.22456/1982-8136.130730

Thomas, Deborah A. *Political Life in the Wake of the Plantation: Sovereignty, Witnessing, Repair.* Duke University Press, 2019.

Thompson, David C. "Evangelical Christianity as Infrastructure in Brazil's Penal System," *Journal of Latin American Studies* 54, no. 3 (2022): 457–479. https://doi.org/10.1017/S00 22216X22000426

Varella, Drauzio. *Estação Carandiru* [Carandiru Station]. Companhia das Letras, 1999.

Vargas, João H. Costa. "Gendered Antiblackness and the Impossible Brazilian Project: Emerging Critical Black Studies," *Cultural Dynamics* 24, no. 1 (2012): 3–11. https://doi .org/10.1177/0921374012452808

———. *Never Meant to Survive: Genocide and Utopia in Black Diaspora Communities.* Rowman & Littlefield, 2010.

———. "Taking Back the Land: Police Operations and Sports Megaevents in Rio de Janeiro," *Souls* 15, no. 4 (2013): 275–303. https://doi.org/10.1080/10999949.2013.884445

Vianna, Adriana, and Laura Lowenkron. "O duplo fazer do gênero e do estado: Interconexões, materialidades e linguagens" [The double making of gender and the state: Interconnections, materialities and languages], *Cadernos Pagu*, no. 51 (2017). https://doi.org/10.1590/18094449201700510001

Wacquant, Loïc. *Body and Soul.* Oxford University Press, 2004.

———. *Punishing the Poor: The Neoliberal Government of Social Insecurity.* Duke University Press, 2009.

Walcott, Rinaldo. *The Long Emancipation: Moving Toward Black Freedom.* Duke University Press, 2021.

Wilder, Gary. "The Promise of Freedom and the Predicament of Marronage: On Neil Roberts's Freedom as Marronage," *Small Axe: SX Salon*, no. 24 (2017).

Wool, Zoë H. "In-Durable Sociality: Precarious Life in Common and the Temporal Boundaries of the Social," *Social Text* 35, no. 1 (2017): 79–99. https://doi.org/10.1215/01642472-3728008

York, Sara Wagner, Megg Rayara Gomes Oliveira, and Bruna Benevides. "Manifestações textuais (insubmissas) travesti" [Travesti textual (ungovernable) manifestos], *Revista Estudos Feministas* 28, no. 3 (2020). https://doi.org/10.1590/1806-9584-2020v28n375614

Zaluar, Alba. "O crime e a não-cidadania: Os males do Brasil" [Crime and non-citizenship: The evils of Brazil]. In *O Mal à Brasileira* [Evil, Brazilian style], edited by Patricia Biram and Regina Novaes. Eduerj, 1997.

Zamboni, Márcio. "O barraco das monas na cadeia dos coisas: Notas etnográficas sobre a diversidade sexual e de gênero no sistema penitenciário" [The cell of the *monas* in the jail of the *coisas*: Ethnographic notes on sexual and gender diversity in the penitentiary system], *Aracê: Direitos Humanos em Revista* 4, no. 5 (2017): 93–115.

———. "Travestis e transexuais privadas de liberdade: A (des)construção de um sujeito de direitos" [Travestis and transsexuals deprived of liberty: The (de)construction of a subject of rights], *Revista Euroamericana de Antropologia*, no. 2 (2016): 15–23.

Index

Penitentiary Council, 172–73

People of Israel, 8, 151–52, 196n13

Periodic Home Visitation, 40, 204n1; evasion and, 159–60; reforms to, 208n20; requirements, 124–25

Police: archives, 151; blitzes, 175, 186, 188, 209n5, 209n17; correctional officers as, 197n36; destruction of documents, 54; expansion of, 3; 6; factions and, 195–96n10; history of, 33, 148, 162; homicide and, 2, 17–18, 88–89, 110–11, 181; lock-ups, 29, 96; masculinity and, 145, 167; militias and, 196n12; PRONASCI and, 69, 138; racial profiling, 196n14; testimony, 99–100, 203n20; theatrical representation of, 110–11; travestis and, 156. *See also* UPPs.

"Postscript on the Societies of Control" (Deleuze), 74

Poverty, 138, 209n9; evangelical Christianity and, 94–95, 100–101, 103

Prison: architecture, 16, 23, 159, 198n48; history of, 5–6, 32–36, 95, 147–48 (*see also* House of Correction); location of, 3, 5–7, 29; names of, 22; social science and, 21, 52; gender of, 145–46; in geography, evangelical 105; as system, 6, 195n6

Prison administration. *See* SEAP

Prison population, growth, 3, 6–8, 39, 56, 93

Prison sentence: correctional officers, influence on 43, 157; evasion and, 148–49, 160–61; length, 2, 18, 22–23, 197–98n37; objective of, 35, 55; structure, 12–13, 30–36, 38; temporality of, 32–33, 38–39, 160–62, 165

Progressive imprisonment, 12–14, 24, 30–32; criteria, 31, 40, 43–44, 173, 200n33; day release and, 148; delays, 40, 45, 54, 56–57, 165; evasion and, 20, 149, 160–

61, 163, 168–69; history of, 11, 32–36; paperwork and, 37–39, 57–59, 131; praise for, 18, 55; temporality of, 33, 58–59, 149, 165, 190; travestis and, 157–58

Project Life, 1–2, 23–24, 26–27, 60–89; critiques of, 73–74, 78–79; evangelical Christianity and, 91–92, 153; graduation, 86–69, 91–92; history of, 61–62; LGBT Group, 153–54; multipliers, 63, 81; pedagogies of, 60–61, 63, 77, 85, 88; psychology and, 60–63, 73–74; theater and, 80–86; violence, concern with, 77–78. *See also* Peaceball; Mutual aid

Project Overcome, 16–18, 109, 126

PROJUDI (Digital Judicial Proceedings), 55–56

Promise: of emancipation, 18, 149, 162–63; evangelical Christianity and, 19, 102, 107, 122, 140; incarcerated people, framed by, 18–19, 63, 69, 117–18, 134–35; of paper, 31, 41, 57–59; refusal of, 154, 189–90; of release, 1–4, 41, 59, 165, 173; resocialization as, 3, 11–12, 15, 154, 189–90; unfulfilled, 9–15, 19, 122, 149; whiteness, as embodiment of, 117–19

PRONASCI (National Program of Security with Citizenship), 67–69, 137–38

Protestantism: 93–93, 104. *See also* Evangelical Christianity

Psychiatry, 35–36, 45, 113, 128, 139

Psychology, 26–27, 60–89; criminological exam and, 45–53; critique and, 10, 73–74; Elias and, 129–30; ethics, 60–61; evangelical Christianity and, 93, 102; Federal Board of, 52–53; numbers of, 61–62, 91, 201n2; Project Life and, 60–63, 73–74; training, 60–61, 70, 73–74

Public defenders, 13–14, 23, 29–31; clients, relationships with, 39–41, 93, 125, 158, 161; convictions, report on, 203n20;

The authorized representative in the EU for product safety and compliance is:
Mare Nostrum Group
B.V Doelen 72
4831 GR Breda
The Netherlands

www.ingramcontent.com/pod-product-compliance
Lightning Source LLC
Chambersburg PA
CBHW020857270326
41928CB00006B/745

* 9 7 8 1 5 0 3 6 4 4 5 6 4 *